The Immigrant Heritage of America Series

Cecyle S. Neidle, *Editor*

THE PENNSYLVANIA DUTCH:

A Persistent Minority

By WILLIAM T. PARSONS
Ursinus College

TWAYNE PUBLISHERS
A DIVISION OF G. K. HALL & CO., BOSTON

Library of Congress Cataloging in Publication Data

Parsons, William T
    The Pennsylvania Dutch

    (The Immigrant heritage of America series)
    Bibliography: pp. 289–305
    Includes index.
    1. Pennsylvania Germans. I. Title.
F160.G3P36   974.8'004'31   75–22044
ISBN 0–8057–8408–X

For Gottfried Grünzweig (1731–1821)
and Judy Parsons (1966–)
who both surmounted obstacles
and share a common heritage

Contents

About the Author

William T. Parsons is Professor of History and Director of the Pennsylvania Dutch Studies Program at Ursinus College, Collegeville, Pennsylvania. His major field of interest is Colonial Pennsylvania history. He took his graduate degrees at the University of Pennsylvania, where he studied with Roy Nichols, Richard Shryock and Arthur Bining. He has also studied dialect and folklife with Earl Moyer and Clarence Reitnauer. A Pennsylvania Dutchman himself, Parsons now attempts to gain proper recognition for his ethnic group.

He has contributed numerous scholarly articles to such publications as *The Pennsylvania Magazine of History and Biography, Quaker History, Pennsylvania History* and the *Bulletin of the Historical Society of Montgomery County* (Pennsylvania) and served briefly as editor of the latter publication. Currently he is Assistant Editor of *Pennsylvania Folklife.* Recently he has written monographs on *Ethnic Tradition: The Legacy of the Pennsylvania Dutch* and *The Preachers' Appeal of 1775.*

The author has held local elective office and is active in the Pennsylvania German Society, Pennsylvania Historical Association and Goschenhoppen Historians, Inc. He participates in the Kutztown Folk Festival and heads Bicentennial activities. He is chairman of an advisory committee for a Pennsylvania PBS television special on Dutch Country Life. He sings with *Die Sivva Schwowe,* dialect folksong group, and is a member of *Grundsau Lodsch Nummer 7* and of the *Barricks Caunty Fersommling.*

Preface

It is not easy to imagine how a minority group which is not particularly visible could persist over a span of three hundred years within a society which applauds conformity and adaptation to majority values. Yet the Pennsylvania Dutch have achieved that distinction, to their own satisfaction and to the despair of many of their neighbors. These people, essentially German immigrants, arrived in the New World and settled in Pennsylvania between 1684 and 1835. They have experienced recurring success and failure from then on to our own time. They did not constitute a single cohesive group at the time of arrival and have diverged even more as a result of their response to an essentially English society in Pennsylvania. They enjoyed neither a sense of unity nor the right to participate in the decisions of a fiercely divided Germany from which they emerged. They rejoiced in their differences as they competed and contended in the New World.

This book attempts to deal with both main segments of Pennsylvania Dutch settlers. The so-called Church Germans were composed of Lutheran and German Reformed settlers. Smaller pietistic sects, many of them Anabaptist or Brethren, who opposed formalistic religion, were the "Plain Folk." There were also Swiss, Alsatian, and Holland Dutch, though in smaller numbers, and they intermixed with the main body of Palatine and Württemberg Germans to form subgroups of the larger Pennsylvania Dutch settlement. A few migrants who arrived after 1835, and settled in already established Pennsylvania Dutch villages or rural communities, became absorbed into the Dutch culture, but since most of the later arrivals emanated from different areas of Germany and from a higher social level, they remained an urban High German settlement, separate and distinct from the essentially agrarian Pennsylvania Dutch Folk.

In this essay, I use virtually interchangeably the terms Pennsylvania Dutch, Pennsylvania German, Dutch, and German, as all these terms are used in Pennsylvania's Dutch country, remembering that Dutch is English for *Deitsch*. Such use will surprise few in Pennsylvania, where we have subjected the Scots-Irish to the same treatment, often inaccurately calling them Irish. Explanations for the loose terminology identifying the Pennsylvania Dutch will appear at a more appropriate location in the text itself but the reader should be forewarned of that use of terms. Because so many of the Pennsylvania Dutch originated in the Rhineland Palatinate, the term Palatines is also used occasionally, mainly when Palatine origins are actually of some significance; the author recognizes that the use of the term "Palatine" as a class noun to indicate all Germans is much more a New York term than one current in Pennsylvania usage, a distinction which will be honored in this book.

The great mass of migrants who composed the Pennsylvania Dutch minority were farmers, peasants, or agricultural workers in their homeland. Many of them were thus required to travel to America as indentured servants, with only a few (but notable) members of the upper class or German nobility as exceptions to the rule. I shall give first consideration to the small farmer, his status and his problems. The importance of the Dutchmen as a link in Pennsylvania frontier development (*die Iwwerbarriyaleit*, as they called themselves) receives appropriate attention here, though they have been generally overlooked elsewhere. The reader will note that the participation of Pennsylvania Germans in American life is not limited to Pennsylvania, although obviously it is most evident there. Pennsylvania Dutchmen can be heard today (and it is not difficult to perceive distinguishing verbal characteristics in a Dutchman's pronunciation of the English or in his grammatical lapses) from the farmlands of Ontario to graduate classrooms or faculty offices from Cambridge to Berkeley and from Kutztown State College to Arizona State University. In rural Pennsylvania today, the visitor will still hear some Pennsylvania Dutch spoken, although less frequently than twenty or twenty-five years ago.

In addition to the lack of unity among the numerous component groups of Dutch, the other great problem faced by the Dutch was an inability to retain advantages granted temporarily by the dominant majority around them. Thus political advantage, concessions in education, and local recognition of language or custom were quite often extinguished by passage of time, change, and the inexorable advance of technology. Each generation among the Pennsylvania Dutch that attempted to hold on to concessions and advantages or to the old ways has been forced to repeat the struggles of preceding generations, in a diminishing spiral of costume, custom, and language use. Yet in today's idiom, the Dutch folk cannot be considered a disadvantaged minority.

At last in the final third of the twentieth century, America seems willing to concede to minority groups the apparent advantages of cultural pluralism. The quaint ways and appearance of the Plain Folk, and the remnants of the *Muttersproch*, receive both scholarly attention and vocal approbation of visitors and customers at Folk Fairs and other types of *Fersommling*. Even so, many Anglicisms have crept into the language.

Old rules and restrictions of custom of the Dutch Country are reviewed and sometimes bent by their leaders to avoid alienating youth altogether. The Dutch have their admirable features, certainly including frugality, tenacity, warmth, and an unusual sense of community; but they can be irritating, petty, obstructionist, and just plain thick-headed, as many of their neighbors will testify at length. They tend to be provincial but have nonetheless assumed world leadership in private benevolent projects. In short, the Pennsylvania Dutch present not just one paradox but a veritable interlocking puzzle of paradoxes.

For information and ideas and a host of illustrative examples in this work, I owe a debt of gratitude to friends, family, and neighbors too numerous to detail. I acknowledge also the valuable assistance derived from useful collections housed at the Perkiomen School, Ursinus College, the Historical Society of Montgomery County, the Historical Society of Pennsylvania, and the American Philosophical Society. To Doris Albright for typing the manuscript, Cecyle S. Neidle for editorial guidance, and Phyllis Parsons, long-suffering wife, I express my thanks as well. Errors are, of course, my own.

WILLIAM T. PARSONS

Ursinus College

Chronology

1517   Martin Luther challenges church hierarchy at Wittenberg.

1531   Death of Ulrich Zwingli at Morgarten.

1555   Peace of Augsburg: Territorial concessions to Lutheran princes.

1563   Heidelberg Catechism of Zacharias Ursinus and Casper Olevianus.

1618–   Thirty Years' War in the Germanies.
1648

1648   Peace of Westphalia: Catholic, Lutheran, or Calvinist princes determine the religion of their own territory.

1682   William Penn's Pennsylvania: invitations to Germans.

1683   Germantown Mennonite settlement.

1688   Germantown petition against Negro slavery.

1709–   Palatine resettlement in England.
1712

1710   Palatine economic experiments in New York.

1717–   Great Migration to Pennsylvania.
1754

1725   First German Reformed Communion at Falkner Swamp.

1727   Oath of fealty required by law of all German immigrants.

1742   Henry Melchior Muhlenberg arrives in Pennsylvania. Bloody Election in Philadelphia. Moravian settlement at Bethlehem under Count von Zinzendorf.

1744   Valentine Haidt at Bethlehem.

1747   German Reformed Coetus founded by Michael Schlatter.

1754–   French and Indian War.
1763

1755   Gnadenhütten Massacre.

1756–   Chain of Forts from Stroudsburg to York.
1757

1764   German Society of Philadelphia (Pennsylvania) founded. Election defeat of Franklin and Royal government.

1765 The Stamp Act.

1775–
1783 War for American Independence.

1775 Preachers' Appeal for the Patriot Cause.

1777–
1778 Winter at Valley Forge: von Steuben drillmaster.

1781 Yorktown battle.

1783 Peace of Paris.

1789 Frederick A. C. Muhlenberg first Speaker of the House.

1798 Alien and Sedition Acts. Fries Rebellion, or Hot Water Rebellion.

1808 Simon Snyder elected first Pennsylvania Dutch governor.

1809–
1851 Era of German governors in Pennsylvania.

1811 Jacob Eichholtz, painter.

1817–
1832 Pennsylvania politics, the Game without Rules.

1834 Free public schools established under Governor George Wolf.

1837 "The Buckshot War."

1849 Earliest publication of Rondthaler's *Pennsylfawnisch Deitsch* poetry.

1850 Thomas U. Walter, Capitol architect.

1853,
1858 North Pacific Maritime Explorations.

1860 Voyage of the *Kanrin Maru* to San Francisco.

1861–
1865 The Civil War.

1863 The Emancipation Proclamation; Battle of Gettysburg.

1870 *Harbaugh's Harfe.*

1877–
1895 Kress, Kresge, Woolworth, and Wanamaker business leaders.

1891 The Pennsylvania German Society founded.

1904 Thomas Harter, *Boonastiel.*

1914–
1918 World War One.

1917 United States' entry. German language removed from school curricula. General John J. Pershing, Commander, A.E.F.

Chronology

1918–1923	Joint Occupation of the Rhineland.
1923	Classroom restrictions on German language ruled unconstitutional.
1936	Pennsylvania German Folklore Society founded. Preston Barba, *'s Pennsylvaanisch Deitsch Eck.*
1939	Outbreak of World War Two.
1941–1945	The United States in World War Two.
1943	Army Specialized Training Program—Language and Area Study.
1944	General Dwight Eisenhower, Supreme Commander in Europe.
1945	V-E Day.
1949	First Kutztown Folk Festival: Pennsylvania Folklife Society.
1974	First Institute on Pennsylvania Dutch Culture, Ursinus College.

CHAPTER I

Background in the Germanies

THE STATUS, CONDITION, AND OUTLOOK OF THE PENNSYLVANIA
Germans (familiarly called Pennsylvania Dutch) were determined by centuries of experience in Germany and in neighboring areas of continental Europe. While the validity of speaking
in terms of national outlook may be questioned, social and
economic organization on the local level included definable
differences based on geographic location and political structure.
A realistic appraisal may be found in the law code of Prussia
as late as 1791: "Civil Society consists of many small societies
and estates, connected to each other, by nature or law, or by
both together."[1] Ordinary experiences close to the individual,
the organization of everyday life and its restrictions, determined
his attitude and set his values in a way that no national or
international concepts had managed to do.

The farmer (*bauer* in Germany) in 1500 continued to be
the major factor on the European scene, living in the countryside or in country villages, under traditional forms which
stretched back for centuries. Many of them had achieved the
status of free farmers, competing for available land, and were
able to raise cash crops. Those farmers had emerged from the
great agricultural period of medieval feudal Europe with its
hordes of serfs and unfree agricultural workers who were tied
to the land by custom and contract. Even in the face of changing
conditions, many traditional relationships from the medieval
period remained intact. Nobility, or *Grundherren*, still subjected
the peasantry (free or unfree) to their will, collected landrents,
fines, and dues from them in a way totally beyond the ability
of the agrarian worker to oppose. Life was controlled by
important men, a factor which changed little with the passage
of time.[2]

17

In many ways the traditional means of control rested with the landowner or nobility. The farmer at the base of social and economic institutions continued to witness a working alliance between the estates of nobility and clergy. As for many years past, he found little means (and little hope) that basic forms and basic relationships would change. Yet, had he but known, in 1500, the forces of change were closer at hand than nobility and peasant realized.

Towns and cities, on the other hand, offered some consolations such as leadership in guilds and churches, not available in the open countryside. But the main attraction of urban life was opportunity. Often that opportunity was more theoretical than practical, but it drew myriads of hopefuls from farm and country village. The townsman (*Bürger* in German areas) had the future on his side. Some German cities, like Hamburg, forbade the nobility to live within town walls, although small groups of families controlled the burgeoning cities, as in Lübeck or Frankfort. In the German area, the cities tended to be among the most privileged areas for free populations and additional rights.[3]

Counter to the great tradition of freedom in the cities was the corresponding prevalence of poverty. Many times, half the town or city population was free to struggle, free to starve, or at least to live in conditions of deprivation and scarcity. True, they also had mendicant rights and the cathedral as hospital, but for many that was small consolation. In most of the towns of Europe, the majority of the dwellers had very few advantages. Slums were as extensive as they were dismal; sanitation was virtually nonexistent in cities only beginning. For many the difference between death and survival was the town garden plot for the family food supply many managed to operate even in the larger urban concentrations. However, to some, tenements in the cities closed even that survival possibility, as greater populations occupied increasingly valuable areas.

Drawbacks such as these appear to us a great hindrance to progress; yet the city provided opportunities for social advance and economic success. Church, army, and overseas colonization afforded an alternate means of ascending the social ladder, but cities were nearer at hand. Furthermore, at the turn of the sixteenth century, they offered an easier and more comfortable way for individuals to try their luck. As a rule, the most commercially active towns were also the freest, so that greater opportunity came to those who migrated from rural areas to Lübeck, Nuremberg, Augsburg or to other free imperial cities often located in South Germany. Only a miniscule percentage of the German population had this opportunity, so the majority remained rural, socially static, and without new economic opportunities.[4]

Then, to climax a century or more of vigorous criticism of the worldliness of the clergy and radical suggestions of reform, in 1517 Martin Luther openly challenged the Roman hierarchical church from German territory. Population growth and the revolutionary rise of prices in the fifty years preceding Luther's attack had put further economic pressure upon the ordinary people of northern and central Europe. The response of the church had been the call for more vigorous collection of tithes and an expansion in the sale of indulgences, plus a firm insistence that wages should remain steady, even if prices ran to double their previous level.

Martin Luther's appeal for a reform in head and body of the church thus fell upon responsive listeners, for it seemed a direct solution to the financially oppressed. Luther's doctrine of the universal priesthood of all believers suggested fewer prerequisites and less advantage to the mighty. His absolute insistence upon a readable Bible in the vernacular language, available to all the faithful, likewise struck a responsive note among ordinary people who had long since tired of social distinctions and economic advantages of a wealthy upper class. In the face of assurances that all Christians would be equal before the eternal judgment seat, many disadvantaged or underprivileged preferred an equality among true believers here and now.[5]

A strange coalition immediately sprang up. Not only did the aspirations and hopes of peasant communities emerge, but their long standing resentment of feudal remnants and the exactions of the nobles led them to radical action. Combined with this was the scholarly call of teachers and learned doctors in the universities for a "total reformation." Older documents such as

Reformation Sigismundi reappeared in print in 1520 and 1522, eighty years after its first appearance. This spearheaded the appeal for revolutionary change in the structure of society, reduction of a wealthy church hierarchy, the end of the clergy as a separate social and political class, elimination of financially powerful interest groups, and an end to serfdom and poverty. The poor made rich, the clergy humbled, Jews restrained in trade—all these characteristics of a golden age would be climaxed by a peasant emperor. As if to give credence to this radical dream, Andreas Bodenstein von Carlstadt, associate and fellow professor of Luther's at Wittenberg, bought a farm, briefly assumed peasant attributes, and stated the demands for radical transformation of the religious institutions of Europe. With this sort of logic, peasant and intellectual surged forth in the name of the Reformation.

Luther cut it short. He planned and sought changes of policy and worked for alterations within the ecclesiastical structure. He found the secular princes and the great nobles of North Germany interested in backing his program; some of them were worthy exponents of reform policies within the German church. Carlstadt's preachments notwithstanding, Luther had no inclination to foster peasant ambitions. Peasant revolt endangered his efforts. He worked best with the true friends of religious reform, the dissident fellow churchmen, scholars, and territorial princes. Peasants and their scruffy associates continuously complained of the failing of others and the treachery of nobles who were bound to protect them, but offered little real protection. They sought relief from their obligations wherever authority seemed threatened. Luther sent forth the nobles to smite down the peasant usurpers, to wage war against the agrarian upstarts, "the murdering, thieving hordes of the peasants." As he watched the stream of "Prophets" ranging across the Germanies in the name of spiritual reform, Luther found his most dependable followers in those who exercised power.[6]

Sharing with his contemporary in Wittenberg the conviction that the Roman church had failed, Ulrich Zwingli proposed similar, but more thorough, reforms. He would return the church to the people. In some ways, over a period of time,

Zwingli's greater simplification of form and his further involvement of the laity, carried his program to a larger audience than had Luther's. Removal of many of the miraculous elements of religion and an insistence upon local economic controls made Zwingli's Reformed church tradition most appealing in Switzerland and the western German lands, particularly along the Rhine. Because of the many similarities of doctrine, belief, and program, Reformed Swiss and Germans (following the early death of Zwingli in 1531) gradually coalesced with Calvinists in Geneva and western Europe. Zwingli and Calvin shared similar predestinarian beliefs and both attempted practical working reforms which could immediately be translated into the everyday life of church members and citizens.

This Calvinist Reformed element urged a simple religious worship while they vigorously opposed the concepts of the older religion, which seemed idolatrous to them. The new sermons and prayers were long; the church service, like the church edifice, was plain. Music seemed appropriate only when it reinforced worship, unlawful when it interfered. The middle-class town merchant or master craftsman found solace in the rigid logic and devastating certainty of John Calvin's predestinarian religion. Instead of a sanctified priesthood, energetic Calvinists of the Reformed religion saw God's hand in everything. Even greater was the sense of satisfaction when business successes and abundant harvests certified God's approval of their efforts. Predestinarian aspects of the religion emphasized harsh judgment.

The German Reformed tradition was best exemplified by the young scholars at the University of Heidelberg on the Neckar River, but it also drew upon the simpler beginnings of Ulrich Zwingli in the Swiss cantons. These youthful interpreters of religion held much in common with the systematic Jean Calvin of Paris and Geneva. Theologians and scholars like Zacharias Ursinus debated and argued on a theoretical level, while the peasant understood the likelihood of damnation and eternal torment in store for him and his fellows. He worked under the exactions of an economic and social system scarcely less demanding than his Calvinist religion.[7]

Congregations of both Lutheran and Reformed faiths continued to meet in church edifices for worship and prayer services. In many cases, this was the same building used for Catholic worship before the Reformation. The change which had occurred was legally recognized by 1648. If the lack of a church building, or because of its destruction, forced meetings of the faithful in buildings of a secular nature, or in homes, it was only briefly, since the construction of a sanctuary was of the highest priority.

The great variety of "sect Germans," or those organized on a religious base of pietism or mysticism, and particularly those who were not Lutheran or Reformed, were styled "House Germans," a title only partly accurate. Distinctive characteristics of the sects were often based on literal reading of particular scripture verses. They worshipped in their homes, at times to the exclusion of church buildings altogether, as did the House Amish, some of the Mennonites, and a few others. For some of them, the practice was an effort to imitate early Christians, whose meetings and worship took place in a clandestine fashion in homes. Sixteenth- and seventeenth-century Plain People who worshipped in private homes and maintained secrecy about their religion, did so by choice rather than by necessity. Still, in the states of Reformation Germany, many rulers were exceedingly strict, requiring conformity to their religion. Of course, neither Mennonite, nor Amish, nor Dunkard, nor Brethren had means to achieve recognition, because there were no German princes of these denominations. These groups were shut out first by the Augsburg peace terms, which granted Lutheran and Catholic princes territorial religious rights, then by those of Westphalia, which conceded the same territoriality to Calvinist rulers.

Numerous other pietist Germans did worship in meetinghouses or church buildings, but those buildings tended to be completely plain. While many of their Lutheran or Reformed German neighbors retained some degree of liturgy in their worship, the Plain Sects had almost none. So they were House Germans by comparison with their Church German relatives and neighbors.

Each of the small sects of Plain People had their own set of rules, characteristics, and requirements. Regulations of that sort often originated in one verse of scripture or one particularly important act of piety, or of principle. Thus the Dunkers thought adult baptism to be efficacious, emulating what they understood as the example of John the Baptist and Jesus Christ. Gatherings of Brethren of several varieties emphasized brotherhood, the community of believers, humility, piety, and personal devotion. Many sects valued piety in general, but sometimes they considered important a particular act or incident, as the love feast, ceremonial laying on of hands, kiss of peace, or ceremonial washing of feet. Often they emphasized the importance of prayer. They avoided pride at all cost, including outward signs of pride in clothing or embellishments. They dared not love worldly possessions for themselves, but instead looked upon them as gifts of God.

A great many of the pietists were pacifists, based on scripture, on their own desire to live in peace, and because of the carnage of repeated wars around them. Toleration also became characteristic of pietist groups, though they did not find the beliefs of others to be as valid as their own. As tiny minorities, they survived better on the tolerance of the more powerful around them. Gradually, they saw merit in mutual toleration.[8]

Likewise, many of the pietist groups found value in the ideals or teachings of a particularly saintly, renowned, or noble member. In many cases by the same token, they took their name from the honored leader. Hence, the Schwenkfelders acquired their identification from Caspar Schwenkfeld von Ossig, the Mennonites from Menno Simons, the Amish from Jost Amman, and the Herrites from Christian Herr. The latter was a branch of the Church of the Brethren. The Amish were a splinter group of Mennonites who emphasized ostracism or "shunning" (*Meidung*) both of members who broke rules, and of outsiders.[9]

A religious society prominent earlier were the Moravians, or *Unitas Fratrum*. Pietist in belief but episcopal in organization, they traced their spiritual heritage to the teachings and ideals of John Hus, martyr to the Protestant cause a hundred years before Martin Luther. More directly, the Moravian church was organized by Jan Comenius. They emphasized simple forms, personal piety, and a vernacular Bible. Having struggled against imperial authority for many years, they developed an organization which was effective in both large and small groups, and held ritual and dogma to a minimum. Like other pietist groups, they objected to the fact that the Church Germans seemed to them to retain too many ways and traditions of the Catholic church. Within the Moravian movement were to be found both simple farmers and sophisticated scholars. Moravians who came to Pennsylvania followed devious routes to reach the New World, but consolidated rapidly upon arrival here.[10]

Of all national areas of Europe, Germany had produced the widest range of religious organizations or denominations in the course of the Reformation period. More thoroughly than for centuries past, the new religious forms wrought a bond between people and minister. The local priest, preacher, or pastor seemed infinitely closer to his flock than ever before. No more than peasants or craftsmen of his own congregation could the priest of the Old Order aspire to close contact with bishop or with God.

Religious forces at work in the German states splintered into a thousand independent groups, each certain of its special insight as it competed with other local sects. Most of these small gatherings of the faithful drew inspiration from a vernacular scripture, rather than from dogma, liturgy, or ritual.

Political control was exercised by the upper ranks of the noble class which directed the daily lives of the people in the numerous states, a fact which most nonnobles tried hard to ignore. For the German princes, political opportunities offered by the Reformation were too important to ignore. Breaking the domination of the Austrian Hapsburgs was even more important than breaking the domination of the Roman church. Wars, sieges, and the need for foot soldiers, combined with a new, fierce competition for trade, caught all Germans in a massive squeeze.

Those ambitions of North German princes led them to appreciate Luther and the force of his movement. They were aided by German-speaking Swiss Calvinists in challenging the imperial Catholic armies. Combined forces wore down the resistance of fighting men led by Holy Roman Emperor Charles V as defender of the Roman church. Just before his abdication in 1555, Charles V proposed concessions in order to ensure a peaceable succession.

In the Peace of Augsburg of 1555, territories of Lutheran and Catholic rulers were recognized as separate and legal entities, and their local rights were guaranteed. It recognized the status of rulers who accepted Lutheran doctrine as enunciated in the Augsburg Confession. It also stated the principle of *cuius regio, eius religio,* whereby each ruler, Catholic or Lutheran, established the religion for his state. The entire arrangement was so favorable to the non-Catholic leaders, their heresy now politically excused, that they chose not to contest minor ecclesiastical reservations of Charles V.[11]

Political boundaries shifted during the sixty-odd years that followed as individual states rejoiced in their newly found power and no succeeding emperor ever achieved the level of power that Charles V had built.[12] As time passed, local princes and population grew discontented. Continued disturbances, the ambition of local princes, such as the Calvinist Elector of the Rhineland Palatinate, and the question of imperial succession, combined in 1618–1619 to produce a war situation in central Europe. It culminated in the Thirty Years' War, one of the most debilitating wars in the history of Europe, bringing terrible destruction to southern Germany. In the end, a weakened Holy Roman Empire did concede territorial adjustments. The principle established at Augsburg was extended to local princes who held Calvinist beliefs by terms of the Peace of Westphalia of 1648. This modification placated German Calvinist rulers and the Reformed populations who inhabited territories ruled by princes of compatible faith, but it still left a great many other Germans without the advantages of that choice.[13]

Large numbers of Germans remained faithful to the established Catholic religion of the empire, especially in South Germany. Some returned to the faith after experiments as Protestants or brief flirtations with other religious forms. Peasants who heard of equality before God and reports about the priesthood of all believers were unwilling to wait any longer and plunged into social revolution. German princes brought retaliation and destruction to ambitious peasants, in accord with Luther's injunction, "Smite them, strike them down." The Peasants Revolt in 1524 and 1525, reminiscent of the earlier unsuccessful *Jacquerie* in France and Wat Tylers' Rebellion in England, brought added death and destruction to rural Germany. It also disillusioned the frustrated peasants.

Differing Anabaptist groups gathered in the old West German ecclesiastical town of Münster. They preached and prayed, but in the end, their great hopes deteriorated into civil strife. Instead of seeing the millenium, they succumbed to imperial armies. New visions of religious prophets had brought renewed violence, death, and destruction.[14] In areas of South Germany, Protestants returned to the Catholic fold in great numbers, especially after the Peasants War ensured favored status for the Protestant nobles.

The conditions of life, involving working rules and the right to hold land, remained so chaotic in seventeenth-century Germany that for many the only hope lay in work and prayer. Because of the relative insecurity of their daily life, peasants found comfort in a religion which promised serenity and rest in life-after-death. Pietism, which offered specific salvation, appealed particularly to these relatively simple folk. Peasant workers stood lowest on the social scale of their day. They worked land that they never owned, using simple tools which were usually their only possessions. They had no hope of ever owning any parcel of land. Unable to fight in their own behalf, they were forced to arms as a matter of state policy. Small wonder they continued to seek a release from that system.

Few areas of Germany escaped without loss of life or property during the Thirty Years' War. Invading troops, a majority of them not native to the German states, chewed up crops and homes and killed off civilians in the path of the armies.[15] After the Westphalia settlement of 1648 placed some German-speaking population under control of young Louis XIV of France, renewed outbreaks on the French-German border shattered the quiet of the countryside again. One Martin Rinkert, even though desolated by losses in his family, his village, and his church, found sufficient strength in his faith to write:

> Now thank we all our God,
> With hearts and hands and voices,
> Whom wondrous things hath done,
> In whom this world rejoices.[16]

For those who faced hardship in Pennsylvania that hymn came to represent the same kind of faith under tremendous odds.

In addition to the Rhineland, Württemberg and Baden suffered extensive damage from the excesses of the Thirty Years' War, but not so complete as in the Palatinate. The accession of a new elector, Karl Ludwig, who returned to rule his homeland from exile in England, promised improved conditions. Yet even the effort of the new leader was unable to produce a major change in a land so devastated by war, though he attempted economic and social improvement. Then Louis XIV of France renewed the attack. Suffering Palatines hesitated to carry on even routine aspects of farming as the probability of enjoying the harvest diminished.[17]

Nor did this prove to be the end of the wars. In 1688–89 French troops again invaded the Rhine provinces with the result that the agricultural fabric of Germany was further torn apart. Eventually many fled the constant wars, violence, and destruction. Even the relatively isolated Swiss cantons were rocked by repeated local wars from the late seventeenth century through the first half of the eighteenth. For many, the religious and political restrictions were too great, and they found no relief anywhere on German territory. Thoughtful citizens, concerned about their families, considered other solutions. As princes required religious conformity, the dissenters found little opportunity where they lived.

In 1726, for example, in southeastern Germany, Melchior Schultz advised his sons that choice could no longer be postponed. Either they remained in Silesia and converted to the Catholic faith, or they held to their Schwenkfelder principles and moved out. Remaining in Silesia while retaining a dissident faith had by then become absolutely untenable as a solution. Common folk had little pride in being German under those conditions. They merely plodded along, residing in a given locality, working the fields their predecessors had tilled before them. Except for differences in language, custom, and religion, the lot of the unfree worker, and even free workers without land, remained relatively the same throughout western Europe.

At the same time, population growth throughout Europe placed additional pressure upon the individual near the bottom of the economic scale who was trying to hold his place. When religious oppression was renewed in the smaller German states, it proved too much for some persons who had previously remained despite the difficulties.[18]

For thousands of families, escape from the European scene became the only viable option and America offered the most attractive solution. But even that had its darker side, since peasants who had achieved free status rarely had funds sufficient to pay their passage to the New World. Thus they were forced into contract labor as indentured servants, which made them unfree once again, at least until the costs of passage had been paid.[19] At least their hopes of improvement were greater in America and many who came felt liberated by the separation from Old World limitations. Of course, many died in the wilderness of the back country before they had a chance to realize their goals.

CHAPTER II

To the New World

DURING THE LAST QUARTER OF THE SEVENTEENTH CENTURY, AN experiment that had political and religious implications gradually took shape. Originating in the ideas of George Fox and William Penn, it proposed a way out to one of the most harassed of the pietist groups, the Society of Friends. The trials of these plain-thinking English Quakers during the Restoration period of Charles II had forced them to look for new solutions to the old problem of conscience and the matter of religious uniformity. In basing their beliefs on the relations of man to God and consequently of man to man, the English Quakers appeared stubbornly determined to return to the joyless austerity of Cromwellian England. On the other hand, most Englishmen seemed just as decided that austerity should not again be the hallmark of English life.

When the requirements of their plain faith pitted the Quakers against royal officials and the English law, many Englishmen felt that their very presence in England smacked of treason. Friends believed in a God who cared for his children on earth and who communicated with them directly by means of an Inner Light. By the special understanding Friends had of the Bible, Holy Scriptures insisted that man should not kill his fellow man, even under the guise of war or capital punishment; that plain speech and plain words allowed them adequate opportunity to express the most complex ideas and emotions; that oaths were as unnecessary as they were blasphemous, for every man should tell the truth in all he said, not just when under legal oath to do so.

Indeed the criteria set by the Society of Friends provided a statement of conduct in an ideal society, a state of being that was not a feature of Restoration England. To most of their

29

fellow Englishmen, the Quakers seemed impossible and more than a little peculiar. Friends stood firm on principle, refusing to concede even the niceties of conduct in the English court. Friends insisted their Society follow rules of conduct which set them apart from the common English customs of the day. Thus it became absolutely necessary to find a place to live where they might exist in peace according to their own conscience.

Among the early converts of George Fox and the Society of Friends in England was the young and impressionable William Penn. So attracted to Quaker principles was young Penn that he left his studies at Oxford, much to the chagrin of his father, Admiral William Penn. The elder Penn, highly indignant at his son's outrageous behavior, first pleaded with him to no avail, then cut young William out of his inheritance. Admiral William Penn had served England under King and Commonwealth and had loaned money to the restored Stuart royal family. As the admiral aged, he mellowed, and finally restored his son to full standing in family and estates. At the admiral's death, his son William, at a relatively early age, inherited the family estate, fortune, and legal rights. The royal family owed a debt of some sixteen thousand pounds to the young Quaker.

At the beginning of the decade of the 1670s, George Fox and some other leading Quakers undertook an experiment to settle Friends in western New Jersey. For the most part, Quaker holdings in West Jersey lay along the Delaware Bay, the Delaware River, and its tributaries. The Quakers did not achieve peace and contentment there, because the land they settled was contested. These territories were claimed and partially occupied by Swedes and Finns in 1638. The Dutch ruled the area briefly from New Netherlands, issuing new deeds to land already allocated by the Swedes. After English conquest, even newer land claims competed with those previously authorized.

Quakers were forced into court to determine the legal status of the land. For a given property, as many as three warrants or patents existed. But Quaker claimants attempted to avoid litigation as much as possible, because of the requirement of sworn testimony.

Some Quaker inhabitants in western New Jersey did retain

their estates without court proceedings, and a few others did successfully establish legal title through the courts or by negotiation. To the majority of Quakers, however, a less involved solution was preferable. Providentially, issues were settled in a simple manner. In return for a parcel of land west of the Delaware River, William Penn agreed to cancel the outstanding debt of sixteen thousand pounds the Stuarts owed him. New York and New Jersey bounded this grant on the north and east, as Maryland did to the south. In recognition of the sovereignty of the king, Penn had to pay an annual quitrent: "Two Beaver Skins to be delivered at our said Castle of Windsor, on the first day of January in every year."[1]

To the new Province of Pennsylvania, William Penn, as Proprietor, invited Friends and non-Quakers he termed "freemen and adventurers." Territory was available to Quakers and others of similar thoughts and ideals, but Penn did not restrict settlement to any one sect or religious group, nor did he deny to any the right to settle and participate because of the religious concepts they held. Those who purchased property and made improvements also acquired the privilege of participating in the government.

Pennsylvania furnished an opportunity for Friends to dwell in peace and tranquillity. Their landholdings were to sustain them and they were free to follow their religious tenets with as little interference from worldly government as possible. As advanced as he was for his time, Penn did not attempt to eradicate all functions of government. Indeed, he reminded all settlers of the rational view he held: "Governments, like clocks, go from the motion men give them, and as governments are made and moved by men, so by them are they ruined too. Wherefore governments rather depend on men, than men upon governments."[2] He then spelled out the interdependence of man and government in a very brief equation: "That [people] may be free by their just obedience, and the magistrates honourable for their just administration: for liberty without obedience is confusion, and obedience without liberty is slavery."[3]

This young Quaker showed amazing foresight for a man who in many ways vacillated between medieval and modern concepts. In spirit and ideals, he was years ahead of his time.

In 1681, William Penn advertised for settlers who would take his experiment seriously, but he warned off idlers and gold seekers. Two promotional pamphlets described the steady, industrious, frugal adventurers he would welcome to purchase or rent land in the new province. Servants who came into his province would also have an early opportunity to become landholding citizens upon completion of bonded duties. One of these tracts, *Some Account of the Province of Pennsylvania*, was translated into the Dutch and German languages and circulated on the Continent. Penn hoped to attract like-minded persons, even if they were non-English. He promised a new kind of adventure to all, climaxed by a government in which "the people and governor have a legislative power, so that no law can be made, nor money raised but by the peoples consent."[4]

Thus William Penn challenged the newcomers to establish original economic and social forms under the benevolent, compatible government he would provide. Within the year he promulgated his *First Frame of Government*, granting early settlers participation in the legislative process. It was original. Over a twenty-year period, Penn made several efforts to improve his Frame of Government. Meanwhile, Pennsylvania attracted a wide variety of people, drawn to the province by the very opportunities that existed there.[5]

Whether the proprietor was content with the initial settlement is not clear. First arrivals made the most of their opportunities upon landing and began the green country town of Philadelphia forthwith. That settlement lay, for the most part, to the north of earlier Swedish and Dutch concentrations, although the three Lower Counties of New Castle, Kent, and Sussex were superimposed upon the area of prior New Sweden.[6] The Lower Counties formed virtually a separate settlement. Many initial Philadelphians spent their first winter in caves along the Delaware River. Still, those adventurers and Quakers who shared the earliest experiences were eminently successful in their efforts to build a colony which was unusual if not unique in formula and in content. William Penn's Dutch and German invitation to join his colony based on religious toleration, good government, and social and individual morality brought an immediate response from German and Dutch Mennonites gathered near Frankfurt. Their agent and advance planner, Francis Daniel Pastorius, came to Pennsylvania. From there, by March 7, 1684, he was able to send first reports to Frankfurt concerning the settlement in the New World. Pastorius, whose pietism so resembled that of the Society of Friends that he became renowned as "the German Quaker," bought lots near the new town of Philadelphia. He asked that weavers, vintners, coopers, and other artisans be among the first to come. An order for farm implements, iron boilers, copper vats, and brass kettles accompanied that request.

Within eighteen months, Francis Daniel Pastorius reported plans he and Penn had formulated. The new settlement north and west of Philadelphia "we called Germantown or Germanopolis, in a very fine and fertile district, with plenty of springs . . . , well supplied with oak, walnut and chestnut trees, and . . . excellent and abundant pasturage for cattle."[7] In Pennsylvania's towns and farms, these German and Dutch settlers found the fulfillment of their hopes. Here existed opportunity to an extent they had never deamed of in Europe. They enjoyed freedom to practice their own interpretation and understanding of religion under no coercion. In this Quaker province, Pastorius specifically reported that Penn would "compel no man to belong to his particular society, but he has granted to everyone free and untrammeled exercise of their opinions, and the largest and most complete liberty of conscience."[8] New settlers, even though they spoke no English, had equal access to land that was virtually free. Many chose their occupation, which was simply unheard of in Germany. Even servants might come with every prospect of earning free status in a short time, as little as five years, and not exceeding seven years at the longest. That ability to advance in rank and station represented perhaps the most astounding opportunity for all who had found themselves trapped in a hard and fast social rank system on the European continent. From the first settlements in Pennsylvania, they were assured social mobility by Penn's "Holy Experiment."

Germantown and Frankford developed concurrently with Philadelphia. Neighbors included the mixed Dutch, English, and Swedish community of New Castle, forty miles to the south, and the old Swedish village of Upland (near present Chester,

Pennsylvania). Forty-one individuals, members of twelve families, composed the initial group at Germantown. Before a score of years had passed, their town earned a reputation for their excellent woolen and linen cloth. Pastorius held high hopes for a great future for his Germantown. In his adopted Pennsylvania, he made good friends among Penn's Quaker associates as well as among other Germans who joined him there. He exercised much the same leadership as did Thomas Lloyd, Isaac Norris, Samuel Carpenter, Samuel Preston, and the proprietary family.

Much of the confusion and misunderstanding which has surrounded the German settlements of Pennsylvania, arose from their own identification of themselves. Dutchmen from New Netherlands had seized power in the Delaware Bay area from Swedish initial settlements. Almost half the Frankfurt Company of Mennonites in early Germantown were Lowland Dutch. But the Germans who arrived in Pennsylvania spoke their provincial dialects, though most commonly the dialect of the Rhineland—Palatinate. In that dialect, immigrant Germans referred to themselves as *Deitsch* rather than the more formal High German *Deutsch*. Either way, their non-German speaking neighbors ordinarily called them "Dutch" or "Pennsylvania Dutch." Philip Mackenzie, a Virginian traveling through a thoroughly developed Pennsylvania shortly before the American Revolution, described it thus:

Do you know that about one-third of the People in Pennsylvania are Dutch? I mean German but they call them Dutch here. They do not mix in much with the English speaking Settlers. They keep their own Language and the Street Signs here in town [Philadelphia] are in both English and Dutch.[9]

Many and loud have been the debates over relative merits of the designations "Pennsylvania Dutch" and "Pennsylvania German." Both terms are appropriate. "Pennsylvania German" may be technically more accurate, but "Pennsylvania Dutch" from *Pennsylfawnisch Deitsch* is the more common usage.

As time passed, Germans in Pennsylvania were drawn not only from the Mennonite pietists but from other religious groups

as well. The Church of the Brethren, a Baptist sect organized
in the Rhineland in 1708, became known as Dunkers in Pennsylvania. Some came from more highly organized Lutheran,
Reformed, and Evangelical church denominations. Mennonite
and Brethren held their services in plain, austere meetinghouses, whereas the more liturgical Lutheran and Reformed
Germans built Lutheran and Calvinist church buildings in
Philadelphia, Germantown, and the surrounding countryside.
Church Germans often built union churches, that is, church
buildings which held alternating Lutheran and German Reformed services, often on alternating Sundays. Other sects,
especially the smaller groups, continued their German habit
of meeting in members' homes rather than in formal church
buildings.

Among the arrivals in the German settlements at the beginning of the eighteenth century were printers and bookbinders,
so that Germantown was as liberally furnished with craftsmen
as any major town in America. Philadelphia and Germantown
served as centers for the printing and dissemination of German
language tracts and publications. In the mideighteenth century,
English-speaking Pennsylvanians complained that in the province there were more magazines, pamphlets, almanacs, broadsides, and newspapers printed in German than in English. Since
most Germans considered the Bible in their vernacular German
language as basic to religious learning and worship, Pennsylvania
printers produced German Bibles as readily as English ones.

William Penn had promised religious independence to those
who would populate his province. Pastorius and his German
compatriots took Penn at his word. Imitating the English experience, they set up local governmental bodies, often with personnel who did not speak English. Yet Pastorius so admired
William Penn that his call for further German settlers followed
the Penn advertisements almost to the word. Both called for
industrious, ambitious craftsmen and farmers, which benefited
not only the province but also the newcomers. While Pastorius
emphasized that unencumbered land was available, Penn made
certain he had completed purchase arrangements with the
Indians, though by his charter from Charles II that was not
necessary. Pennsylvanians thus were able to avoid the long

and costly litigation which obstructed settlement in New Jersey and other American colonies.

By the year 1700, virtually the whole population of Germantown was European-born. German ways flourished and the wool and linen trade expanded at a rapid rate. Craftsmen in other industries in home and shop created a booming settlement of some "sixty-four families in a very prosperous condition." Pastorius was impelled to purchase additional ten-thousand-acre tracts of land on the outskirts of his new town. That was an unbelievable quantity of land for people who had lived in land-poor Germany, where many farmed steep mountain slopes in a desperate effort to find usable land not already in possession of an owner.[10]

These farmers and artisans had been continually stymied in the German states by a combination of class stratification, feudal landholding, and disruptive wars. Small wonder that they rapidly accepted Pennsylvania as their new home. Few would go back to the Old Country, even for a visit, and still fewer returned to their places of origin to retire. Possessed of lands in their own name and legal right, why should they jeopardize their holdings or their position by even temporary return to the old way? Within fifty years of initial settlement, the Pennsylvania Dutch farmer had made himself indispensable to his New World associates. Their farming skills justly earned them proper appreciation.

As an independent farmer, the Pennsylvania German hired farm laborers from the continuing supply of workers arriving almost daily from Rotterdam. He tended to hire his own countrymen, although Irish or Indian farm workers were not unknown. But Celts were often too independent and Indians proved to be unsuited to farming in the white man's way. Reliance upon German compatriots became the ordinary method. The German farmer worked best where he tilled a soil with a limestone base, which he found beyond the perimeter of English, Welsh, and Irish Quaker settlements. He improved upon methods from the old country and came to rely heavily on both natural fertilizer and limestone for his fields. He shared with the experimenting Quaker the development of clover and legume crops in order to replenish the nitrogen content of the soil, although he remained ignorant of the technical explanation why the new processes succeeded. When a process worked, he wasted little time questioning why.

Linen manufacture in Germantown, from the blue-flowered flax plantings which appeared in the vicinity, compared favorably with the best of German linen from the weavers at Krefeld. Blacksmiths and ironworkers were no less successful in assuming their rightful place in the life of the province. Pennsylvania was by no means self-sustaining by 1700, but she was able to supply more of the wants of life than were many of the colonies which had preceded the settlement of the Quaker province. Certainly German inhabitants contributed significantly to that achievement.

In 1688 the German pietists issued their strong objection to the practice of slavery. They saw it growing insidiously in Pennsylvania, which, they feared, might soon resemble other provinces to the south. Francis Daniel Pastorius voiced the near-unanimous opinion in Germantown:

These are the reasons why we are against the traffick of men-body, as followeth: Is there any that would be done or handled at this manner? . . . Now, tho' they are black, we cannot conceive there is more liberty to have them slaves, as it is to have other white ones. There is a saying, that we shall doe to all men like as we will be done ourselves; making no difference of what generation, descent or colour they are. And those who steal or robb men, and those who purchase them, are they not all alike?[11]

The Pennsylvania Germans emphasized mutual community assistance, the gathering of neighbors at harvest time, or for barn raising, house building, or the fencing of properties. The farm element in the Dutch Country of Pennsylvania continuously resisted the use of Negroes as slave workers, sometimes for reasons not entirely unselfish. Nevertheless, they desired to rid the country of slavery.

In general, German workers and farmers were as dependent upon American English Quaker merchants and traders as they had been upon the ship captains who brought them to America. For essential goods—tools and salt, which were not native to, or suited to, cultivation in the province—the German farmer in the new world had to depend upon his commercial neighbors. Francis Daniel Pastorius acted early and Christopher Sauer later as spokesmen for the German interests. More often, someone like James Logan, or William Parsons, provincial officials who paid little attention to their Quaker background, provided for the Dutch. On other occasions, Richard Peters, William Allen, or Nathan Levy carried out legal or commercial functions on behalf of German-American neighbors. With English values predominant, the Germans of colonial Pennsylvania occasionally found their interests overlooked. Still, landlords and officeholders sought them as dependable workers who would trade their efforts or their votes for guidance.

Essentially, then, Pennsylvania Dutch relations with their English, Welsh, and Irish Quaker or Anglican neighbors proceeded best when each ignored the other and each left the other alone. These people were willing to put up with some inconvenience in return for the essential rights that Pennsylvania granted to all settlers. It mattered not what faith they practiced. Pennsylvania was, as William Allen put it some years later, "the best poor Man's Country in the World."[12]

In the wake of the Glorious Revolution, the earlier friendship between the Penn family and Stuart rulers of England proved to be embarrassing. Indeed, for a two-year period William Penn's government was removed from his control. He faced charges of involvement in the Jacobite movement. In the end, the fealty of William Penn was confirmed and in 1696 the Quaker Holy Experiment was returned to him. Penn and his provincial assistants agreed at that time that a visit by the Proprietor to his lands and people on the Delaware would prove mutually advantageous. So almost literally as the old century gave way to the new, William Penn again arrived for a brief stay to resume his dual role as Proprietor and governor.

Between 1699 and 1701, while residing once more in Pennsylvania, William Penn was plagued by doubts. With all the efforts he had put forth to guarantee rights and privileges in Pennsylvania, was it possible that, some day in the future, the basic freedoms he had assured might be reduced, restricted, or annulled? With that thought nagging at him, he attempted to create a social contract in 1701. Consequently, after appealing to members of the Provincial Assembly and to his political and financial advisers, he set out to rewrite Pennsylvania's basic Frame of Government. A change in the constitution was not unusual, since the original frame of 1682 had already been revised in 1683, 1685, and 1696. After consulting with those individuals he most trusted in government and business, he came up with an entirely new document, the Pennsylvania Charter of Privileges of October 28, 1701. Government was the responsibility of William Penn, the original Proprietor of Pennsylvania, and this product was the culmination of his work. It was even more in advance of his time than was John Locke's novel interpretation of the political basis of English government in the second of his *Two Treatises on Government* in 1690.

In nine major articles, Penn restated all his previous assurances and instructions, but couched them in new language and in a nearly ironclad guarantee of rights for the province. These rights he promised to "all the freemen, Planters and adventurers, and other inhabitants in this Province and Territories." With clear-sighted intent, William Penn struck the keynote in his initial article:

FIRST: Because no people can be truly happy, though under the greatest Enjoyment of their Civil Liberties, if abrig'd of the freedom of their Consciences as to their Religious profession & Worship . . . I do hereby Grant and Declare that no person or persons, inhabiting in this Province or Territories, who shall Confess and acknowledge an Almighty God . . . shall be in any Case molested or prejudiced in his or their persons or Estate, because of his or their Consciencious perswasion or Practise, nor be Compelled to frequent or maintain any Religious Worship, place or ministry contrary to his or their mind. . . .[13]

Renewing his assurances to the inhabitants of Pennsylvania, he emphasized in the last paragraph of the charter that the guarantees of the first article were irrevocable. Neither he nor his heirs, nor anyone acting for them, might legally infringe upon these rights. Should any in power attempt such revocation, "it shall be held of no force or effect."[14]

Legislative decisions were invested in a unicameral assembly, to be called the "House of Representatives of the Province of Pennsylvania," acting with the governor. The appointive Provincial [Governor's] Council had acted as an upper house under previous frames of government. It now stood as an advisory council to the executive, possessing no legislative power in the internal affairs of the province.

By the granting of such extensive rights to the inhabitants of Pennsylvania, Penn closed the first phase of the "Holy Experiment." In the 1690s, the ban against capital punishment was lifted, though only a dozen or so crimes became subject to capital punishment. Penn, now weary of the obligations of personally directing the colony, granted his authority to the Assembly and the lieutenant governor. He sent his oldest son William to assist in the operation of provincial affairs. The son fell in with bad company and never fulfilled the expectations his father held for him. The old proprietor lamented, "Pennsylvania has cost me dear!"[15] Among the citizenry who benefited from Penn's actions were the Germans and Dutch who had settled Germantown and who were, by 1701, as Pastorius indicated, prosperous freemen of the province.

Fellow Germans arriving after 1712 stood to gain the same kind of advantages. Other Germans came into Virginia back counties where they found the soil rich and the climate mild. Palatine settlers there maintained contact with the Pennsylvania Germans. But in some ways, living in Virginia posed more problems. Certain members of the German American community fared well in the South, but to a majority of them, Pennsylvania offered the most compatible conditions.[16]

During the reign of Queen Anne, hard times and economic problems exploded in the German states of Europe, and, as a result, great numbers of Germans, especially from the Palatinate, took advantage of Anne's offer of British protection. After 1712, large numbers of Palatines landed in England, where they maintained a kind of tent city existence. But that palled on both Germans and English, and finally the queen suggested these Palatines emigrate to America. There, these workers might well produce valuable naval stores, badly needed for the extensive maritime ventures of the British Empire. Land was available for such settlement in the upper Hudson and Mohawk River regions of New York province. Palatine Bridge, Stone Arabia, and German Flats are reminders of an experiment which never quite succeeded.

The Germans found upper New York under the influence of Dutch patroons and a thoroughly medieval Dutch land system very unattractive. Many of them moved within a decade or two, traveling southward, from Schoharie or the Mohawk to join a new wave of German Palatine settlement on the Pennsylvania frontier at Tulpehocken. Encouraged by Queen Anne, and the Hanoverian George I after 1714, whole families of displaced refugee Germans came to America. Contrary to royal plans, the vast majority headed directly for Pennsylvania, some of them after a brief stay elsewhere.[17]

Germans and Swiss settled in North Carolina as well, some near the coast, others in the interior. They found a more casual operation of government in that province. Farming was more difficult for them as they found less flat land or slightly rolling hills than in Pennsylvania. Throughout the colonial period both economic and political advances in Carolina lagged behind Pennsylvania developments.

As for Georgia and Nova Scotia, the last two English provinces founded in America, they also welcomed some German settlement, though neither achieved a particularly sizable German population. Throughout the colonial period, the German element in both Georgia and Nova Scotia maintained contact with the Pennsylvania Germans.[18] But German settlements in colonies other than Pennsylvania remained small in size and limited in rights. Germans elsewhere compared their situation with that of the Pennsylvania Dutch. Not only did other provinces suffer by comparison, but many Germans from other provinces gravitated to Pennsylvania. Nonetheless, German settlements continued to have some influence on the history of New York, North Carolina, Virginia, and Nova Scotia.

The early Palatines, Württembergers, and other Germans in Pennsylvania enjoyed the bounty of good land and became the envy of refugees in Europe and elsewhere. German people in Pennsylvania found it profitable to fall in with plans of William Penn, William Allen, Isaac Norris II, and others who vigorously encouraged their settlement in the province. They required very little persuasion. The result was that they flourished and multiplied.

CHAPTER III

The Great Migration: 1717–1754

AFTER THE INITIAL MENNONITE SETTLEMENT OF GERMANTOWN, John Kelpius, Daniel Falckner and other German Mystics arrived in 1694 and settled just west of the now-thriving town of Philadelphia. Others in occasional companies or boatloads continued to arrive sporadically. Scattered German settlements from Germantown to the Ridge, from Falls of Schuylkill to farm villages twenty miles north or sixty miles west of Philadelphia, extended the area of their occupation to much of southeastern Pennsylvania. Henry Muhlenberg later lamented that most of the arrivals before 1710 were "disinclined" to the doctrine of Lutheran or German Reformed churches, but rather consisted of "Baptists (Dunkers as they are called here), Mennonites, Schwenkfelders, or similar kinds."[1] Muhlenberg also noted that many of the sect Germans had embraced Quaker principles either upon landing, or gradually. Few of the migrants seemed capable or desirous of retaining principles of Lutheran or Calvinist German theology. To the Lutheran pastor who, for all practical purposes, founded the German Lutheran Church in America this represented backsliding of the worst type. He proposed much more direct relations between parent churches in Germany and the Netherlands.

In the year 1717, three shiploads of German Palatines arrived, sailed by Captains Richmond, Tower, and Eyers, who supplied provincial authorities with a list of those three hundred sixty-three persons imported from London. Governor William Keith was scandalized by the arrival of so many non-Britons, of whom scarcely a half dozen could speak or understand English. Keith felt constrained to take official cognizance of this threat, which he described in detail as he listed his objections to the Provincial Council. He warned, "This Practice might be of very dangerous Consequences, since . . . as well Enemys as friends might throw themselves upon us."[2] Since the travelers had stopped over in London, his objections carried less weight than Keith intended. But the governor did conclude that all such arrivals, in particular those who spoke no English, at the very least posed a serious threat to the province. They should be required to register with proivncial authorities. He also suggested that they take an oath of allegiance to His Majesty George I, or other oaths or affirmations suitable to the occasion.

Another decade passed before ship lists and Oaths of Allegiance and Abjuration were required by law, but Governors William Keith and Patrick Gordon agreed that some controls were urgently needed. By the time the laws were fully operative (i.e., by 1730) the Reverend John Wilhelmius, a Dutch pastor in Rotterdam, estimated that "15,000 Reformed confessors of the Palatinate" had settled in Pennsylvania. In Philadelphia, however, the number of fifteen thousand German arrivals was confirmed, but with the sad statistic that only about three thousand "truly Reformed people" remained faithful to their principles. Denominationally sound or not, the figure of fifteen thousand German arrivals in Pennsylvania is probably too low, but it will serve as an absolute minimum figure.[3]

Again, the explanation for much of this migration from central and northern Europe lay in the sadly unsettled conditions which prevailed in the Holy Roman Empire, Württemberg, and the Rhineland Palatinate, as in French-held Alsace and Zweibrücken. As the word spread across the face of middle Europe regarding opportunities in America, more and more of that continent's excess population found they needed less and less reason for abandoning the struggle in the old world to set out for fortune and adventure in the new world. In fact some of the most imperative calls to migrate came from North America, from whence the early arrivals wrote enthusiastically to friends and relatives in Germany. They told of vast stretches of land and the ability of each individual to control his own life and to direct the lives of members of his family. Hardships existed and quite a number of the new arrivals failed in their glorious expectations. But it was the successful farmer and new landholder who wrote, extolling the virtues of the new life; few felt impelled to describe their failures or the cost in human lives of the transatlantic voyage.

Commission agents called "newlanders" appeared throughout Germany to arrange travel to America. They were propagandists and occasionally bankers for the projected trip. Departing from German or Dutch port cities, touching always in an English homeland port, emigrants arrived in Philadelphia after four or six or fifteen weeks. Many newlanders charged fees, often exorbitant, for their information, directions, and services. Numerous cases later came to light, where they charged the prospective traveler an amount equal to all the cash he had raised. Then he had to fend for himself when dealing with ship captains, provincial officials, or Pennsylvania merchants or employers on the far side of the water. In lieu of cash, some of the economic leeches who passed themselves off as newlanders took clothing or trunks with the traveler's valuables packed inside as their fee for very dubious services rendered. The young, untrained, inexperienced, and often illiterate voyager found little protection from that kind of confidence man. Despite those who would milk the passengers of their few belongings, most of the travelers who set out for the promised land of Pennsylvania considered that hazard to be one of the final exactions of a European system they detested. Hadn't they been stripped of other values through taxes, fees, or dues in their old semifeudal status?

Some of the adventurers heading for the new land came financially prepared. They moved from positions of mercantile or agricultural self-sufficiency in Europe to an America which offered religious and political opportunities. To many this risk seemed worthwhile. Younger sons had limited prospects under English and continental systems based on primogeniture; consequently many turned to the New World. It was also true that the voyage to America was sometimes the last refuge of a scoundrel. It sometimes offered an escape from an unbearable arranged marriage. To some degree it was the misfits of Europe who made the trip. What resulted was frequently a mixture of religious idealists on one hand and the dregs of society on the other.

But by far the most numerous of those who ventured to

America were the landless farmers (often younger sons, too) and the rural laborers, who were giving up little or nothing of economic advantage. They quite simply risked their lives in that American adventure. Better to take a chance, no matter how farfetched, than to continue the struggle against landlords, petty princes, avaricious churchmen, and the whole of the establishment under which they lived. Most numerous of the prospective passengers for the new world were the redemptioners who chose to sail into a world of indentured servitude rather than struggle any longer in Europe. Their bargains with ship captains were often pitifully brief, as the redemptioner found he had to accept whatever terms the mariner offered. For a ship's passage costing three pounds English currency they might find themselves bound servants for a period of three, five, or seven years in Pennsylvania or New Jersey. A few of them had to pay extra service, costs or damages they incurred while indentured on the American side.

Tens of thousands of the lower ranks of German people joined Irish and other landless persons in this unfree labor service. They served as the major import addition to the labor force in the Middle Atlantic colonies. Because of the eighteenth-century English emphasis on the sanctity of the contract, these white indentured servants found that the courts actually protected their rights, even though they were unfree workers. Since they were indentured, the very document of indenture served as a legal guarantee that they would not be required to labor longer than the time specified. At the termination of their legal temporary servitude, they were assured the tools, clothing, and other possessions of goods provided for by contract. Almost always the tools of his trade and a financial grant for his new free life were promised by the employer.[4]

Early in the eighteenth century the English government, particularly Queen Anne, felt an obligation to large numbers of Palatine Germans and promised them shelter and security. New York was the original destination but soon proved unsatisfactory for a number of reasons, although several thousand Palatines were resettled there. To the present day the characteristic German architectural style is visible in old buildings. Many of the Germans of New York province moved to Pennsylvania, where they found congenial neighbors, also Germans, settled along an agricultural frontier. Conrad Weiser became the most prominent (or the best known) of those who lived a few years in New York province and then later moved south into Pennsylvania.

Large numbers of prospective migrants to America met at Rotterdam, a site very suitable for travelers who had come down the Rhine from their towns and farms upstream. The Neckar River valley had been home for many of them. Rotterdam was a sizable flourishing trade center, one of the two major shipping centers in the Low Countries. In many ways, Rotterdam was the typical trading port of its time. Cluttered dock and shipping facilities and bustling street markets with very crowded living quarters were an indication of its prosperous condition. The addition of thousands of Germans, fleeing from districts their families had inhabited for generations, placed a great strain on the city. Merchants and shippers looked upon them as living cargo, to be accommodated the same way any other cargo was.

Germans found the surroundings strange yet congenial, although for most of them this was merely a stopping place on the way to America. Some few remained in Rotterdam, becoming a part of the varied population of that trading center; but most of the Rhineland travelers, on their way to the promise of the New World, found it too commercial or just too worldly, much as English dissenters a century earlier had felt about the Low Countries. The little substance these poor wanderers had gathered for the voyage to America was dissipated by even a brief spell in or near the port. Many who left their German homes in a solvent financial condition departed Rotterdam without any funds (and very few goods) at all.

Most had found their way down the river valleys of the Neckar and the Rhine by available river transportation. Many others simply walked or pulled their carts of possessions along the paths which fed into the river valley system of roads, highways, and bridges. Whether they brought their families with them depended somewhat on local and personal circumstances. Usually the father of the family tended to make the voyage alone. When it became economically feasible, he later sent for his family. Yet a surprising number of the Palatines and other minority Germans brought all or most of the family with them, uncertain as they were of the prospects at the American terminus of the trip.[5]

Refugees and adventurers from the eastern provinces of Germany ventured down the Elbe to its port of Hamburg. Over the years, Hamburg stood as a distinctly second-choice port, with as many gravitating to Rotterdam as possible.

From the several detailed accounts of the ocean crossing which have come down to us, it seems quite evident that the voyage was the chief hazard or obstacle of the flight from Europe to America. Many who had never sailed before crowded the small vessels with poor sailors and rotten accommodations. They lived for six to eight weeks in cramped space on board, holding fast to the trunks, chests or baggage which contained all their worldly wealth. They were fortunate to find deck space.

Many of the ships which called at Rotterdam were North American vessels looking for return cargo. Among them were some that called Philadelphia home port. Ships, brigs, sloops, brigantines, and pinks were included in the vessels which were used as carriers for the North Atlantic crossing. Of course the masters followed the simple procedure of carrying as much cargo as they could load aboard.

Many of the families on their way to Pennsylvania were crowded onto ships that carried double the number of passengers the vessel could theoretically accommodate. In those cramped and crowded conditions, numerous passengers died at sea. So extensive was the list of casualties that ship captains finally settled upon a formula on how to avoid an excessive number of deaths which reduced their cargo. Occasionally fatalities also made them subject to quarantine regulations in the American ports. They agreed (and by the 1740s made it part of the verbal contract with prospective passengers) that the halfway point of the voyage was the critical time. If a passenger died before the vessel had traveled half the distance to Pennsylvania, then the captain would bear the expense and the corpse was reckoned as no fare. If, on the other hand, a passenger died after the halfway point of the voyage, then his family must pay full fare to America, even though he was buried at sea.

Various accounts of the passage have survived, leaving us a literature of frustration and suffering. Few of the accounts make the experience appear pleasurable; most of them summarize weeks and months of hardship and deprivation. One such description by John George Jungmann of a sea voyage of the ship *Love and Unity*, in the years 1731–1732, relates the problems in detail. Originating at Rotterdam the vessel made port in Falmouth, adding supplies and food there. Twelve days out of Falmouth, the captain declared half the journey had been completed; five months later the ship had not yet sighted land in America, but after nearly sixth months on the high seas, they came ashore at Martha's Vineyard. The emaciated passengers told tales of intense suffering. After eight weeks their bread and water had to be rationed, but during the last six weeks before Christmas, no bread ration was distributed and water was apportioned at a pint per family per day. Ship rats sold at a shilling sixpence and mice at sixpence each, when available. Deaths on this terrible voyage ran exceptionally high. Only four dozen persons reached American soil of an original passenger list of one hundred fifty-six. Barely forty, represented by a mere thirteen heads of families, eventually reached the original destination of Philadelphia, and that by the compassion of a Quaker master who happened upon them at Boston. The survivors claimed the only final choice they had was mutiny, whereby they forced the ship to make a landfall.[6]

Ordinarily, for a six- to eight-week voyage, the captain's costs were modest. To feed hundreds of passengers cost him a few pennies per week. In return for the food he supplied, the master was ordinarily well reimbursed. Cash customers paid from three to five pounds when they landed. Mittleberger claimed that in 1750 adults paid ten pounds for passage. Ten to 20 percent of the passengers paid cash fares. Time of the year, conditions in Rotterdam, and the particular individuals transported determined passenger distribution. Prospective employers (or occasionally, prospective husbands) bought up indentures or contracts of the remaining mature arrivals, at profits which exceeded the cash fares for the masters or ship captains. Underage passengers without families were nearly always apprenticed or bound out.[7] Philadelphia ship captains late in the 1740s generally agreed that human cargo was more profitable than cloth or hemp. Many captains could scarcely restrain themselves as they shipped from Rotterdam with a 100 percent overload of such human cargo. But Quaker captains were apt to find the trade troublesome and not at all to their liking.[8]

Johannes Naas in 1733 and Gottlieb Mittelberger in 1750 provide us with similar discouraging descriptions of the ocean passage under conditions far more normal than Jungmann's. Naas was favorably disposed toward the American venture, while Mittelberger spent four unhappy years in Pennsylvania prior to his return to the German homeland. Yet they thoroughly agreed as to the crowded conditions on shipboard, discomforts and hazards of the voyage, and the toll of women and children who died in transit. Naas wrote of a mother and three children buried together at sea, with the bereaved husband their only survivor; Mittelberger of the generally poor conditions jeopardizing the health of pregnant women passengers and the deaths of parent and newborn as childbirth casualties.[9]

Perhaps due to their different outlook assessment of responsibility also differed. Naas attributed most of the problems to the difficulty of passage and the length of the ocean voyage. He did take the precaution of keeping watch on the ship's compass to assure they were heading directly toward America. Mittelberger, on the other hand, more openly blamed the avarice of newlanders and captains. He insisted all passengers were victims of unfamiliar surroundings as well as sufferers in an economic squeeze.

The ocean passage required six weeks under favorable conditions, but even then preliminaries at Rotterdam and Cowes added days or weeks to the voyage. Debarkation at Philadelphia was sometimes delayed because of wind and tide, or due to mercantile or port requirements and official red tape. Food consumption from the traveler's own stock was apportioned for a six weeks' crossing. When that was gone, they subsisted on meager rations from ship's stores, at inflated prices. Occasional suffering from storm delays or navigational miscalculations, as described above, affected both crew and passengers, but especially the latter.

Journey's end caused loud celebrations and extended rejoicing among the weary passengers. Those who had, weeks earlier, given up all hope of ever reaching port, now offered up thanks to God for their safe arrival after their journey across "the very big sea."[10] Even the broad Delaware River reminded many of them of the familiar Rhine River in its lower reaches, broad, smooth-flowing, and bordered by impressive natural growth on both banks, with occasional dwellings and outbuildings visible.

Philadelphia was an eye-opener for the migrants who arrived between 1717 and 1754. The majority of Germans came from farms or rural villages. Philadelphia was a major population center, although in 1717 its population numbered under ten thousand. Penn's capital was a very young city, just beginning to grow, with much space for development and improvement. The leading Quaker city had been built to accommodate trade, as the number of docks, shops, and taverns particularly illustrated. On the whole it contained broader streets, larger lots (although many tiny ones existed as well), and newer construction than that of any town or city they had passed through on their way to America.

Construction of houses and outbuildings, stores, wharves, and public facilities continued throughout the year. Only a few months of heavy winter slowed building projects. Brick kilns, tannery yards, sawyers' rigs, and blacksmith shops all contributed to industry and the smells in the bustling, busy town. Above all, the fish, salt, pitch, and distinctly maritime odors pervaded the dockside area and often wafted back over Philadelphia.

Wide streets and broad thoroughfares were particularly evident in this model town, although narrow back streets and alleys could be found. At the insistence of William Penn and because of its recent development, Philadelphia was much more a planned town than the ancient and often archaic villages the German migrants had left. Implementation of the Proprietor's plans was often imperfect, but the effort to provide "a green country town" bore results. It was true that new streets and roads under harsh weather conditions became virtually impassable quagmires.

Still, the overall impression was a favorable one, however novel and strange to the migrant in transit. Philadelphia grew rapidly during the great Palatine migration boom. It had a population of perhaps thirteen thousand in 1740 and nearly twenty thousand by 1754; the population of forty thousand by 1776 turned Philadelphia into the second largest British city in the empire, second only to London itself. It had surpassed Boston and all the other port towns of the Atlantic coast in a remarkably short time. Before the end of the high migration of Palatines, Philadelphia enjoyed streetlights and the beginnings of paved cartways and sidewalks along the major streets of the town. It was a source of wonder and pride to the Philadelphia population, who nonetheless complained about the costs of public construction and public buildings.[11]

To the immigrant from Württemberg or the Palatinate, confined to shipboard in the harbor, nearby Philadelphia was both awesome and welcome. In many ways it represented the New Land, no longer far off. Yet, standing as an achievement of English Quaker colonization, it posed obstacles of language, custom, and organization. To a majority of the immigrant Germans, Philadelphia was a symbol of new opportunities, not a reminder of hardship. From the decks of the ships in the river, they literally looked up to the new city, built on high ground, a gateway to the interior river system and the land they coveted.

However, after the hardship and trials of the long sea voyage with its memories of hunger and burials at sea, some of the travelers felt bereft and confused. For the discouraged or the solitary voyager, it was especially gratifying to be greeted by fellow Germans, who were sufficiently organized and concerned to row out to the ship to see who had arrived and where they came from. Often they offered assistance. During the autumn months they brought apples or other fruit of the province and gave them to passengers as a sign of concern and of welcome. Less enthusiastic was the welcome for ships rumored to be arriving with large numbers of passengers ill or dying, even though the need might be far greater under those conditions.[12]

A few, particularly older persons, or those of some rank or

status at home, to whom the prospect of heavy physical effort did not appeal, changed their minds and arranged to return. Others carried out an initial term of obligation and then returned to the more settled procedures of the old country. Gottlieb Mittelberger, for instance, was so disenchanted with the Pennsylvania scene that he tried to discourage possible emigrants from undertaking the journey by pointing out that the cost was too high in money, service, and life itself. Some arrived in such a state of exhaustion or shock that they did not grasp the meaning of indenture as local employers or farmers bid for their service.

Still, in contrast to the number of objectors, the overwhelming majority of arrivals found the balance vastly in favor of Pennsylvania. The port city represented to them an opportunity to break with a past weighted down by obligations and restrictive conditions. Many soon found temporary employment and some permanent jobs. For them Philadelphia was strange but wondrously different from what they had previously experienced. It was an open settlement, where town lots were available and the streets clear and accessible. The port city had no town wall nor fortifications, nor any ruins or semblance of any.[10] More than that, it was hard to tell where town ended and individual farms or plantations began. For most of the arriving Palatine, Swabian, or Württemberger migrants, the roads inland to Germantown, Skippack, Reading, Lancaster, or Easton provided the means to find the farms they sought. In a year, Philadelphia sometimes received migrants numbering more than its own total population. It could provide for only a few of those arrivals, so the destiny of most lay in the interior. These settlers were *bauern,* farmers by training, experience, and social condition, who arrived fully intent on continuing in agriculture.[14]

An initial hazard for many, if not for a majority of the German arrivals, was the settlement of accounts for passage across the Atlantic Ocean. Diffenderfer makes a major distinction between redemptioners and freemen. The former were so handicapped by lack of funds that they signed indenture contracts with the ship captains in Rotterdam. Their status was fixed before departure. The "free willers" were slightly better off. They sailed as free men but submitted to indentures after arrival. However, the new world disapproved of convicts and felons sent from England to become settlers to Maryland and Pennsylvania. But those released from jail on condition that they emigrate constituted a very minor fraction of the whole number of colonists.[15]

Getting off the ship usually proved difficult for those who still owed their passage. Masters were not only reluctant but downright unwilling to see these freights depart, to be swallowed up by back country Pennsylvania, before the debts were collected. Such restriction while at anchor in the Delaware River or even while tied up at a dock seemed to be the ultimate in carelessness or in cruelty. When Peter Kalm landed as an honored passenger with Captain Lawson of the ship *Mary* in 1748, he was shocked to hear orders to the second mate who stayed aboard. "Let no one of the German refugees out of the ship unless he pays for his passage or someone else pays for him."[16] As much as two months might pass awaiting completion of the work contract. Occasionally in the purchase or assignment of indentures, parents and children were separated, a cause for concern and sorrow. Some Germans pointed out that being in service was advantageous for the young. Servants obtained meals and shelter, whereas on their own it might have been much more difficult.[17]

Redemptioners came as early as 1728, although the British use of unfree indentured servants in a relatively free-labor province dated back almost to the establishment of the colony. Most fortunate of all were those persons indentured into rural households of fellow Germans in the upper reaches of the province. There congeniality and the ring of familiar speech prevailed. Familiar social custom helped ease the cultural shock of the change from Palatinate German conditions into those of English custom and tradition.

At any rate, the vast majority of new arrivals found their way into rural areas and agricultural situations. Bypassing the already developed English and Welsh farm tracts, they settled beyond, where they found themselves filling out territory stretching to the Blue Mountains in Lancaster, Berks, and Northampton counties. In that process, a great change in cultural patterns took place. Whereas most immigrants chose to develop farms on open meadow land, the Pennsylvania Dutch were apt to choose land where the woods were thick. Clearing the ground was hard work, but where trees flourished they might expect rich soil. So extensive was the available land that each farmer could build his house, barn, and outbuildings directly on the land of his own farmstead. Thus farm villages with farm fields fanning out like spokes of a wheel beyond the hub of homes at its center did not fit local need and did not develop. Where the religious principles of a brotherhood sect emphasized ownership in common, village settlement did occur. But virtually all farms were individual family holdings. One farmer, with a solitary building or a few small buildings, was separated from his near neighbors by field, forest, valley, or mountain. Common pastures and village greens were absent in Dutch farming areas. The self-contained independent farm represented a major change in agricultural style.

In attachment to the land, diligence in working the farms, and firm faith in the values of an agricultural life, the Pennsylvania Dutch farmer was among the best producers of salable crops, especially foodstuffs, in America. Despite the tendency of agricultural elements to resist change and to hew to old, established formulas, these men adapted to the soil and to the conditions they found. They were happily at home using limestone soil with the conditioning built into the very composition of the soil itself. As did other national groups, these Dutch husbandmen proceeded to build their houses, barns, and outbuildings in an architectural style resembling dwellings in Germany. Shape, height, and floor plan showed the German influence; in a few rare cases the combination of human habitation and animal shelter under one roof solved a problem of space utilization, while saving on material and the cost of extra construction.

With surprising speed and thoroughness, the Dutch farmer did accept and use early innovations of experimental agriculture, particularly where he had English farming neighbors. Many adopted the new methods. In some cases Dutch and English farmers stood in vigorous competition in the growth of grain crops and processed products (wheat and bread, for instance). In other cases, especially when a Quaker farmer lived on the next plot or plantation, or in instances where Pennsylvania farmers farmed for the English Quakers on a rental basis, cooperation (at least in the field) was thorough and productive.

However, many of the English-origin farmers tended to look down socially on the Dutch, and sometimes described them only as "The Dutchman," "Old Dutchman," or "wife of the Dutch miller." But the very same Quaker farmer-merchant, in the course of his daily tasks, shared information as to mixture of crops and efficient field use to improve yields of his fellow Dutch farmers. In many cases both English and German farmers sent their grain to the same mills for grinding into flour, but so great was the need for grain and flour that competition remained friendly, open, and cooperative.[18]

The Pennsylvania Dutchman learned local crop procedures also from the Indians and absorbed other useful information of Indian origin by way of the English Quaker farmers who had associated closely with Indians. The Indian simply abandoned much of his agricultural know-how as his association with the white population grew; hence much practical information was lost. In great measure, the extent of agricultural sharing and borrowing reflects the relative significance each group attached to agriculture. Indians found farming tedious, degrading, and a great waste of time, whereas the Dutchman, with few exceptions (city dwellers, craftsmen, or merchants), found in agriculture his real interest and true occupation.

Dialect differences continued to exist in German as in other languages of the eighteenth century. German and Swiss settlers of Pennsylvania spoke a dozen dialects of German. In a way, German particularism strengthened language distinctions and differences. As for English-speaking Pennsylvanians and their German-speaking fellows, there was a barrier of language. Although many in both groups found it advantageous to learn a few words or phrases in each other's tongues, this casual approach also resulted in misunderstandings through inaccurate or erroneous translations.[19] English remained the official language and the language of the majority of Pensylvanians. As a practical solution, Germans tended to congregate geographically with other Germans, a situation which became very familiar in later American minority experience.

Still, non-English-speaking arrivals were able to retain their own tongue, for Pennsylvania laws, unlike those of other provinces, did not force them all to learn English. Of course, even those Germans who continued to speak their own dialect at home found the use of English was required once they passed beyond the limits of their local community.

Among the Germans of Pennsylvania some used their language abilities quite profitably as interpreters on the frontiers or as guides or agents for the government in Indian areas.[20] Such men as Conrad Weiser and Daniel Claus for Pennsylvania and New York served in the best interests of the province and the Indians. Not only were they fluent in numerous Indian tongues, but they were also equally adept in English and German. Conrad Weiser clarified and explained nuances and shades of meaning in Mohawk or other Iroquois languages, or in Delaware, at numerous conferences and in treaty terms; Claus followed somewhat the same pattern, especially in New York, and eventually translated the Book of Common Prayer into Mohawk for use in New York and Canadian areas of Anglican influence. Frederick Christian Post and David Zeisberger carried German usage deep into Indian territory while still retaining contact with their Pennsylvania Dutch constituency.[21]

The vast majority of the Pennsylvania Dutch remained content in their own section, carving out their livelihood and their economic and social patterns in the forests and lands of interior Pennsylvania. Most spoke nothing but their own German dialect, requiring no other language for their daily needs.

However, the presence of non-English-speaking Germans caused anxiety to some of their neighbors. The Germantown settlers had seemed content to remain within the bounds of a large but nonetheless well-defined space. Not so the eighteenth-century arrivals, who spread out into entire valleys and claimed much of the good farming land still available. Moreover, after establishing a farmstead, they often applied for and purchased additional tracts of neighboring land, or they encouraged other friends and relatives to do so.

The major influx of German settlers which began in 1716 or 1717 caused little concern at first, for all understood that in order to prosper the province must gain in population. But the increase was so steady that their large numbers came to be viewed as a threat by provincial officials. Moreover, the German migration increased decade by decade well into the eighteenth century. Even the most careful estimates of entering Germans are subject to error, but by the clamor against them we can judge that by 1727 they were considered a major threat. Fear that the numerous Germans would engulf the original settlement led the new governor, Patrick Gordon, to call for regulations. He asked that arrivals declare their good faith by an oath of allegiance to the king and a promise of fidelity to the Proprietor, "and that a List shall be taken of the Names of all these People, their several Occupations, and the Places from whence they come."[22] Shortly, to add assurances of political reliability, a renunciation of the Stuart pretenders was also required of them.

While these lists, oaths and registry were restrictive, and for a time accompanied by a duty of two pounds per alien entry, the requirements seem not to have slowed Palatine arrivals to any great extent. The duty on German servants entering Pennsylvania was double the duty on Irish servants. This is another instance of official discrimination against the Germans. Quaker merchants and farmers, speaking on behalf of the imported Germans, demanded and finally achieved removal of that financial imposition.[23] Many Irish and Scotch-Irish servants and freemen also swarmed into Pennsylvania with the additional Germans, thus reminding established inhabitants of the growing competition for preferable locations.

Particularly among the Palatines who had arrived early in the reign of George I, and who had established farms and demonstrated their economic value to the province, the desire to attain citizenship rights through naturalization began to mount. Mild requests for a naturalization bill as early as 1721 failed to bring forth legislation until several years later, and then in a form (requiring sworn statements of their religious faith and value of property) that Governor William Keith refused to approve.

Aware of the increasing public concern, the Pennsylvania Dutch once again raised the issue, this time successfully. In October 1729, the Pennsylvania Assembly passed a bill, soon approved by Governor Patrick Gordon, extending the same "privileges" which the native-born subjects of Great Britain" enjoyed in the province, to those "various Protestants," German, who took an oath of loyalty. General requirements included ownership of one hundred acres of land, of which ten acres were improved or cultivated land, or possession of an income of ten pounds per year. The new subject of the Crown must also be a freeman to qualify. Naturalizations needed approval of the Provincial Council, so for a time lists were included in the *Colonial Records*.[24] Initially German petitioners were few in number, but as the migrants became acclimated to the Pennsylvania scene, they gradually availed themselves of their rights and privileges. Most of them had to be educated slowly, and in pragmatic ways, to qualify for advantages and opportunities their English counterparts took for granted.

The large number who entered Pennsylvania from German-speaking areas of Europe indicate just how attractive Penn's Province was, especially at the peak of migrations from 1749 to 1754. During the first of the heavy years, twenty-two ships carrying more than six thousand "Palatines" debarked at Philadelphia. In the five years of the most intensive movement, no less than seventeen thousand Germans arrived, and early estimates ranged as high as thirty thousand in the half decade.[25] To be sure, some of these voyagers settled on New Jersey soil, at least temporarily, while a few strayed off to Maryland, Virginia, or Delaware. Crowded ships and poor conditions on board also meant that casualties of the crossing ran high during the peak period. It was then that Gottlieb Mittelberger made his observations, complaining strenuously of the unfavorable aspects of the passage.[26]

Leading men in Pennsylvania also took note of the excessive numbers of German immigrants. Benjamin Franklin in 1751 wrote his asides on populating Pennsylvania with "Palatine boors," a concern which received more prominence in later political struggles. William Smith, Anglican priest and educator, issued additional warnings in 1754, when he charged that the close-knit groups of Germans were probably subversive.[27]

Agglomeration of Pennsylvania Dutch in the province continued at a reduced rate for another twenty years. Newcomers never equaled the pace of the years 1749 to 1754. The natural increase in population continued to add to these German-speaking Pennsylvanians at a rate that sent their numbers well over one hundred thousand by the early 1770s. The combination of continued immigration, large families among the Dutch, and their skillful and successful tilling of the soil served to underscore the threat posed by this foreign settlement, especially to the non-German, English-speaking elements of Pennsylvania's population. The Pennsylvania Assembly, concerned for the health and safety of the province, as well as for the German migrants, received a petition against "the overloading of ships bringing German immigrants to Philadelphia."[28] The Assembly passed bills regulating the importation of Germans and required ship captains to be more accountable. Governor James Hamilton agreed with the Assembly and presented his arguments to Thomas Penn, reminding the proprietor of the political strength Pennsylvania's Germans might someday muster. The Assembly bill which he signed "arose intirely from the Principal Men of the German's Side, on account of a prodigeous mortality on board some of the Ships." In the end, the Pennsylvania laws were invalidated by the Board of Trade.[29]

CHAPTER IV

Pennsylvania Dutch as Settlers

As THE MOST CONTROVERSIAL GROUP OF ADOPTED PENNSYLVANIANS, the Dutch had their sympathizers as well as vocal opponents. Their tendency to settle in areas that were separate and quite thoroughly German, and their continued use of their own German dialect, made them unpopular neighbors to vast numbers of English-speaking inhabitants of Pennsylvania. Although we now understand that this was one way of keeping their identity while adjusting to the new surroundings, their contemporaries did not take such an objective view. Benjamin Franklin hedged. He wavered between compliments and criticism, although he seemed most earnest in 1751 when he insisted that the government should "Anglify" these devotees of the *Muttersproch* as rapidly as possible; else they would surely "Germanize" Pennsylvania.[1]

Considering the status of the German language as a legal language in the province (from the efforts of Francis Daniel Pastorius and others), most of the Pennsylvania Germans showed no tendency to abandon their old speech. Accepted in law in the form of deeds or wills, the dialect of the Pennsylvania Dutch exhibited a remarkable tendency to survive, even though the Dutch were surrounded by English-speaking neighbors. Continued use of the language became a matter of importance to the Dutch. Carried over to the twentieth century, it became "the oldest immigrant language still in daily use in the United States."[2]

In general the association between Pennsylvania Dutch farmers and craftsmen and the English Quaker establishment of the province was a mutually beneficial one. As successful and productive agrarians, the German-speaking population added considerably to the wealth of the colony, expanding the settled

61

area and increasing the value of properties held by earlier arrivals. As the Dutch (and, slightly later, the Scotch-Irish) expanded the concentric arcs of settlement further and further away from Philadelphia, they not only increased the colony's production by extensively farming those lands but expanded the trade of the province.

Their English, Irish, or Welsh fellow provincials tended to lump all "Dutch" into a single stereotype, usually defined as "Dumb Dutch" by some of their Scotch-Irish associates. Several distinctly different groups of Germans were in many cases as mutually antagonistic as the English and the Scottish Presbyterians. The one common factor was the language used by these German emigrants, even though they brought a dozen dialect variations with them, and in Pennsylvania settled into a half-dozen local valley dialects as well. The admixture of English words tended to make *Pennsylfawnisch Deitsch* a distinctive language, never to be incorporated into *Hoch Deutsch*.

The greatest differences in style, outlook, expression, or even costume, centered in the religious types. After all, great numbers of them had left the familiar surroundings of their German valleys in order to assert their own beliefs and values. They would not easily relinquish those particulars of religion once they became established in the New World.

Most adamant in their ways, or most insistent upon retaining specified and fixed procedures in both religious and secular affairs, were the German sects, the Plain People. Just as in the German states before their migration, each sect clung to its own literal interpretation of beliefs. They set their daily tasks and their worship in harmony with those particular concepts or scriptural principles. They punished their own numbers who strayed from the revealed way, and they resisted attempts of "nonsect" neighbors to investigate, or even understand, the source of those differences. Regulation of dress or costume was certainly no rarity in the eighteenth century, but the absolute rules of dress and the penalties for any departure from those rules seemed unduly harsh to many of their contemporaries in Pennsylvania. By the twentieth century the exaggerated differences appear even greater.

Limits were most often determined by the sect itself. One

means of reinforcing the values of the particular religious sect was an insistence upon marriage within the denomination. In a Quaker province where Friends were read out of the Society for marrying outside its limits, this did not seem a particularly exceptional requirement. In fact, some of the small sects exerted considerable pressure upon the young people, virtually forcing them to marry within the bounds so set. It was both socially and economically disastrous to contemplate marriage outside the religious circle. As a result, among Amish, Mennonite, Dunker, or Schwenkfelder groups ten or a dozen family names became almost identifying labels, showing the sect to which a person or family belonged.

Of course, as religious bodies, they continued to argue theological interpretations. The values of adult baptism, the status of the eucharist, and other aspects of the relation between God and man were topics hotly debated, at least by the leaders. But even among the members, buckles or buttons, plain cloth or decorated fabrics, bearded or clean-shaven visages often engendered disputes and limited the course of their actions. But again, such minute variations in principle and style were causes that had led many to Pennsylvania; to overturn such regulations in America would be as unthinkable as to have accepted princely mandates in the Europe they had left.

Most important to their own security and status was the right of each group to set its own rules and regulations. So long as they did not break the laws of Pennsylvania they were allowed freedom in their religious exercises. It did not mean that non-Germans understood them. It did not even assure the plain sect freedom from provincial interference. But it did offer them far better guarantees than they had ever enjoyed in their home countries, and for the most part the small religious organizations survived and sometimes flourished in their American experience.

Except for those few who settled in the towns of Philadelphia, Germantown, Reading, Easton, and Lancaster, the plain folk almost unanimously followed agrarian pursuits. They tilled the soil with religious devotion, and they harvested the bounty of the land accompanied by prayers of thanksgiving to God who had led them to this land of promise. In time, entire valleys were settled by members of a single group, Amish in one distinguishable area, Mennonite in a neighboring valley, Dunkers in yet another, and other sects just across the ridge in the valley beyond. Sometimes denominations mixed together, but the tendency was separate settlements within a limited area.

Benjamin Franklin shared the view of some more cosmopolitan Pennsylvanians that such clannish practices were not unqualified blessings. Indeed, in 1751, Franklin suggested that it was time to start spreading the Pennsylvania Dutch throughout the province. That would leaven Dutch ways and language by forcing them to associate with, and to deal with, less likeminded neighbors, and to force them to use English for their transactions.[3]

The Amish and the Old Order Mennonites passed religious and folk customs orally from one generation to the next, for the very keeping of church or religious records was considered unworthy. This further tended to concentrate settlement in a given area. Even after two centuries, some cohesive remnants exist with distinguishable groups of Schwenkfelders in the Perkiomen Valley, Mennonites in upper Montgomery County (old Philadelphia county) or in the Oley Valley of Berks, and the Amish quite visible in the Conestoga Valley and in Lancaster and Lebanon Counties.[4]

The Plain Dutch lived by church regulations which seemed to outsiders to be more anachronistic with each passing generation. Change in religious structure was severely limited. But in their farm procedures, the Amish, Mennonites, and Schwenkfelders seemed willing to accept some new ideas as to crops, tools, and methods of harvesting, at least in the early decades of their settlement in Pennsylvania. This tendency soon slowed, and by the late nineteenth century, they became less adaptable than in earlier years. The result is somewhat confusing. Amish and Mennonites built barns in the New World which were almost the same as in Germany, yet they soon accepted corn they had never grown in Europe. They gradually introduced tobacco culture in south central Pennsylvania as a money crop, though it had never been a product of the Germanies, and despite Amish and Mennonite rejection of the use of tobacco among themselves. They did sustain their general suspicions concerning education and remained content with a basic, quite minimal schooling, appropriate for their practical farm life. Some New Mennonites, desirous of more education, split away in the nineteenth century. They not only established schools, seminaries, and colleges but also broke with Old Order Mennonites on the matter of church records, which the New Order began to keep.

The plain sects gained such a reputation for industry, frugality, and abstention from wasteful living that many of their neighbors assumed their members to be wealthy misers. In some cases the description was justified, but it was by no means universally true. Wherever Amish families lived they tended to remain as much aloof from other Germans in the vicinity as they did from the Englishmen or Indians nearby. Virtually all the Amish, Schwenkfelders, and Dunkers settled on farms.

Many of the so-called Church Germans also adhered to the rural life they knew. But a larger percentage of Lutheran or German Reformed found it feasible to live in the growing towns of southeastern Pennsylvania. Quite early in the eighteenth century, "German Lutheran" and "German Calvinist" church buildings were erected in Philadelphia, Easton, Reading, and Allentown. These edifices, basic to a congregation that was partly urban and partly rural, served as centers of social life as well, quite in the spirit of the eighteenth-century American church.

Although in some respects they were competitive, the Lutheran and Reformed Germans found they had a great deal in common in the colony. Theological differences existed, but the two groups of Church Germans found few pragmatic disagreements to mar their relationships. After all, on major matters, Lutheran and Reformed congregations were in accord: a trained, educated, consecrated ministry led their worship, an elected church council or consistory assisted the pastor in practical, mundane matters of the church, and the service was conducted in German, the vernacular language of their Bible, hymnbooks, and prayerbooks. They were both somewhat apprehensive of their English Quaker and Anglican acquaintances. The Church Germans felt general scorn and disdain for the splintering, quibbling sects of the province. A working agreement existed among Church Germans of the New World fully half a century before the Prussian attempt to combine these elements into an Evangelical Union in the post-Napoleonic German lands of Europe.

Over the years the Lutheran and Reformed Church elements in Pennsylvania began to dispute who could claim to have been first on the local scene. In point of fact, after a 1683 German settlement which was almost entirely Mennonite in form, and the experiences of several solitary German mystics along the Schuylkill and Wissahickon around 1700, Church German origins in the period of 1717 and 1726 were simultaneous, so that arguments over priority have been generally futile. What they have chiefly revealed is that, in the absence of the trained clergy, church members of both denominations undertook the organization of congregations themselves, with relatively successful results. With the arrival of clergymen, congregations more effectively organized and fewer local churches failed to survive.[5]

Thus among the Lutheran elements, congregations established by Daniel Falckner and John Caspar Stoever remained tenuous, and their church did not achieve a firm foothold in Pennsylvania until Henry Melchior Muhlenberg arrived in 1742. Gradually other trained and dedicated clergy helped organize local congregations from Philadelphia to the Susquehanna and from Chester County on the Maryland border to the wilds of what became Northampton County on the upper Delaware. Convincing qualified clergymen to take on the American problems was no easy matter, and fellow clergymen regarded Henry Muhlenberg as somewhat odd when he became enthusiastic about possibilities in Pennsylvania.[6] Muhlenberg's efforts to raise his Augustus Lutheran Church to European standards brought Gottlieb Mittelberger to Pennsylvania as church organist, organ builder, and choirmaster in the mideighteenth century. The experiment proved abortive when Mittelberger returned to Württemberg in 1754, unable to accept frontier conditions or the colonial population any longer.[7] Success in recruiting brought other pastors to the difficult work here, although the Lutheran church in Pennsylvania received no state support as in Saxony, Prussia, and other German states with Lutheran rulers. Muhlenberg diligently organized Pennsylvania congregations and also coordinated Lutheran churches in Virginia, New Jersey, New York, and even Nova Scotia and Georgia.[8]

Just as complicated were the efforts of the German Reformed (or German Calvinists as the Philadelphia newspapers of the time referred to them). Their local organization in Pennsylvania began in 1725. To be legitimate, their sacraments must be administered by consecrated clergy; thus both the efforts and credentials of John Philip Boehm were questioned, though he founded no less than four churches. Not until the Reverend Michael Schlatter arrived at the end of the 1740s did the Reformed element have a leader to rival Muhlenberg. Nevertheless congregations organized between 1725 and 1747 continued to function despite doubts as to the qualifications of their pastors. Schlatter alienated many of the Reformed German members by his zeal to cooperate with English authorities in matters of schooling and use of the English language.[9]

German Reformed congregations in Philadelphia city and county and from Bucks to Lancaster counties had been formed by 1750, though some of them consisted of only a few dozen members. To the problem of small, scattered congregations, three solutions appeared. First, the minister rode the circuit, visiting numerous outlying small churches and often holding worship service, baptizing, and marrying as he traveled. These itinerant preachers shared an experience common to practically all rural denominations of eighteenth- and nineteenth-century America. A second solution was pragmatic: Sunday's minister also served as weekday schoolmaster in many of the Lutheran and Reformed congregations, a procedure also practiced by Mennonites and Brethren. That not only kept the minister occupied on weekdays as well as the Sabbath, but it also gave him an income to supplement the meager returns (often in kind rather than cash) from the congregations he served.

The third solution was singularly Pennsylvanian, possibly because of the concentration of Church German populations in that arc of settlement beyond English, Welsh, and Irish Quakers around Philadelphia. Beyond the Germans lay frontier settlements of the Scotch-Irish in the west, or the Connecticut Congregationalists in Pennsylvania's Wyoming Valley to the north.

Their unique solution was the Union Church. It really meant that separate Lutheran and Reformed congregations would share the same church building, burial grounds, and property. Worship services met in the single edifice every Sunday, simply alternating Lutheran and Reformed services. Both denominations survived, even though lacking in members, by a single effort of construction. Naturally some haggling followed, and pragmatic questions of prior right or of predominance arose occasionally. Although both congregations met under the same roof, ordinarily each had their separate liturgy and Bibles. They sometimes shared psalters or hymnals, since both continued for years to use the German language for worship.[10]

Although the incidence of the Great Awakening has been examined in detail for many denominations in many provinces, its effect among the Pennsylvania Dutch has not yet been thoroughly studied. One difficulty in such analysis are the sparse records and the primitive organization of Lutheran and Reformed Congregations by 1740, although a specialist in that area, John Frantz, is now prepared to show that the Great Awakening had a major impact in the Dutch country. The liturgical denominations in America were scandalized by the activities and emotionalism of the Awakening. The Germans, tending to avoid emotional outbursts in public, looked askance at unusual (and seemingly unsuitable) conduct of the Sects and were greatly concerned about these other new emotional religious disturbances.[11]

Palatines of the Mohawk Valley of New York, who made Pennsylvania their home eventually, were of Lutheran and Reformed origins. Conrad Weiser was surely one of the more prominent men who traveled overland from central New York to central Pennsylvania. Pastor Henry Muhlenberg married Weiser's daughter, Anna Maria, who had been born at Schoharie, New York. In Pennsylvania, Reformed and Lutheran Dutch settled not only in established counties but also in new counties erected on the northern and central frontiers. The Blue Mountain frontier of Northampton County, settled mostly by Church Germans and Moravians, occupied former Indian territory.[12]

The Moravians were among the most intriguing as well as the most unusual of the Pennsylvania Germans. Under Count

Nicholas von Zinzendorf, they came to northeastern Pennsylvania near and above the Forks of the Delaware (confluence of the Delaware and Lehigh Rivers). Heirs of the oldest attempt at Protestant Reformation, Moravians enjoyed a revival under Zinzendorf in Saxony. In 1741 and 1742, he led them to Pennsylvania, founding experimental towns and schools near the Lehigh from Nazareth to Bethlehem and present-day Allentown. Zinzendorf experimented with community living and the performance of assigned duties in the model towns he set up at Nazareth and Bethlehem. In Pennsylvania, the count had a far larger dream: he planned to unite all the Protestant German groups in the province. The plan failed because there was no mutual response from the groups he attempted to amalgamate. The Moravians followed episcopal organization and kept extremely thorough records. Even though Nicholas von Zinzendorf returned to Saxony, he assured the experimental communities in America of his continued support. The last of the bonds between the Moravian church and the town of Bethlehem were not severed until 1845.[13]

A particularly gratifying aspect of the Moravian program in Pennsylvania, and later in Ohio, was their enthusiasm for the conversion of the Indians to Christianity. In a variety of missionary travels by John Heckewelder, Christian Post, and David Zeisberger, these and other Moravian leaders attempted to show by their own living examples what Christianity offered the Indians. They also looked upon the Indians of Pennsylvania and Ohio as heathens especially placed there by the Divine Power to encourage mission work in the New World. Moravians adopted an astonishingly modern concept of Indians as children of God. They literally regarded the Indians as men, whereas most other European settlers in America continued to class the Indian as an animal who had some human traits.[14]

One of the major achievements of the *Unitas Fratrum*, or United Brethren of Moravians, was the much needed but exceedingly difficult project of bridging the gap between New World Europeans and the native Indians. By reason of their benevolence and their concern for the welfare of individual Indians, the Moravians achieved a position of greater trust among the Indians than did any of their neighbors. Pennsylvania's Quakers, who granted the Indians status they did not enjoy in other provinces, happily watched the Indians depart as their lands were purchased by Penn or his successors. The Moravians on the other hand, almost from the moment of their arrival, attempted to win the Indians to a Europeanized style of living. In a way and to a degree that was quite unusual, the Moravians attempted to convert the Indians to a way of life and a state of mind that approached the Moravian ideal of cooperative living.

Moravian preachers and teachers met the Indians on their home territory and on terms of equality. At Gnadenhütten, just above the Lehigh Gap, beyond the Blue Mountains, a small but flourishing colony of Indians attempted to live in a community with white advisers. Some of the Indians were brought there from the New York border and were resented by the Delawares. Mission posts to the Delawares were also set up at Meniolagomeka and Wechquetank, slightly to the north of their original experiment at Gnadenhütten. Twenty years later in the wilds of eastern Ohio, a second series of settlements, including a new Gnadenhütten, attempted to rally the displaced Delawares and Shawnees to Moravian standards once again. Above all, Moravians attempted to provide the Indians with the tools and the experience needed to survive in an increasingly white man's world. Experiences at both Gnadenhüttens were promising, but both failed when beset by armed fighting in the two wars for empire. The lasting settlement so earnestly desired by Moravian leaders was not forthcoming; white and Indian affairs had already deteriorated too far. Failure did not result from lack of effort or enthusiasm among the Moravians.[15]

Moravian community experiments at Bethlehem produced far more lasting results, possibly because they required a transitional or novice service that weeded out temporary enthusiasts. A few Indians were brought to Bethlehem for training, but only minor success and few lasting results among the Indians were achieved. The Moravian experiments at Bethlehem attracted other Germans, not only Sect members or those who tended toward pietist or mystic explanations. A good many distressed or dissatisfied Church Germans also found new solutions to old doubts there. Those individuals may have fled from the more traditional ways of the Lutheran or the Reformed church. Reformed and Lutheran pastors looked upon such conversions as spiritual body-snatching by the Moravians. Nazareth and Bethlehem stood as monuments to the Moravian principles, but were looked upon with suspicion by Dutch and English neighbors alike. The very success of their community living and the exclusiveness of their work aroused doubts and jealousy among the more orthodox in their vicinity. Zinzendorf and the Bishops Cammerhof and Spangenberg ran a highly organized movement, and no member subjected himself to greater discipline than any of the three.

Specialized religious music, most spectacularly the trombone choir, contributed to the *Unitas Fratrum* as a unique religious achievement in Pennsylvania. Doubts, suspicion, and misunderstanding greeted their efforts, but then some of the most violent critics, such as William Smith, objected as much to their German forms and language as he did to their hidden past. Moravians were accustomed to adversity through three full centuries of European misunderstandings; more of the same in the New World affected them very little. In Pennsylvania they found rich opportunity, available land, and a productive soil. With the expression of God's bounty to them, why should they be concerned with the reactions of petty jealousies around them?

Moravians did not lend themselves easily to grand generalizations; yet they hold a rather unusual place in American life. Although they appeared to be mystics, they were not; they worked in an episcopal framework quite different from the Anglican episcopacy; they experimented with the idea of religious community which ran counter to majority religious assumptions. For these and other reasons they were suspect. Especially through the person of Nicholas von Zinzendorf they retained their association with the German scene. They were truly, as a recent writer explained, men "of two worlds."[16]

Another Pennsylvania German experiment in communal living was the Ephrata Cloisters of Johann Conrad Beissel. This community arose and collapsed within a period of fifty years. Beissel was a mystic, albeit an authoritarian one, and his base at Ephrata was regarded as a local scandal by most of the surrounding countryside, and apparently by some within the Cloister itself. He nearly succeeded in making Ephrata a self-sufficient community; he certainly tried hard enough to make it a success. Male and female separation was the general rule, although with some exceptions, but Beissel was a sufficiently controversial pioneer in social forms to make himself and his associates suspect. That Johann Beissel attempted to be pragmatic as well as mystic is adequately demonstrated by the forge and shops for making tools and utensils, and in the print shop where the community's needs in books and printed materials were also provided. Most of his converts were from the Seventh-Day Baptists, also called Dunkers, but at Ephrata converts were welcomed from any and all sources. They were required only to indicate their sincere concern for their soul, a willingness to work within the framework of the community, and a renunciation of past errors.[17]

Unfortunately for the success of the Cloisters at Ephrata, dissension appeared both early and late. Beissel himself was the main cohesive force. While he lived, despite numerous problems, he managed to keep the experiment hanging together. After his death the members lacked any figure to rally around. Perhaps some challenge to Beissel's motives was inevitable, but he did run a very restrictive community. Some of the converts had presumed they would experience a relief from the daily pressures of work and family. Many left disillusioned.

In a way that Beissel would have considered unimportant, one of the great contributions of the community is the reminder of Old World architectural style which the *Saal* and other buildings provide. With all his efforts to bring a fresh, positive alternative to the outdated religious and social forms he saw around him, Beissel, or rather the Ephrata Cloisters, are remembered for their building style, suspended, as it were, in time.[18]

Ephrata represents one of the alternatives in socioreligious solutions which Pennsylvania offered. Beissel was kin to Zinzendorf in that respect. One of the old complaints, uncomplimentary to both social experiments, was the charge "that the Moravian Brethren have too high a regard for marriage and the people of Ephrata have no regard for it at all." Beissel attempted to change too much too rapidly. That always arouses opposition, as it surely did in mid-eighteenth-century Pennsylvania.[19]

Only a few German Catholics ventured to America in the eighteenth century. Even those small numbers split into two groups in Pennsylvania. One group settled in Philadelphia, where they built and staffed a German Catholic church near the heart of the city. Another handful of Catholic settlers headed for the open spaces and rolling farmland of the upper end of Philadelphia County (later Montgomery County). They spilled over into southeastern Berks County and in both jurisdictions enjoyed their religious rights. They were, of course, looked upon as a singular nuisance by most Protestant Germans.

Pennsylvania Dutch settlements were essentially German with some Holland Dutch and a smattering of French Huguenots. But one additional European source of settlers was Switzerland. Many Swiss, virtually all of them German-speaking, joined the pilgrimage from the European scene to Pennsylvania. They, too, found Pennsylvania the land of opportunity, producer of plenty, and the locale of rich farmlands such as they never dared to dream of while in Switzerland. In recent years, particularly throughout the twentieth century, Switzerland has earned the reputation of being peaceloving, isolated, and easygoing— a pastoral dream, in short. The Swiss of the eighteenth century would rapidly remind us that such descriptions in no way belonged to their seventeenth- or eighteenth-century homeland. Rather they faced recurring petty wars, skirmishes, and dynastic struggles then so familiar in central Europe.

Whole settlements of Swiss bunched together in the heart of the rural segment of Philadelphia County, especially between the years 1716 and 1735. Since all arrivals in those years were lumped into the designation "Palatine," Swiss origin is not indicated in the ship lists. However, research into the names and family origins provides evidence of Swiss background. Lederachs, Hunsickers, and Leibenguths (or Livengoods as Anglicized) staked out claims to some of the best farmland in the midst of Mennonite and Lutheran German settlements; yet they continued to regard themselves as distinctive in origin.[20]

Four colonial governors of Pennsylvania, Keith, Gordon, Thomas, and Hamilton, in turn expressed their concern over the large number of Palatines entering Pennsylvania. Yet each argued the necessity of population increase, for Pennsylvania needed more people to develop its potential. Governor James Hamilton, in 1750, stated that "German settlement was indeed necessary," although he would have preferred "persons who understand our Laws and our Language."[21] William Parsons, district judge for the newly founded Northampton County, wrote in December, 1752, "I don't mention Dutch People from any particular Regard that I have for them more than for other People. But because they are generally more laborious and conformable to their Circumstances than some others amongst us are."[22] Even Benjamin Franklin, with his concern already expressed in print, by 1753 privately conceded the value of these immigrants: "I say, I am not against the admission of Germans in general, for they have their virtues;—their industry and frugality is exemplary. They are excellent husbandmen and contribute greatly to the improvement of a country."[23] And yet, withal, reactions against the Pennsylvania Dutch did appear. Adverse comments did not deter them, and as time passed the Dutch became accustomed to their surroundings and adapted to the new experience more thoroughly than ever before.

CHAPTER V

Political and Economic Participation

ALTHOUGH IT IS EASY TO SUCCUMB TO THE NOTION THAT PENNSYL-vania was one vast democracy in the eighteenth century, it is not an accurate portrayal. Like every other American province, colonial Pennsylvania had a property qualification for office and for suffrage. Not until the radical Constitution of 1776 were all property qualifications abolished. Beyond that, the requirements in Pennsylvania were relatively simple. In theory the suffrage was rather more extensive than in other colonies. By 1727, voting rights were extended to every free white male adult who was also a "freeman" of the province. Freemen included those who had purchased one hundred acres of land, regardless of its condition, renters who paid their passage and took up one hundred acres or more at a penny an acre rent, with at least ten acres under cultivation; freed servants or bondsmen who bought or rented fifty acres of land, with at least twenty acres under cultivation, and every "Inhabitant, Artificer or other Resident" who paid scot and lot tax to the government.[1]

On the practical side, since they had only one polling place per county, it meant that voters who lived at the other end of the county, or even in a less remote section, hesitated to make a three to five day trip to the county seat simply to cast the vote (or vote a ticket as they called it) each October first. There were no province-wide elections, but county assembly-men, sheriffs, clerks of election, and a few other local offices were at stake. By the 1740s eight hundred to a thousand votes were cast in a county which had a heavy population of twenty to twenty-five thousand inhabitants; less populated counties had proportionately fewer voters.

From the time of the first Frame of Government of 1682,

the voters of Pennsylvania literally chose the representatives to make their laws. Provincial statutes were subject to parliamentary limitations, and were regularly reviewed. The governor had a right to negate laws by failing to approve them, but that occurred infrequently. During the early years, Germantown leaders served with English Quaker leaders in the Provincial Assembly. After 1701, William Penn's new Charter of Privileges provided for an unusual unicameral legislature, the House of Representatives of the Province of Pennsylvania, commonly called the Pennsylvania Assembly. This provided a more direct, popular participation in lawmaking than in any other colony. Pennsylvanians, old and new, were aware of these advantages, although quite often the Assembly spent much time bickering over details rather than tending to the very real problem of lawmaking.

By an intriguing combination of law, custom, and voters' habits, the Quaker segment of the provincial population, even though a minority of less than 20 percent of the population of the province, continued to hold majority control of provincial and county politics. As a tribute to William Penn and the leadership of the Society, it seemed natural to elect officers and Assembly members who were Friends. After 1711, Penn's obvious financial mismanagement and his disabling illness raised doubts in the minds of some voters. But with disproportionate strength in the three original counties, Quakers remained virtually unchallenged in political office.

With the death of the founder in 1718, new factions grew and in the 1730s even the Speaker of the Assembly was non-Quaker. As the second generation of Proprietors grew away from the Society of Friends in England and by the 1750s returned to the Anglican faith, factional differences grew stronger in Pennsylvania politics. The Quaker party and the Proprietary party, far from being synonymous as they had been at the beginning of the century, now found themselves in vigorous political competition. Use of the term "party," carrying with it later connotations of unity and organization, is questionable here; rather the political groupings were loose factions generally adhering to the personal political outlook of one or two of the most vocal and most convincing leaders.[2]

During the decade of the 1720s Quaker faction leaders, James Logan, Thomas Lloyd, Samuel Preston, Richard Hill, Isaac Norris I, and the proprietary governor found themselves less politically united. As secretary to the Proprietors, Logan could overlook the differences; others gradually reduced their political participation. Then in the 1730s a growing number of non-Quakers, such as Andrew Hamilton, Jeremiah Langhorne, William Allen, and several others, achieved political eminence. Andrew Hamilton was chosen Speaker of the Assembly. Quaker leaders looked at the political situation much more cautiously.

Then, essentially by chance, the Quaker faction in politics found itself more and more antagonistic to the governor and the so-called "Gentlemen's party," and cast about for means of holding on to political advantages. In those circumstances, the German element and the Quaker party leaders found increasing reason to cooperate. The loose, informal coalition which developed, became a very real factor. Quaker assemblymen like John Kinsey or the Isaac Norrises (Senior and Junior) assisted German settlement and helped Palatines and other Germans to gain land, recognition, and naturalization. In turn, the new arrivals traded their produce to the business Quakers and thus formed a market for Quaker trade goods as well. In short, adequate economic and religious bonds existed to recommend a basic political understanding.

"The country Dutch" were extremely reluctant to enter politics themselves, as their Germantown predecessors had done, for they were not familiar with legal procedures, nor were they comfortable with the English language. The Dutch found it very convenient to help elect Quaker assemblymen and other Friendly officials, who made it perfectly evident in their political actions that they would safeguard the interest of the German and the Quaker population. It was not even a matter of political claims. Without campaigning as friends of the Germans, the Quaker legislators simply insisted upon mutually beneficial legislation, even though at times it meant challenging Parliament and the Crown. Palatine request to be exempted from the forty shilling per head duty was noted by the Quaker legislators, who in a very few sessions repealed the bill entirely.[3]

Leading Quakers with large country estates, particularly the two Isaac Norrises, Richard Hill, Thomas Harrison, and others, found the incoming Germans to be particularly productive tenants and agrarian business associates. In the 1725–35 decade, the senior Isaac Norris settled numerous Palatines on his land in and around Fairhill and Norriton Manor. He noted that the diligence of the workers increased perceptibly when he himself found time to act as overseer.[4] In return for consideration or assistance in obtaining valuable farmland in the midsection or the far reaches of Philadelphia County, the newly arrived German farmers also sold their produce or their surplus grains through Isaac Norris and Company. Many of them regularly had their wheat or rye ground into flour at the Isaac Norris flour mills in Norriton or elsewhere.[5] In Chester County, and later in Lancaster County, other Germans made similar arrangements with other Quakers.

The concern of the Quaker plantation owners or merchant traders was also evident in their assistance to those Germans who desired to be naturalized and thus to be able to participate fully in provincial political and economic affairs, if and when they chose to do so. After the death of Isaac Norris I in 1735, his sons Isaac II, Charles, and Samuel continued the practice of extensive dealings with the Germans in the restructured Isaac Norris and Company. Isaac Norris II also built more houses annually for German and Irish farmers. Land itself was in heavy demand. In his opinion, land, even without houses, "at Conostogoe, will, I suppose, be worth what we ask to let it lye for Sale among the Dutch, who are settled around it."[6] Less than six months later, the deal was completed, including some land previously offered to Lawrence Williams, and Norris reported to him, "We have [been] induced to part with that land to some Dutchmen here at the price we offered thee."[7] Debts were rapidly repaid by the Pennsylvania Germans. "What remains unpaid, I believe will not remain long because the Dutch are uneasy while they pay Interest," said Norris.[8]

Norris advised Williams of the great potential for profit, despite the fact that "several Palatine Vessells came in ... very sickly and having carryed 'the Distemper' among their countrymen. If thou hast any Inclination to lay out Mony that way, while the Palatines come Over as they do now, there is scarcely any Place in this Province where Lands will more readily raise Mony."[9] Norris saw to the erection of grist mills and saw mills, which he then also rented out; in the Norris Workers and Tenants Accounts the Dutch figure prominently. Some of them were William Hauk, tanner; John Tiel, starchmaker; and Conrad Righter, bookbinder.[10] Johann Conrad Steiger harvested hay and grain crops for the Norrises, who, in turn, paid Conrad's provincial tax, then entered that debit against him in the ledger. Norris received rent payments in kind, that is, specified number of bushels of wheat per annum in lieu of cash rent.[11]

In 1740–1741 disputes arose over military requirements in the pacifist Assembly. One of the major points at issue was the potential enlistment of three companies of "servants." In all, Governor George Thomas requested eight companies to be authorized, provisioned, and supplied by Pennsylvania. Quaker leadership in the Assembly (especially Kinsey and Norris) fought against the bill, using the argument that "three hundred servants" and "five hundred freemen" was a highly improper ratio, which would cause hardship. Norris declared that the Assembly might possibly offer four companies, but no servants, if only New England "long settled and full of people" would send more than its allotted five companies. That stand raised Norris even higher in the esteem of Dutch servants, who had no more intention of doing military service here than they had in the Rhineland.[12] Many were the attractions that drew German and Quaker factions together and, as one historian recently noted, "the thrifty and economical government ensured by Quaker rule pleased the Germans, who supported Quaker demands."[13]

In the contested Bloody Election of 1742, the status of naturalized Pennsylvania Dutch voters became a key issue in the balloting. In 1740 and 1741, after the resignation of Andrew Hamilton as Speaker, a vigorous political struggle ensued. It pitted the Hamilton-William Allen-James Logan-Conrad Weiser governor's faction, essentially non-Quaker despite the presence of James Logan, against the John Kinsey-Isaac Norris-Samuel Preston Quaker faction. Issues included taxation, the militia, Assembly power, and the prerogatives of the Proprietors, among others. Despite the lack of any modern party organization (or even structure), two distinct "tickets" of candidates faced the voters, representing the two factions described above. To some degree at least the naturalized Germans held the balance of power measured against relatively equal Quaker and Proprietary blocs.[14]

Before the election of October 1, 1741, Conrad Weiser wrote a two-page blast against the Quaker Assembly entitled "A Timely and Earnest Advice to our Countrymen, the Germans," warning fellow Germans not to be taken in by the Assembly's propaganda. At the 1741 election, some bitterness erupted, but it died down after a bit of pushing and shoving at the Court House above the vending stalls at High and Second Streets in Philadelphia.[15]

With a year to consider the implications of the situation, the Quaker faction came to the 1742 elections a great deal better prepared. Even after two centuries, the facts concerned in the fall 1742 election remain as disputed as ever. It appears that the Allen-Logan-Plumstead Proprietary faction prepared for a physical contest to control access to the stairs up to the polling station, using sailors from Philadelphia dockside as a goon squad. Certainly the Quaker faction also was prepared for some sort of political (and perhaps physical) skirmish, for they did encourage many upcountry naturalized Germans to come and vote even though many of them had rarely, if ever, voted before.

The initial fracas centered about the question of Inspectors of Election, contested under an archaic law ever since a reform election law had been allowed to expire by the Assembly. Norris and the Quaker faction easily carried all Inspectors of Election. Balloting was scheduled to begin at nine o'clock in the morning. Assured that Germans who appeared to vote were naturalized, the inspectors certified them and allowed them to vote. Clubs and cudgels were introduced in a battle royal which pitted sailors against Dutchmen. After some serious injuries, order was restored, blame was publicly cast upon William Allen and several town magistrates of his faction, and the Quaker Party won a handy victory at the polls.[16]

Much of the Quaker opposition centered about the Friends' objections to war and war measures. Most Quaker leaders of this time, with the chief exception of James Logan, were pacifists, and they wanted to protect their position. It would be shortsighted to imagine that the Quaker political figures endorsed the rights of naturalized Dutchmen simply as a matter of principle. In fact, nearly every up-country Dutch vote was a vote for the Kinsey-Norris Assembly. In the process this debate also strengthened the position of successful and prominent Pennsylvania Germans, who perceived their advantage clearly enough. Just as in the matter of enlistment of indentured servants, the Quaker position was one of enlightened self-interest, but the practical result was to the advantage of the German element as well. They remained in Pennsylvania, not participating as soldiers, and they gradually exercised their franchise; as in 1742, the Dutch vote did determine the winners in some later contests. Mutual benefits to Quakers and Germans obviously recommended a continuation of their understanding; few events even suggested the existence of problems.

Less affluent Germans, those who found themselves under indenture in rural areas also benefited from some unusual legislation passed by Quaker Assemblies. Perhaps it seems farfetched to assume that antipest regulations would have any bearing on the Pennsylvania Dutch population. Legislation sometimes produced serious results. As early as 1734, settled inhabitants of the original counties, distressed by the nuisance created by excess numbers of squirrels, petitioned the Assembly for a bounty law to destroy some of the animals which became quite irritating in the developed segments of the province. No law was enacted then, but by the late 1740s, the Assembly in its wisdom passed a bounty law on "squirrel scalps." On presentation of the ears of eradicated squirrels, the persons who turned in the evidence received a small bounty from the treasurer of the county in which the hunter resided.

Many scalps and hundreds of pounds in bounty money later, the landholders of the Lancaster County area petitioned successfully to have the law rescinded. The result of the squirrel law, a law which came to the attention of naturalist Peter Kalm while he was in Pennsylvania, was the neglect of the duties assigned to indentured servants. They found they could earn sufficient bounty money to pay off the cash balance of their indenture. On the other hand, the landlords had to pay tax money to the county which their servants then used to buy their freedom. The law was in effect only briefly, but it had a lasting social effect. Eventually colonial Pennsylvanians found they simply had to endure the presence of squirrels. Meanwhile, Kalm was informed that a year's bounty cost not less than eight thousand pounds. "Many people, especially young men, left all other employment and went into the woods to shoot squirrels."[17] The bounty was first halved (from three pence to three half-pence each) but was then abandoned entirely. This was another case in which indentured servants, many of them German, benefited, even though unintentionally, from the activities of the Quaker legislature. After buying their freedom with bounty payments, many of the Pennsylvania Germans supported the Quaker party members who had made it possible.

The assiduousness with which Quaker Assemblymen objected to bills limiting German immigration by placing harsh taxes upon the incoming migrants, suggests that a Quaker-German political agreement was very real. Among the leaders of the Quaker faction, only Benjamin Franklin declaimed loudly against further mass arrivals of Germans. Even he hedged from time to time when he needed German support. Just before he became Speaker of the Assembly, Isaac Norris II noted the paradox, "It is remarkable that the Frontier county of Lancaster, composed of all sorts of Germans and some Church of England Electors, have chosen their Representatives out of ye Quakers, tho' there are scarcely one hundred of that Profession in the whole county." For the Germans, few spoke more succinctly than did Christopher Schultz, who saw the Quaker candidates as "qualified men [to be] your Representatives" who will protect "your beloved Freedoms."[18]

Isaac Norris served as chairman of an Assembly committee of five members to investigate and report on the shipboard conditions of the German migrants. No German sat on that committee because none had been elected to the Assembly. But Norris and his committee were so affected by the appalling conditions they saw that they brought in a strongly worded report demanding regulation of the trade. The Assembly translated those recommendations into law. Subsequently the law was disallowed in London because it placed limitations on British captains and vessels. Nevertheless Norris and his Assembly associates had again amply demonstrated their political concern for the health and welfare of German arrivals from Rotterdam. Supreme Court Justice Thomas Graeme of the Proprietary faction had a different solution, restriction of German rights. Governor James Hamilton stood somewhere on middle ground, but he had to enforce the wishes of the crown in this matter. He lost support in Lancaster and Berks counties as a result.[19]

Though the Pennsylvania Dutch did not think in terms of their own political ambitions, they did not hesitate to speak out when they saw their position or their privileges threatened. In 1752 Christopher Schultz wrote numerous letters and spoke out publicly to his Schwenkfelder kin, friends, and neighbors. His message was clear. He recalled the oppresion they had faced in Silesia. For some of his younger cohorts, born in Pennsylvania, it was a story they had heard from parents or uncles. Now, when the green countryside of Pennsylvania was threatened (as much from within as from French or Spanish America) Schultz insisted that Friendly faces be restored to their position in the Assembly, "lest we lose our place."

While German-speaking residents were reluctant to run for office, they were not reluctant to sign their names to petitions. Literally hundreds of petitions still bear the slow and painful signatures of Pennsylvania German farm inhabitants, who were more than willing to go on record in a way that would have invited retaliation in the old country. But they continued to be suspicious of military organization, and therefore had almost totally ignored Benjamin Franklin's Volunteer Militia in 1747. Franklin complained aloud of their neglect. The German citizenry of Pennsylvania was almost as suspicious of a volunteer force raised by Franklin, which elected him colonel, as were the Crown and Parliament, who negated the entire scheme.[20]

By way of crafts and production on the American scene, the Germans supplied both old world know-how and the ingenuity of those forced by the lack of tools and commercial products to experiment. In construction, the German style so resembled their European homes that today houses or barns can be found in Pennsylvania that are the twins of those in the Rhineland, Württemberg, or Switzerland. Similar construction is to be found in Ontario, where Pennsylvania Germans settled after the American Revolution. Wooden tools and utensils were fashioned on the spot, sometimes using nut woods familiar to them in Germany, or experimenting with trees and wood products indigenous to Pennsylvania. William Allen reported in 1761 on a commercially successful Pennsylvania Dutchman.

No other than Wooden Bellows are now used among us, either at our Furnaces or Forges. By experience we find that the Blast from them is much better than those made of Leather, for which reason [those] are universally disused, A *German* introduced the Wooden Bellows amongst us, and by constructing them at ye different Iron works, has made a pretty good Fortune. He has now a Forge of his own and rents a Furnace.[21]

The Pennsylvania Dutch brought strength and vitality to the New World in the realm of farming. They did not hesitate to settle on the frontier, where land was available. In east-central Pennsylvania they occupied land the Indians were still reluctant to give up, even though Pennsylvania authorities had bought the land by treaties of purchase. In short, the Dutchmen brought with them an economic stability which was at times stolid. They were slow to change, slow to speak, but they were also slow to concede defeat in agricultural ventures. They were an advance guard of settlement which provided a balance to the Quaker adventure in America. They were as solid as the stone and half-timbered houses they built. They achieved these things without Negro or Indian slaves, by utilizing their own large families as work force.[22]

That some of the Pennsylvania Dutch became involved in Indian affairs was inevitable. In the 1720s, many of their newly established farms were virtually in Indian territory, particularly in the Lancaster-Lebanon area, along the Tulpehocken Creek and by the 1740s, beyond the Forks of the Delaware. To the west, the Scotch-Irish served as buffers between a developing

Pennsylvania and the still primitive Indians. In the northeast it was German settlement which took the brunt of Indian reaction.

Many of the Pennsylvania Dutch farmers considered the Indian question totally beyond their realm of responsibility. Others, most notably the Moravians, felt a special obligation to the Indians, sometimes mistaking Indians for the wandering tribes of Judah. But whether they felt responsible or not, the German population was directly affected by the Indian question, for it most affected their lands and their security.

Pennsylvania's experience in Indian matters was generally salutary. Indians in Pennsylvania were consulted on trade and were notified of official land policies. Proprietors purchased additional land from the Indians instead of simply appropriating it, though under the charter, Penn need not have done so. In Penn's province, the Indian (if he was a Christian convert) was allowed to give legal testimony in court cases; on the whole, the attitude toward Indians was benevolent. To be sure, the status of Indian and white was never entirely equal, for it rapidly became a white man's world.

Early in the experience of the province, sale of liquor and gunpowder to the Indians was forbidden. A trade developed anyway, in spite of government restrictions. Provincial officials then attempted to regulate and control it with stringent enforcement. They appointed agents familiar with both the white and the Indian way of life. The Dutch country population tacitly agreed with the Pennsylvania Assembly that Indian affairs and treaties of friendship or purchase were really executive responsibilities of the governor and Provincial Council, or of the Proprietor himself. But by the very nature of things (including Indian discontent and the land question) both the Assembly and the local population were drawn into the complex relationship between Indian and white.

Up to and including treaty purchases of 1732, negotiations conducted in a spirit of fairness led to the acquisition of approximately the southeastern one-sixth of the land area Pennsylvania eventually called its own. Indians of course did not receive trade goods equal in value to the land they ceded, but, compared to land acquisition in other provinces, treatment of them was relatively fair, and they did agree to abandon the land they had just sold.

More scandalous, in the eyes of the Indians of Pennsylvania, was the treaty cession of lands in the Walking Purchase of 1737. In a province temporarily without a governor (Gordon had died and George Thomas had not yet arrived) the Provincial Council acted in executive status, with James Logan, chairman of the council, standing in as acting governor. The Walking Purchase did twist the meaning of a phrase in a 1686 treaty to justify the purchase of land, "as much land as a man could walk in a day and a half" into an unrecognizable form. Following a path blazed through the woods and valleys in advance, Edward Marshall and his white and Indian companions ran a virtual marathon up through Bucks County in a line roughly parallel to the Delaware River. From a point thirty miles further north than the Indians had expected, the northern purchase line was drawn northeast along the upper Delaware River instead of measuring on a directly easterly course. The Walking Purchase claimed for Pennsylvania about 40 percent of the actual area of habitation of the Lenni Lenape, or Delaware, Indians.

For years the treaty was justified by the simple observation that no Indians objected at the time. Therefore, later complaints could be interpreted as false claims made by Indians who had reconsidered. In fact there was a sizable reaction by Indian walkers, even while the walk was being run. "You Run, that's not fair, you was to Walk" surely is one of the understated complaints of history. Lappawinzoe, whose town at Hocindoquen was lost in the purchase, put forth his well-nigh literary objections:

[Marshall, Yeats and the other walkers] should have walkt along by the River Delaware or the next Indian path to it. . . . the Walkers should have Walkt for a few Miles and then have sat down and smoakt a Pipe, and now and then have shot a Squirrel, and not have kept upon the Run, Run all Day.[23]

More important and of larger consequence, it appears, was the judgment by Teedyuscung, chief of the New Jersey branch of the Lenni Lenape, after he removed from Jersey to north-eastern Pennsylvania. Many disputes followed, and the whole matter of the 1737 purchase became a political football a score of years later.

Since the Lenni Lenape were a subordinate tribe to the Iroquois Confederacy, presumably some of the Iroquois tribes should have been consulted as well. In 1754, therefore, when a further land purchase was contemplated, the preliminaries and negotiations were held at Albany, New York. There John Penn specifically bargained for nearly half of today's extreme northeastern portion and nearly all of western Pennsylvania. The Albany meeting had many items of business, but one of the specific reasons for the meeting was the clarification and adjustment of lands and boundaries. In 1737, James Logan had been specifically concerned with the status (and the future) of his Durham Furnace, just south of the Forks. In 1754 John Penn was anxious to purchase land not only to expand Pennsylvania Territory but to prevent French occupation.[24]

Although the Pennsylvania Dutch did not participate in the treaties as a delegation, they were presumably represented by all the officials negotiating in 1737 or in 1754. Weiser as inter-preter was a German in a very critical position. In subsequent treaties, particularly at Easton in 1757, 1758, and 1762, Christopher Schultz joined Quaker leaders who attended treaty gatherings as private citizens.

Both 1737 and 1754 purchase agreements cleared the way for an expansion of settlements in the north and west. In a study of the Dutch, those aspects of the treaty dealing with lands in Bucks and Northampton Counties are of chief interest. Palatines and other Germans held land in Bucks County as early as 1718, whose title presumably was officially cleared in 1737. Within a half-dozen years, Pennsylvania Germans had already staked out land claims beyond the Lehigh Gap, on the north side of the Blue Mountains and, in some instances, had immediately constructed houses and outbuildings there.[25] Little impressed by the imminent danger of Indian attack, the number of farms increased spectacularly in the 1740–1755 period. Just as Weiser had deliberately built his home on the then Indian frontier near present-day Womelsdorf, so Conrad

Mehrkam, Nicholas Oplinger, Andreas Beyer, and Friederich Klein established their farms and built barns on the unprotected far side of the Blue Mountain in the 1740s.[26] Land was land, so virtually as soon as treaty purchases made open land freely available the German farmers moved in. Ordinarily they moved onto the land as soon as a land warrant had been issued and then had it surveyed after actually occupying it. In many cases they failed to have the deeds recorded, because they believed the land warrant itself was sufficient proof.

Legal goods for the Indian trade included trinkets and beads, frying pans, pots, and other iron ware. Counter to provincial law, and over the repeated objections of the provincial Indian agents, rum, iron tomahawks, guns, and powder were also bartered. That brought a splendid financial return to the traders who traveled out among the Indians, but it also provided the means whereby atrocities were made possible especially during the 1750s. Some enterprising Pennsylvania Dutch also took advantage of the rising market and the inflated value of furs and pelts traded by the Indians. No doubt, some of the sales were made by resident farmers also. For a time, in theory, all Indian trade goods passed under the scrutiny of Conrad Weiser, who was Pennsylvania German, or later under the supervision of George Croghan, who was not. In fact many goods were sold to the Indians in their own territory by itinerant peddlers or trading companies who had no intention of submitting to provincial inspection. As a result, the relations between frontier Indians and frontier settlers, Scotch-Irish or Dutch, were badly strained. Even the Moravians, on good terms with the Indians through their mission work, were unable to restrain Indian attacks entirely. Every day, Moravian missionaries recognized the danger of carrying the gospel message to the aboriginal Americans.

For some time Moravians compiled an enviable record, but many of their accomplishments were lost with the onslaught that was the French and Indian War of 1754–1763. Indian attacks increased after the initial skirmishes. The physical isolation of the farms, with no organized agricultural villages as Europe would have offered, made the defense against Indian raids a futile gesture. Considering the duration of the war and the scattered farmsteads, the number of Indian incursions was remarkably low. Usually such raids brought sudden death to farmers or to members of their family caught in the fields away from the house, or, on rare occasions, they were burned while taking refuge in a solitary cabin. Also, a number of women and children were taken away as captives. Their plight and the disposition of such cases will be treated in the next chapter.

Even more traumatic to Germans who had ideas of expanding or taking up new farms farther north in Pennsylvania were the reports in 1754 and 1755 of incursions of Connecticut Yankees into the Wyoming Valley of northeastern Pennsylvania. Men from Connecticut claimed they had made a legal purchase from Indians who had all rights to that land. The Connecticut Charter specified development rights from sea to sea, or thus to the Pacific. Indian claims were difficult enough for the Pennsylvania Dutch to swallow; the new Yankee claims appeared to be some trick or practical joke. The Wyoming Valley was considered by them a western extension of Litchfield County, Connecticut. This menaced the farm element who had broken trail into Delaware Indian territory above the Forks of the Delaware River.[27]

Pennsylvania's legal title to the Wyoming Valley was clearly restated in the series of Indian treaties which were negotiated and adopted at Easton in 1757, 1758, and 1762. Initially they dealt with the Lenni Lenape and their leader, Teedyuscung. But they also cautiously verified the whole matter through Iroquois chiefs in 1762, when Teedyuscung stayed away. Political leaders and ordinary citizens of Penn's province remained convinced that Connecticut claims had no merit. New Englanders persisted in their occupation, so Pennsylvanians mounted an armed invasion of the disputed territory in 1774.[28] Most Northampton County settlers agreed with John Penn, William Allen and William Parsons, all Proprietary spokesmen, who felt force must eventually be used. Sect Germans on the other hand were of Christopher Schultz's opinion. He was a member of the private Friendly Association, an organization which seemed intent in their desire to maintain the peace, even if they had to do it unilaterally.

Political and military crises came to a spectacular climax in

1755. Quaker Assemblymen refused to run for reelection; others who did and were elected resigned after serving part of their terms. After November, 1755, the government was effectively no longer a Quaker Assembly. Quakers now gave up domination of Assembly affairs which they had controlled for fifteen years. Quaker hegemony in the legislature had ended. Some Friends refused to listen to advice sent from London with Samuel Fothergill, that all Quakers resign from the government. Isaac Norris II continued as Speaker despite such suggestions. As far as many of the Pennsylvania Dutch were concerned, Norris continued to represent their interests as he stood up to the Society, to a persuasive Benjamin Franklin and to a home Parliament which exerted major pressure to force a change.[29] In effect, the Quaker-German coalition continued. They embarrassed William Allen and William Parsons at the polls in October, 1756. That year William Allen charged that many "unnaturalized Moravians and other Germans who have no right to vote" went to the polls and cast votes anyway, accounting for his defeat.[30]

Germans would have more to say in October, 1764, when that coalition elected Allen and Norris but defeated Benjamin Franklin, who ran for reelection from the Speaker's seat. A pamphlet war followed, with scurrilous allegations on both sides. Christopher Sauer, Jr., clarified the position of the Dutch, as he lauded "Our Friend Norris," "the honest friend, Isaac Norris," or "Father Isaac Norris" for his stand. The Speaker still protected and guaranteed German votes. Sauer explained that Pennsylvania's Dutchmen had always been willing to send Quakers into the Assembly as their spokesmen. They would continue to do so as long as the Quakers kept their part of the bargain. This was to allow the German areas to elect from their own people, the Sheriffs of Dutch counties, who could, when needed, serve the official papers they must, with explanations and calm assurance in the *Muttersproch*. Sauer bitterly rejected the role of second-class citizenship which less sympathetic public officials seemed to recommend: "For we Germans will be used as hewers of Wood and bearers of Water, and it will be Honor enough that we be allowed to pay our Taxes." All that, he said, would follow, if they elected the wrong ticket to the Assembly. If the Pennsylvania Dutch really cared for their own welfare, they would rather "with a calm and watchful Heart on Election-Day, . . . vote for the true Friends of our old Freedom, namely Messers Isaac Norris, [John] Dickinson, [Richard] Harrison, [Henry] Keppele, &ca." Clearly Sauer contributed to the major turnout of voters.[31]

CHAPTER VI

The Great War for Empire
(1754–1763) and Its Cost

THE INJECTION OF EUROPEAN-BASED CONFLICT INTO THE NORTH American scene was not new in 1756. King William's War before 1700, Queen Anne's War directly after the turn of the century, and the sporadic fighting of the 1740s had pitted Britons against Frenchmen. An essentially European struggle, it spread around the globe. Sometimes designated "A Second Hundred Years' War," the sporadic hostilities lasted from 1668 to 1815. The contests of the years 1754 to 1763, whether called the "Seven Years' War" or "French and Indian War," were pivotal for the colonies. Lawrence Gipson's name for this part of the struggle in North America, "The Great War for the Empire," seems most descriptive, in the light of historical events. Empire in America was the core of the dispute not only for the French and English but for the Spaniards as well.[1]

In North America the great military demands cast a shadow upon the freewheeling methods of the American provinces. Great Britain required both manpower and tax money from the American colonies to supplement her own forces and finances. Numerous American Englishmen, including some German-born and others who also had never seen England's shores, nor ever would, took part in the struggle as active soldiers or as modest taxpayers. Great segments of the American colonial population saw little reason for the war and were not in any way personally concerned, other than by the general inflation of prices which nearly doubled in the ten-year period of the war.[2]

To Pennsylvania and its inhabitants, the war of 1754 to 1763 was particularly distressing. It seemed to many Americans to

92

be a fight on behalf of an absentee landlord. Moreover, Pennsylvania attempted to function without an army and with only minimal police and security forces. It continued as a "Quaker Experiment" until 1756. Then the changing exigencies of the time brought that model state to an end, or rather, to a metamorphosis of major proportions. Quakers in Pennsylvania had assumed that they could exist and participate in a peaceable government which allowed more political and economic freedom than any other unit in existence at that time. Some exceedingly difficult problems had been thrust aside prior to the crisis of 1755–1756. Of all the American provinces, Pennsylvania alone stood with no army, militia, or armed local defense of any kind.[3]

Despite their aversion to political action, members of the Society of Friends, particularly those with business interests, had entered into provincial affairs with renewed vigor between 1740 and 1755. Questions of defense and taxation for war purposes had posed major problems, but prior to 1755 legislative Friends had provided funds for temporary relief. Then the need lessened and a showdown was postponed. When the Assembly passed money bills designated "for the Queen's [King's] use," both Friends and Crown understood that royal expenditures were the moral responsibility of the Crown, not the meetinghouse. But in 1755, Spiritual Friends posed moral objections and the Crown required additional revenues. It produced a crisis.

Trouble had begun in the summer of 1754. Young George Washington and other Virginians, staking out land claims in southwestern Pennsylvania, lost a skirmish to French and Indian forces. A year later a Royal Army thrust was fragmented nearby. The situation had become catastrophic.[4]

Quakers had assumed that they could "live in an orderly society that would protect them, their wealth, and also their right to refuse to protect themselves as well as others from public enemies."[5] Those goals, contradictory as they were, had permitted political and social experiments. It was Quaker leadership which held the heterogeneous population of Pennsylvania together.[6]

The political issue was joined: "Can Friends continue in

government while they feel themselves constricted as to revenue measures for arms and defense?" London Friends, who now refused to serve in government, sent Samuel Fothergill to insist that all Quakers resign from the Assembly. Isaac Norris, who regularly voted against defense funds a decade earlier, had completely changed his mind by 1752, "I am satisfied the Laws of Nature, and perhaps the Christian System itself, leaves us a right to defend ourselves."[7] As Speaker, he depended heavily upon Church German support. Pennsylvania Quakers were not united in purpose; they were not all pacifists. Historians have been in error when they assumed a unanimous response.

In the field, the fate of Pennsylvania would largely determine the status of British North America. Penn's province, with no organized defense at all, presented a long, irregular, open, poorly defined three-hundred-mile frontier to the French. Two shallow arcs intersected at the Susquehanna. Pennsylvania's western fringe of sporadic settlement was essentially Scots-Irish. But the defense perimeter east of the Susquehanna, from Harris' Ferry to Fort Hyndshaw at Stroudsburg on the Delaware, had a Pennsylvania Dutch population. Dutch farmers occupied the valleys and some of the upland plateaus, but forests and mountains were Indian territory, where both hostile and friendly bands moved about.[8]

Pennsylvania's northern frontier was a critical defense area. River valleys originating there funneled right down to Philadelphia. Pennsylvania German farms marked the edge of the frontier. Actually, Pennsylvania German groups continued to differ on the frontier as elsewhere. In the valleys on the near side of the Susquehanna River, Amish and Mennonite pietists offered only passive resistance, even when Indian raids took sons and daughters captive. From Fort Henry, near Reading, to the Delaware River, Church Germans stood their ground from fortified farmhouses, retaliating Indian-style against sporadic attacks. Meanwhile, a third force, the Moravians, continued their missionary efforts; David Zeisberger and Martin Mack were sent to convert the Indians by reason and example. The outbreak of violence threatened to nullify those Moravian efforts.[9]

In the heat of the growing political debate, aggravated by

rising French threats, charges against foreign elements circulated freely. As the threat evolved into active war between France and England, a spirit of suspicion and distrust pervaded the province. All who were different, and particularly those who spoke a foreign language, were suspect.

William Smith, educational associate of Benjamin Franklin, anonymously attacked Quakers (as pacifists) and Pennsylvania Dutch (as subversives) with vigor and enthusiasm. His book, *A Brief State of the Province of Pennsylvania*, printed in London, was hard to refute from the province. Smith flailed away at those he judged to be "friends of France." Mennonites (to their surprise, no doubt) might be "Papists" in disguise. For the Moravians, he reserved his harshest attacks. These people continued to send missionaries among Indians, even to tribes still under French domination. And none of this contact was in plain English.[10]

Bishop Spangenberg hastened to explain the Moravian status and defended them against familiar but unfounded charges. Other, closer neighbors than Smith had attacked the Moravians. Very recently William Parsons had tried to prevent them from settling close to his new town at Easton. Smith in his Anglican zeal had simply lumped Mennonites and Moravians into a single derogatory category and blamed the ills of the province upon them. He charged that Christopher Sauer, Brethren printer of Germantown, "was shrewdly suspected to be a Popish Emissary, who now prints a News-Paper *entirely in the German Language.*"[11]

The German element was hurt and surprised by the doubts of their fidelity and by outright charges of disloyalty. Xenophobia increased in the young colony, in sharp contrast with the open invitation issued by William Penn. Even the cosmopolitan Benjamin Franklin had objected to non-English settlement several years earlier. Many of the Dutch, especially those on the northern frontier, had recently arrived. Few of them had been in the province more than a dozen years. Thomas Penn was warned about "the Large body of Germans" in the territory. As these "bad men" spread unchecked along the frontier, they threatened to become "very bad and troublesome Subjects, in danger of growing Savage."[12]

These complaints badly misrepresented the situation. Acquiring savage traits from contacts with the wild Indian (or *Inschin* in Dutch expression) was neither biologically nor socially valid. Rural Dutch settlers sent a petition to the governor. They reviewed the record of German settlement. "Not one single Instance can be proved of any Disloyalty, much less of any Conspirace [sic] against our beloved King George and the Country we live in."[13]

Jersey men brought in to settle land north of the Blue Mountain, near the Lehigh Gap, were German immigrants who had arrived in Philadelphia between 1748 and 1751, but had found initial employment to the east of the Delaware River. Their efforts to shield Pennsylvania from the Indians were greeted by the charges of Smith and other critics.

When Edward Braddock brought His Majesty's Forces to the middle provinces in April, 1755, the Pennsylvania Dutch were the first to respond. Meanwhile, the Virginians and Marylanders flatly refused. The British commander required axmen and wagons to move his supplies toward Fort Duquesne. Benjamin Franklin, on behalf of Norris' Assembly, approached German farmers for the wagons which were needed and promised their return as soon as the campaign ended. These Dutchmen lived near enough to the frontier to perceive the urgency of the matter, and, in response to Franklin's appeal, they supplied the wagons Braddock needed.[14]

The strategy of a French challenge to the Pennsylvania frontier was sound. With no local defense forces available, the British effort rested on the shoulders of Edward Braddock and his veteran troops. Then, in the most important battle yet fought in North America, the French and Indian army of Louis XV annihilated the combined force of seasoned British veterans and inexperienced colonials. Indians adhering to the cause of George II had been alienated by Braddock on the eve of battle, so only five Indian scouts participated. Casualties among English officers ran disproportionately high, including General Braddock himself. Surviving junior officers pinned the blame on their commander. All supplies, including the wagons of the Dutch, were destroyed, captured or abandoned, and Franklin paid farmers for their lost wagons from his own funds. That loss exposed the entire frontier of Pennsylvania to French and Indian incursions, against which the province had no organized defense. The agrarian population of the western and northern fringes of settlement lived in jeopardy.[15]

Quaker spokesmen for peace in Pennsylvania were discouraged; they were discredited by French success. Some legislators resigned, others refused to run at the next election. The Speaker and a handful of "Defense Quakers" continued in the Assembly and voted funds for military pay, supplies, and construction of forts. The numerous false alarms of French attack were now superseded by a very real French threat. War forced reassessments, as Ralph Ketcham has recently observed: "The military campaign in 1755 caused everyone to measure friend and foe anew and to consider what the war meant to each."[16]

Benjamin Franklin, non-Quaker coleader of the Quaker Party, attempted to play the balance wheel in the new situation. Proprietary leaders continued to find fault with existing political irresponsibility and claimed that "these Miserys are chiefly owing to the defenceless State of the province, and Quakers who, by the influence they have over the German Foreigners, get themselves elected as our Representatives."[17] Justice Thomas Graeme of the Provincial Supreme Court had proposed to minimize Pennsylvania Dutch influence by gerrymandering three new counties, as thoroughly German in population as York and Lancaster. By thus segregating the electorate he would sever Quaker-German political ties. Assigning the new counties the minimum two assemblymen each would keep them an ineffective legislative minority. Then five interior counties might "send all Dutch [Representatives, totaling] but Ten Members in 38."[18]

The desperate defensive posture of Pennsylvania in 1755 argued the need for drastic action and the German community in the colony responded affirmatively. Not only did the Church Germans change from their caution and indifference to active support of English arms in the French and Indian War, but they also built defensive forts along the perimeter of their settlement. Many Germans enlisted or founded militia units in affected counties. The pacifist sects, limited to a small number of the Germans, continued to oppose warfare. The Lutheran and Reformed clergy preached "recruiting sermons." A few served as military chaplains.[19]

In autumn, sporadic Indian raids struck at Pennsylvania Dutch on the edge of the frontier in the newly created Northampton County, inhabited chiefly by Church Germans, both Lutheran and Reformed, and by Moravians in and near Bethlehem and Nazareth. The tiny settlement of Christian Indians at Gnadenhütten on the Mahoning Creek was wiped out on November 24, 1755. Captain Jacobs, a Munsee Indian incited by the French, led that attack. Barn, stable, cookhouse, mill, and chapel were burned to the ground. Ten or eleven of the Moravian workers at the mission station were murdered in the general destruction, while other friendly Indians took to the woods. The converts scattered and the tiny remnant of the settlement fled in terror. A few were brought south to Bethlehem; the rest went to the Wyoming Valley Indian lands on their own.

As a result of the raid, the advance mission station to the northeast at Meniolagameka, near the Wind Gap in the Blue Mountains, had to be evacuated as well.[20] Bishop Augustus Spangenberg at Bethlehem cited scripture to remind Moravians that setbacks do occur and they must prepare for chastisement as well as hope. He added, "Those slain on the Mahoning were verily martyrs, to whom God 'spoke roughly.' "[21] The houses of Charles Brodhead and Aaron Dupui, intended as military strongpoints, were attacked by marauding Indians, and the fear extended as far as Easton, where parties were sent out only under guard.[22]

Franklin personally led an expedition from Bethlehem to the vicinity of Gnadenhütten. He designed and supervised initial construction of Fort Allen, on the Lehigh River at later Weissport. It stood a half-dozen miles beyond the Lehigh Gap, and was an eastern stronghold in the arc of twenty forts built between Fort Lowther at Carlisle and Fort Hyndshaw at Bushkill above Stroudsburg.

It was an opportune time for Franklin, who was also called upon to settle some petty squabbles among the military and between military and civilian personnel. From Fort Augusta at Sunbury, two-thirds of the forts erected served to reinforce a Dutch frontier, whereas the western one-third enclosed settlements on an essentially Scots-Irish fringe. Soldiers were stationed at Forts Halifax and Hunter in later Dauphin County, and Fort Swatara at the Swatara Gap in Lebanon County.

Unfortunately for many of the farmers on the newly enclosed frontier line, the forts at twelve- to twenty-mile intervals did little to deter raids on the intervening land. Garrisons were small, mostly from eight to twenty-eight in a fort, with the exception of Forts Allen, Augusta, and Lowther, which housed larger forces.[23] A large percentage of the personnel stationed east of Fort Augusta consisted of Dutch volunteers or rapidly organized militia units.

Also additionally, armed farm houses supplemented the blockhouse forts that were erected, like the so-called Oplinger's Fort. It was simply a stone farmhouse on the flats just north of the Lehigh Gap near the junction of the Aquashicola Creek and Lehigh River, also called the West Fork of the Delaware. On one of his inspection tours, Franklin complained at length about the poor marksmanship of several of the small garrisons. They lacked sufficient powder, flints, and lead to carry out fully his suggestion that the men take extra target practice. By their location along normal routes of travel, the forts did serve as deterrents. Germans living in Northampton County, but south of the Blue Mountain, found little consolation or protection from the forts to the north. A petition asked for "a good guard this side of the Blue Mountain, from Wind Gap to Lehigh Gap."[24]

Many of the German volunteers in regular units and militia companies had lived virtually their whole lives in the forests they had gradually cleared. Expert riflemen, they were disciplined in the hunt and in frontier survival. For the most part, such volunteers found themselves grossly restricted by military requirements and were only mildly successful soldiers at best. In some of the Northampton County militia units, the majority of enlisted men and some officers bore names that indicate Palatine or Württemberg origins. Some journals or soldier diaries of the period have survived and clearly reveal the practical difficulties of these units.[25] The most aggravating situation occurred when officers who knew no language but English were assigned to units whose enlisted personnel understood only German. Captain George Reynolds reported a mutinous condition among the troops of several of the companies in his command. Soldiers were discontented with a captain whom they simply did not understand, "as they are all Duch [Dutch]." Reynolds thought he perceived less friction where their countrymen commanded, "Captain Wetterholdt's company is ready to march. Lieutenant Engel's men won't leave Reading until they are paid, however."[26]

The officers demonstrated much ingenuity. Major William Parsons, on an inspection of troops in June, 1756, reported Northampton County soldiers were sworn in by Captain Nicholaus Wetterholdt. "He has got the 2nd and 6th Articles of War and the Oath and Certificate all put into Dutch, that his Men may better understand them."[27]

Language proved a barrier sometimes among leaders who presumed they were being understood. Jeremiah Trexler had raised a company of men, virtually all Pennsylvania German, to serve with the colonial forces in the war. In the negotiations with provincial authorities, Commissioner James Hamilton asked Trexler how his company would serve. When the intended Captain Trexler replied "Freipartei," meaning volunteers for regular service, his response was understood as militia, or unpaid service. Some time passed before the error was discovered, as the soldiers went unpaid, and it was not until Franklin, with his perception of language gradations, learned of the problem that it was ironed out, and Trexler's company was taken into pay.[28]

Through January, 1756, Indian raids continued at irregular intervals in the valleys just north of the Blue Mountain, and both civilian and temporary military personnel were killed and some additional captives were seized by the Indians. Construction of forts turned Indian marauders away from the most accessible paths toward Bethlehem, Nazareth, Easton, and Reading,[29] but Indian depredations on the northern frontier led to numerous captures of women and children, and a few adult males, who were carried off to live in Indian captivity. Many times, in the Indian custom, the captives were adopted into Indian families to take the place of sons, daughters, or wives who had died sometime earlier.

Specific cases are often poorly documented and frequently

no written records exist. A tale of northeastern Pennsylvania concerned "Esther, the White Queen," a Pennsylvania Dutch girl, captured, adopted, and married into one of the Canadian tribes. She later visited her white family but chose to return to live with the Indians for the rest of her life. Sometimes, but not always, the captives were returned to their original families in German or other white settlements.[30]

Near the western limits of the Dutch frontier, two girls were taken captive just prior to the raid at Gnadenhütten. Marie LeRoy, Swiss-born, and Barbara Leininger, of German birth, found themselves survivors, with two other younger children, when all the adults of both families were tomahawked, scalped, and killed. The young people were marched off on long journeys as captives, beyond the borders of Pennsylvania, to Muskingum in Ohio. Barbara Leininger attempted to retain names and information about her captivity. She did set down all the pertinent facts she could recall, upon her relatively quick release from Indian hands. Among the items she dictated was a list of white captives she had seen or met on her travels and the place where they had been held. Barbara's younger sister Regina was also captured. She is probably the legendary "Regina, the German captive," for many years called Regina Hartmann.[31]

Indian raids did not always spare the children from death. As a result of late winter raids in Albany Township, Northampton County, at least eight of fifteen settlers killed were children. Two adults and one child escaped to spread the word of the attack. As a direct result and without waiting for further advice from Philadelphia, Jacob Levan and David Schultz organized and staffed "the Maxatawny and Allemängle Independent Guard."[32] Burnt homes and abandoned fields stood as mute testimony to the terror of the moment. Three hundred seventy-four plantations abandoned beyond the Blue Mountain and five hundred fifty-four in the Cumberland Valley represent only a portion of the long frontier. Still, property could be redeveloped; the greatest toll was in human life. Pennsylvania maintained better relations with the Indians than did most provinces, and Quaker fair dealings produced results. It is probably true that not a single Pennsylvania Friend was killed by Indians. The Indians were nonetheless busy killing more than three hundred equally conciliatory Germans.[33]

A Pennsylvania German contribution of major proportions was the long rifle, or Pennsylvania rifle, often misnamed Kentucky rifle. Lancaster, York, and Cumberland County gunsmiths made them before the outbreak of hostilities in 1754.[34] The bore of the extra long barrel was provided with spiral grooves, reamed out by the gunsmith using machinery for that specific purpose. It was far and away the most accurate firearm in use during the French and Indian War. The long ornate stock and the trigger, cocking, and firing mechanism were all individually handcrafted for the specific rifle. A powder charge sent the lead rifle ball spinning in a true and predictable trajectory, so that each rifleman who had time to become acclimated to his firing piece could be relatively accurate at distances upward of five hundred yards, whereas muskets and blunderbusses still used by the military were less accurate at ten yards. Individual crafting did result in a production bottleneck when wartime sales increased the demand, but for accuracy and durability no equivalent firearm was available in the whole of the eighteenth century.

German soldiers from Pennsylvania served in a number of units during the war, especially in state militia companies after the initial battles. Most impressive contributions were made by the Sixtieth Royal American Regiment, of which Colonel Henri Bouquet's First Battalion was composed almost entirely of Pennsylvania Dutch. Captain Samuel Weiser and Lieutenant Phillip Martzloff commanded at Fort Northkill in Berks County. One of the most successful of the Dutch officers was Christian Busse of Reading, "the Doctor of this Town, . . . a hearty and very worthy person." Captain Busse raised a German company and built Fort Henry, which he then commanded. Unfortunately, the efforts of this capable and enthusiastic colonial to be commissioned in the Royal American Regiment were unsuccessful. At Fort Manada, in present Dauphin County, Captain Friederich Schmitt noted the arrival of new recruits. "Die Neye leit," he called them, spelling out his dialect pronunciation.[35]

The Reverend Michael Schlatter resigned from the headaches

of school administration in Pennsylvania in 1757 to become chaplain with the Fourth Battalion of the Sixtieth Regiment. British General William Shirley raised old fears during the war, when he granted permission for enlistment of indentured servants, resurrecting an issue the Assembly had outlawed once and for all in 1743. Colorful uniforms marked His Majesty's regulars, whereas colonial soldiers wore their civilian garb. Some enlistees thus served in buckskin, adopted from the Indians as the most durable garments on the frontier. More of the men had linen and woolen clothing of indeterminate color. On the memorable march of General John Forbes to conquer Fort Duquesne in 1758, his kilt-clad Highlanders and scarlet-uniformed Royal American officers easily outshone the nondescript provincial levies. Attempts to get local volunteers to wear green clothing as a kind of uniform failed badly. "Must the men buy green Cloathing? I fear this will hurt us much," wrote an agent from York. "Young men that have Cloathing, (especially Dutch) will not like to lay out their money for more."[36]

When the war had nearly ended, pressure upon the Indians allied with the French resulted in a return of additional numbers of white captives. Of the young men and women who came back to the American settlements, a great many originally lived in Pennsylvania, although some had survived from New York and Virginia raids. Nicholas Silfies, taken in 1755, was returned in 1762, the same time Frederick Boyer, who had been abducted in 1756, was sent back. Both were recorded from Plow Park, as the English American clerks wrote the place names. The returned captives actually said "Blo Barrick" for the High German "Blauen Bergen," the Blue Mountains.[37]

During the nine years of intermittent warfare other Pennsylvania Germans saw action with provincial forces and with the Royal American Regiment. Leadership in those units was essentially English. As the war continued, the complexion of the Pennsylvania Assembly changed drastically. Many officials, including Benjamin Franklin, perceived advantages in changing the status of Pennsylvania to that of a royal colony. Taxes increased in the province, although not nearly as much as war induced taxation in the British homeland. War and the increased population of the colonies, and especially of the

Quaker province, produced a far greater demand for relatively scarce goods. An inflation of fully 100 percent resulted, sending costs soaring while the wages paid remained relatively static.

Merchants found that enforcement of additional empire taxes was just as lax during the war as it had been before. The ingenuity of commercial elements found new ways to circumvent even reasonable restrictions and smuggled goods sold almost openly. In short, English Americans failed to respect governmental regulations. The entire problem was aggravated by the war. British forces bought illegal iron products and material from furnaces and forges which by law were restricted to the production of raw iron only; but the finished products were needed on the spot. Commanders could not countenance a six months' delay for an order to be sent and filled. Clandestine sales and illegal trade proved to be one way to circumvent the general inflation of the time. Americans considered infractions and disregard for regulations to be a part of the imperial game. Even Governor William Denny of Pennsylvania sold flags of truce to French merchant ships, allowing them to bring enemy goods up the Delaware to trade at Philadelphia while the war against France continued in full force.

The commercial community faced the end of the war situation with a mixture of caution and enthusiasm. Victory over France was a great triumph for all Englishmen, wherever they might reside. The return of peace might bring further recognition to colonials as full participants in the British Empire, a condition they had never achieved before. Most American Englishmen felt exhilarated at the postwar mercantile possibilities. But the fiercely high costs of the war and a recognition that the homeland Englishman carried about ten times the taxes borne by the colonials, while the colonies received military protection and the benefits of empire, made an increase of taxes in America necessary and efficient collection of taxes imperative.[38]

Peaceful promise rested to some degree on a continuation of England's salutary neglect of the colonies. But British leaders sought avenues to correct the situation, using closer scrutiny to make tax laws already on the books more effective, and to expand the tax base. Above all, they would ensure more efficient collections by admiralty personnel. The end of the era of homeland nonconcern produced shock waves on the American side. Coordination of Americans in a united action was also new; they had never experienced that before. A growing resistance to customs enforcement followed the discussions about American procedures.

In 1763 as part of the peace treaty terms, the British offered assurances to the Indians in the Proclamation of 1763, which established the western frontier of settlement along the ridge of the Appalachian Mountains. Pennsylvanians had already breached that proclamation line and had no intention of retreating to the settled side of the mountains as English treaty promises required. Scots-Irish settlers and Anglican and Presbyterian traders took the brunt of the force of the measure, but a few enterprising Germans had also helped to stretch the frontier while the war had continued.[39]

In some measure Pontiac's War in 1764 was an Indian response to the Pennsylvanians who refused to retreat. The spread of raids and a reign of frontier pillaging implemented the threats of the Ottawa chief. This was further evidence to inhabitants of the province that Indians were both unworthy and untrustworthy. When Colonel Henri Bouquet counterattacked, he took with him Pennsylvania Dutch among his soldiery again. The defeat of Pontiac relieved the Indian pressure of Pennsylvania for good, with the sole exception of minor Iroquois raids into the northeastern corner of the state during the American Revolution.[40]

Pennsylvania internal politics in 1764 also took some devious turns as a result of the termination of the war and the new imperial policy that followed. The Paxton raiders countered Indian thrusts by selectively retaliating against friendly Indians, then by marching on Philadelphia to protest Assembly inactivity and lack of response. Benjamin Franklin had been in England as agent even while he held a seat in the Assembly from 1757 until 1762. His continued absence and his known coolness toward the Dutch brought forth anti-Franklin expressions in the German counties. Some Pennsylvania Dutch held him responsible for prejudice against them in England, for Franklin had warned against overpopulation of Germans in Penn's province.

Franklin, second in power in the Quaker party, returned to Pennsylvania and in 1764 led the fight to make that province a royal colony. Some years earlier, James Hamilton had warned of the potential political balance in German hands, "[the Dutch] are become the most busy at all elections, which they govern at pleasure, in almost all the Counties of the Province."[41] Hamilton was concerned with local offices as well as Assembly membership.

That the Germans intended to become politically active was evident in the provincial election campaign of 1764. Christopher Schultz expressed the concern of the Dutch six months before the election: "Now we hear that such a misunderstanding breaks out in our Legislature, as [to] threaten a Revolution in our Constitution, that our Charter should be delivered up in the King's hands."[42] The issue was this: Franklin commanded an Assembly majority for his Royal Government Bill, so Isaac Norris II became disabled and had to resign as Speaker. He would not append his signature to the bill. The opposition to the Royal government measure produced the strangest coalition Pennsylvania politics had yet seen. Norris and William Allen, old opponents in bitter contests, joined hands. The combination included Christopher Sauer, Jr., the printer and pamphleteer, and William Smith, "the old libeller," Christopher Schultz and both segments of the German population, Church Germans and the plain sects.

The campaign for Assembly seats in August and September, 1764, was marked by vigorous pamphleteering and vituperative political charges which went far beyond the limits of propriety. Pro and con were stated amidst charges that the opposition lied to support its own position. There was little to choose between in regard to propriety of methods. Both sides conceded that the Dutch voters would play a larger part in the election than ever before. And as if to fulfill Hamilton's prediction, the turnout of German voters in Philadelphia County proved to be critical.

Previous political lines of force were scattered by the magnet issue of change of government. Franklin rammed it through the Assembly in May, 1764. In the summer he was subjected to wildly extravagant attacks, to which his partisans responded with even more slanderous statements. Norris and Hamilton, in different ways, both looked down on Franklin as a political upstart; William Smith, erstwhile friend of Franklin, suggested that his old crony was not above receiving bribes. Smith hinted that a check of the public funds would reveal pertinent evidence. Franklin's morality, long regarded as dubious, was now seriously questioned. Hugh Williamson accused him of selfish ambition, incendiarism, avarice, scurrility, personal immorality, and general wickedness.[43]

Sauer, Williamson, and Dickinson on one hand, and David Dove, Joseph Galloway, and some anonymous assistants on the other, descended to new depths in politics and provided daily grist for the election mill. William Allen found himself one of the accused, specifically that he "had wrote traitorous papers and distributed them among the Dutch," whereas he asserted, "in truth, I never wrote any paper, nor even read any of the Scurrilous papers published on each Side." But he knew what occasioned the charges. Franklin, "the base fellow," had heard accurately "that a great many people came to consult me . . . and that I had advised them against a Change of Government, and consequently to vote against the authors of that attempt."[44] Allen, in turn, was accused of siring children by his Negro servants.

The fury of pamphlet and broadside warfare may be demonstrated by a series of charges hurled back and forth for the citizens to read and consider. *Plain Dealer* insisted that Proprietary government had made Pennsylvania the most free and most prosperous of all the North American colonies. It questioned the move to royal status, since royal colonies had achieved less. *An Address to the Freeholders in Answer to Plain Dealer* viewed the "Design in our present Proprietaries to enslave us . . . under absolute controul." It doubted openly that any royal subject should "Pannick . . . at the Thoughts of a King's Government," or see oppression in the actions of "one of the best of Sovereigns."[45]

In the debate concerning change from Proprietary to Royal government, sessions of the Pennsylvania Assembly were cut short one day when the old Speaker, Isaac Norris, became ill just as Joseph Galloway launched into a speech on the merits of royal status. At the opening of Assembly business the next session, Galloway had no chance to continue. His speech applauding the change was printed as though it had actually been delivered. Dickinson sided with Norris, Allen, and other defenders of the status quo. He responded caustically to the Galloway hoax with a broadside, *Advertisement, and not a Joke* (A SPEECH there is which no man SPOKE). He saw contradictions, "All things they'll *change*, yet keep the *Same*," and accused Galloway of being Franklin's cats-paw as William Smith formerly was: "Thro' Rocks and Shelves our Bark they'll paddle / And fasten G——— in WILL.'S old Saddle; / Just as they please, they'll make him fit it, / Unscrubbed, tho' WILL. they say, be–sh–t it." Dickinson advised his readers to "Keep one Ear open."[46] The real joke may well have been the switch of William Smith to the Norris-Allen-Dickinson New Proprietary line, of which Dickinson was apparently unaware.

Just four days before the October 1, 1764, election, the major challenge to Franklin appeared on the streets of Philadelphia. Leaflets in German reminded voters that Franklin a mere ten years earlier had designated them "German blockhead farmers" [die deutschen Bauerntölpel]. Could Franklin be trusted, considering his backing and his associates? What will he do with people's rights? Does he, on election day, deserve "a solitary German vote" [von einem einzigen Deutschen]? In response another pamphlet in German asked voters to remember Franklin as friend of the Germans. It recalled the riotous events of 1742 and charged that Smith and the Proprietary faction were the real enemies of the Germans. *Scribler* raised the same idea in English, additionally questioning why everyone remembered what Franklin wrote in the 1750s but forgot how Smith excoriated the Germans in his *Brief State* then.[47]

Christopher Sauer asked German voters to express themselves in votes for the status quo, against Franklin and his change of government. In short, if all Germans stood like Norris and *true Friends* in the Assembly, "for our old Rights" [für unsere alte Gerechtigkeit stehen] then the election would have the proper outcome. All would be saved. Franklin forces issued still another sheet of advice to the German voters. For whatever reason, many more Germans voted in 1764 than had ever bothered to vote before.[48]

The election of 1764 was a landmark in Pennsylvania colonial elections, for the German minority did vote as a bloc. Theirs were the telling votes. Franklin, the incumbent Speaker and avowed author of the change of government bill, and Galloway, its floor leader in the Assembly, were both defeated. Franklin, who had been returned to the House for each year of his five-year stay in England, now failed of election by a mere twenty-six votes out of four thousand cast. Franklin estimated his "Palatine boor" reference cost him a thousand German votes. When they chose to act in concert, the Pennsylvania Dutch held the balance of power at elections. The new Assembly reiterated its decision to change to royal government despite the pressure of ballots. The Assembly sent Benjamin Franklin to England to present the petition for change. Pamphleteers had a final word after his departure.

> Drink a health to the Boors
> Who turned BEN out of Doors,
> Who GERMANS was always reviling.[49]

When, therefore in 1765, the home government imposed a stamp tax, the Pennsylvania Dutch joined other Americans in stating objections. Earlier, Franklin had spoken of the advantages of such a broad tax to raise money for the Crown. A special feature of the tax seemed to reflect Franklin's long-term antipathy toward German newspapers, editors, printers, and other things teutonic. The Stamp Act enumerated the articles to be taxed and the scale of taxes on individuals and classes of items. A most objectionable provision was the half-penny tax on penny newspapers. A 50 percent tax was no light burden. As the Dutch became aware of a subsequent provision they became irate.

For every skin or piece of vellum or parchment, or sheet or piece of paper, on which any instrument, proceeding, or other matter or thing aforesaid, shall be ingrossed, written, or printed, within the said Colonies and plantations in any other than the *English* language, a stamp of duty of double the amount of the respective duties before charged thereon.[50]

Where could you find another foreign language settlement if not the Pennsylvania Germans? Of course none existed, so the tax on documents in "other than the *English* language" was clearly intended for the Dutch. For every small penny newspaper in German, a 100 percent tax, for every large size single-sheet penny newspaper, a 200 percent tax, and for every folding newspaper of four pages costing tuppence or tuppence ha'penny, a tax of eight pence. For every advertisement of any size to appear in a newspaper or gazette, a tax of four shillings per insertion. On agreements putting out a clerk or delineating an apprenticeship, the sixpence per pound value was doubled to a shilling in every twenty. Tax indeed! It seemed more like confiscation.[51]

Isaac Norris was so incensed he copied the words of the *Weekly Advertiser*, "An Act which, when it takes Place, ye Evils of it will perhaps be more 'sensibly felt' than at present can easily be imagined."[52] And was it coincidence that Franklin was in England while the tax was formulated by the House of Commons? Half of Philadelphia and most of the Dutch Country blamed Franklin for the act, even though as agent he later argued vigorously for its repeal.

When Parliament finally took note of the massive colonial opposition to the tax and listened to English Whig merchants, the tax was repealed on March 16, 1766. But with the deftness of John Bull in an American china shop, the Parliament in its wisdom immediately passed the Declaratory Act. That stated the inherent right to impose another such tax in whatever form and at whatever time the Commons might see fit. Error compounded previous error. Englishmen failed totally to judge the mood of the Colonials, who, according to John Adams now saw themselves as an American people, no longer English. Courts and daily functions of law and government simply closed shop while the tax was in effect. Several newspapers had suspended publication for the duration. Repeal at least set the wheels turning again.[53]

Dutchmen learned the lesson that a vigorous spokesman for their viewpoint was badly needed, especially after the aging, ailing Isaac Norris died in July, 1766. Achieving that goal and training leaders required time. But they were better prepared for minority participation in the decade which lay ahead.

CHAPTER VII

Printers' Ink and Educational Policies

ONE OF THE UNIQUE FEATURES OF THE PENNSYLVANIA DUTCH settlement was the interest of these people in published works. Bibles, hymnals, psalters, and prayer books in German, were considered essential not only for spiritual guidance, but for initial steps in reading and education. Except for those sects most isolated from the world around them, the Dutch community sought ideas and news developments in any available publications. Many pioneers arrived from Europe devoid of education. Even those who were literate were often limited to their own signature and a few basic German or English words. Many signed their mark on port papers, while a clerk filled in the name as he heard it.

Before 1700, Pastorius, mindful of what was needed, provided a printed guide for young Germans. The search for improvement led some families to engage tutors to instruct children on farms or plantations. Few of the Dutch had the funds to educate their children in the same manner as their neighbors, the Quaker merchants. The English community provided initial schooling facilities in Philadelphia as early as 1696 when the Proprietary government issued formal papers to the Penn Charter School, at least in its primitive form.[1]

The tradition of Johannes Gutenberg was strong in America's German community. Fonts of type seemed to be as easily available in German characters as in English. America's first newspaper appeared in Boston by 1704. Philadelphia did not have a regularly issued paper until the introduction of the *American Weekly Mercury* in 1719. Franklin, the printer, early perceived the sales potential of the German market and included some German and Swedish sayings in early editions of *Poor Richard's Almanack*. Louis Timothée, a French immigrant, after a short time in America, went to work for the Franklin print shop. In 1732,

112

just three years after the *Pennsylvania Gazette* first appeared, Franklin announced that a German newspaper, *Die Philadelphische Zeitung*, would be printed if initial sales warranted it. In seven weeks two issues appeared, but the response was small; thus a newspaper in German appeared to be premature.[2]

By 1739 Christopher Sauer, Senior, ventured into newspaper publication and produced several issues of *Der Hoch-Deutsch Pensylvanische Geschicht-Schreiber*. The Sauer printing establishment in Germantown became highly influential in Pennsylvania's German community and the Sauers, Christopher, Sr. and Jr., leading citizens. In the long run, they wielded more power and influence through the books, pamphlets, and broadsides they printed than through their newspapers.[3]

They discovered early the economic facts of life in German Pennsylvania. Rarely have so avid a collection of newspaper readers lived together in a small community. But few of them ventured to buy copies. They read (or listened to a reading from) copies purchased by one of the few regular customers. The two-fold result was the absence of any profit to the publisher from newspaper sales, and the disappearance of many issues of the German language newspapers, quite frayed and ragged from repeated reading. It never occurred to the readership to save copies, for old news seemed hardly worth saving. Besides, they served so many useful household purposes.

Since Christopher Sauer was a member of the Church of the Brethren, he served the pietist community first and foremost. But the influence of the Sauers as printers was by no means limited to the Plain People. He also printed materials for Conrad Beissel's mystical community at Ephrata and did contract printing for many Church Germans as well. Other local print shops appeared to imitate his success.[4]

So influential and so successful were the German printing houses in Pennsylvania, that Benjamin Franklin complained bitterly in 1753 "of the six printing presses in the province, two are entirely German, two half German and but two entirely English. They have one German newspaper and one half-German." Although he objected to the German press, he rejected the idea of suppressing it.[5] Sauer was not originally a printer by trade. He saw both the need and the potentiality of the print shop, which was eventually a success. The most influential product of the Sauer Press was his annual *Hoch-Deutsche Americanische Calendar*. His readers found in it a calendar, phases of the moon, chronology of events, and other features of the almanacs of that time. For a short while Sauer printed his Almanack in red and black ink, but the cost soon led him to abandon that design.[6]

For bibliophiles and those who are more artistically inclined, the Sauer reputation is more sensibly based upon the three editions of the Bible printed by the family, the first printings in German in the American colonies, achieved before a single Bible was printed here in English. Sauer printed the Berleburg translation, acceptable to the Brethren and other small sects, but well-nigh heretical to Lutherans, Reformed, and Moravians. Controversy seethed about Sauer, his printing and his Bible project, but he persevered. One of a number of clockmakers of southeastern Pennsylvania, Sauer produced tall clocks that were simple but effective, a few of which have survived. He remains far more renowned for his publications. A bibliography of items from the Sauer Press runs to a dozen printed pages. Christopher Sauer, Sr., died September 15, 1758, amid the struggles of the French and Indian War. He was immediately succeeded by his namesake son.[7]

A worthy successor to his father, young Christopher was trained as a bookbinder and considered that his prime occupation throughout his life. He reluctantly accepted the responsibilities of printer on the death of his father, publishing those periodicals his father had begun and, with his brother Peter, expanded the operation. "I had rather have earned my bread by continuing in the bookbinding business," he said, "and so have avoided the burdens and responsibilities of a printer."[8] Christopher, Jr., published the second and third editions of the Bible; his father printed the original. The younger man, just a boy when the family traveled from Germany to Pennsylvania, became an Elder, then Minister, with Alexander Mack, in the Church of the Brethren at Germantown.

The Sauer newspaper was continued by the son, although he adjusted the title slightly when he assumed editorial responsibility, then changed the name to *Germantauner Zeitung* in 1762. The *Hoch-Deutsch Almanack* was the financial mainstay of the print shop, but he produced numerous other items. Since he refused to make a personal profit on the printing of the Bible, Christopher Sauer, Jr., used that income to publish *Ein Geistliches Magazien,* a magazine of religious items and contributions, and the first of its kind on the American scene. Christopher Dock's advice on education first appeared in *Geistliches Magazien.*

As significant as were Sauer's achievements in the cultural life of Pennsylvania's German community, his effect upon the political scene was no less immediate. He attempted to keep the Dutch informed of political developments and presumed to offer advice to influence their actions. At a time when public debate in print reached a most vigorous stage, Sauer published a prodigious quantity of pamphlets and broadsides attempting to sway his readers. In that sense and in those publications, he competed with Benjamin Franklin as successfully as any of his contemporaries.[9]

Christopher Sauer, Jr., also experimented in fields related to printing. He made his own ink for printing, as Christopher, Sr., had done. In addition, the younger man established what was probably the first type foundry in America at Germantown in the early 1770s. This innovation was recognized when a resolution was adopted in January, 1775, in Philadelphia. The Continental Congress' resolution against commercial importations cited the example of "an ingenious artist in Germantown" who cast type in America, an item of domestic production. The same printer, attempting to remain neutral in the Revolution, saw his printing equipment confiscated by the American Patriots and his sons Peter and Christopher declare for the British, whom they served as printers in Philadelphia.[10]

Newspapers were extremely important in Dutch Pennsylvania as a means of informing the community of new regulations and trade opportunities. Prior to the outbreak of the American Revolution, a score of editors and publishers issued two dozen different German language newspapers in seven different towns and cities of Pennsylvania. Several bilingual papers also appeared briefly. By the turn of the century, thirty additional editors in ten towns and cities started publication of thirty-eight more German newspapers, several of which continued publication into the twentieth century.[11] Several of the printers, like the Sauer family who began the process, became influential and relatively affluent members of society in Pennsylvania.

Of the German editors of late colonial times and the era of the Revolution, Johann Heinrich Müller (better known as Henrich Miller) and the Armbrüsters, George and Anton, were the most successful in their field. Henrich Miller rode the crest of the Revolution, disseminating the Patriot sentiments of a majority of Pennsylvania Dutchmen. Miller commenced publication of his *Der Wochentliche Pennsylvanische Staatsbote* in 1762 and continued well into the War for Independence. Like Christopher Sauer, Jr., he experienced difficulty while the Stamp Act was in effect, and upon news of its repeal, printed a special edition. Miller's paper began as the *Wochentliche Philadelphische Staatsbote*, but soon changed to its more familiar title, *Pennsylvanische Staatsbote*. In 1775 and 1776, he printed papers regularly twice per week ("Diese Zeitung kommt alle Wochen Zweymal heraus nämlich Dienstage und Freytage, für Sechs Schillinge des Jahres"). For the last three years of publication he went back to weekly issues.[12]

One of the special services Henrich Miller offered non-German-speaking Pennsylvanians was stated in English in the heading of the *Staatsbote*, "ALL ADVERTISEMENTS to be inserted in this Paper, or printed single by HENRY MILLER, Publisher hereof, are by him translated gratis." Miller possessed a fine sense of the cooperation possible between the German and English segments of Pennsylvania's citizenry. Near the beginning of the Revolution, he suspended publication for several weeks and he later complained that his press and his type were confiscated by the British for the use of Christopher Sauer III. By a combination of editorial alertness and the good fortune of his publication schedule, his *Staatsbote* of July 5, 1776, printed the very first announcement of the Declaration of Independence, then published the first complete text of that document in German. The circulation of Henry Miller's newspaper approached sixty-five hundred. He established a readership throughout Pennsylvania, well up into the Mohawk Valley of New York and extending as far as Georgia and the Carolinas. He was a highly influential editor.[13]

The Armbrüsters, printers for the Moravian community, experimented with a series of newspaper ventures from the 1740s to the 1780s, but the Armbrüster shop made more money from its occasional printing than from newspapers. They never succeeded in producing a paper to rival the *Geschicht-Schreiber* or the *Staatsbote*, but they did produce a best-selling almanac for their German constituency. Anton Armbrüster took part in the pamphlet warfare of 1764 as enthusiastically as any, arguing generally for a retention of the old charter and against the change of government, but at the same time he remained a rival of the Sauer printing house.[14]

John (Johann) Dunlop was a bilingual printer who also competed for the Dutch trade. One of his newspapers carried items in English on the first two pages, then in German on the last two. He wrote much himself during the controversial decade preceding independence.[15]

These printing establishments supplied the Dutch readers with the details of news and politics. Much was reprinted in the German press of Pennsylvania. Each editor had his own interests and his own style, and each left his imprint upon the public scene. Political broadsides verged upon the scandalous and names were often thinly disguised. That was the prerogative of the press, an area in which America led the world, particularly after the Peter Zenger libel trial of 1735 in New York.

The press at Ephrata Cloisters was not only a vehicle for the utterances of Conrad Beissel, but it profitably served the community also. Due to the Beissel personality and his conflicts with other Dutch of the province, other printing houses failed to produce precisely what Beissel desired. Occasionally they added some critical or derogatory comment to the printing they did for him. Consequently the Ephrata Community looked to its own needs.

Beissel justified his ideas and his spiritual community in print; his *Mysterion anomias*, a defense of the Seventh-Day Baptists, was printed in Philadelphia in 1728. Franklin printed two of this mystic's philosophical treatises in German. Christopher Sauer published *Zionitischer Weyrauchs-Hügel*, a collection of German and American hymns, for the faithful at

Ephrata. Sauer guessed that Beissel had written many of the hymns himself, a fact verified by Peter Miller. Thereafter Sauer issued a printed objection to them. Ephrata also furnished some of the paper on which Sauer printed his 1743 Bible, and the Brethren were western agents and bookbinders for that imprint.

All in all the dependence of the Ephrata community upon outside printers proved unsatisfactory in view of the growing self-sufficiency of the cloisters. Mills and craft production made Ephrata an early commercial center, where religion was also dispensed. Few frontier communities had so thorough a range of necessary facilities. A gristmill, an early sawmill, a flaxseed oil mill, paper mills, tannery, and linen and woolen fabric looms all operated at Ephrata prior to 1750.[16] Jacob Gast on behalf of the community received a printing press and type from Germany early in 1743. Gast, Peter Müller, Alexander Mack, and Israel and Samuel Eckerlin had worked with or for Sauer in his Bible project. They were experienced in typesetting and printing; yet no imprints issued from the Ephrata press until 1745. At that time Ephrata possessed what James Ernst called "the only complete publishing unit in the colonies—a paper mill with its own watermark, a press with a trained printer, a tannery, ironworks and cabinet makers, materials for ink, bindery, sales department and men and women capable of writing."[17]

The press published several broadsides by Prior Israel Eckerlin in his 1745–46 dispute with Conrad Beissel, when Eckerlin wished to emphasize economic production and improved methods. He was forced out in a reorganization. With the departure of the Eckerlins and Alexander Mack in 1745, production of printed items slowed, although the press printed several more books for Mennonite use. The most famous result of that collaboration was the translation into German and the printing at Ephrata of the Mennonites' *Martyrs Mirror*. No imprint of the Ephrata press gained for them so great a reputation as printers as did that single item. Yet sales lagged and five years after the book appeared, five hundred copies of a press run of thirteen hundred copies remained unsold.

The effort required to edit and print *Martyrs Mirror* brought a closer coordination of the faithful than they had managed for several years. The 1512-page book required full-time energies of fifteen men for three years. A second press was obtained to assist on this job. Peter Müller (John Peter Miller) was translator, editor, and proofreader. Four compositors and four pressmen worked in the print shop, and the six men in the paper mill spent some of their time in the bindery. Tradition had it that during the three years of the project, Müller slept only three hours per night. The handsome volume eventually sold out, which reimbursed the financial outlay of the community, though not until years had passed.[18]

The press served areas far beyond the religious body at the Cloisters. Within a single decade they published works of a considerable variety. There were German translations of John Bunyan's *Pilgrim's Progress* (which drew a competing edition in German from the Sauer Germantown press within a year) and of Anthony Benezet's *Observations on the Enslaving, Importing and Purchasing of Negroes*. Brethren traveled on missionary tours to New Jersey and New York, down into Virginia through Maryland, and to many surrounding areas. Printing continued at Ephrata until 1790, although the effectiveness of the community was seriously reduced after the death of Johann Conrad Beissel, who had in his last years taken the name of *Friedsam Gottrecht*. John Peter Miller, who came to Pennsylvania in 1730 as a German Reformed pastor, succeeded Beissel as Prior Jabez, director of the Cloisters. The founder had been too tempestuous in his dealings with the faithful. The community expired, barely outlasting Prior Jabez who died in 1796.[19]

Among the Pennsylvania Dutch, many occupations centered about the curing and tooling of leather, from shoemakers and cordwainers to those who specialized in leather trousers or aprons and to the bookbinders who were allied with the printing trade. By 1774, of the 106 artisans engaged in twenty-seven crafts at Germantown, leather working occupied almost a third of them. At York, only five years later, over a score of German shoemakers, tanners, hatters, and breeches-makers worked in leather. Philadelphia was also the center of the largest concentration of paper mills in America. First among these was the mill of William Rittenhouse (or Rittenhausen) of Germantown, joined in time by the paper enterprise of Christopher Sauer, Jr., near the same site.

Of all the trades, the bookbinders stood among the most versatile craftsmen, although the printing trades also demanded many skills.[20] Another German immigrant, Peter Leibert, made his livelihood rebinding old books. Other experienced Pennsylvania Dutch bookbinders in or near colonial Philadelphia included Rupert Bender, Conrad Righter, and one known now only as "The Dutchman." Jacob Reinholdt did custom binding for several influential Quakers whose country seats were near the workshop of this Pennsylvania German master craftsman. He bound ordinary account books and letterbooks for everyday use, working in lightly processed leather bindings as well as finer bindings. Anthony Benezet produced library editions of tooled leather, handlettered. Examples of his fine work exist in books from the Isaac Norris library now to be found at Dickinson College, the Library Company of Philadelphia, and the Historical Society of Pennsylvania.[21]

Many controversies arose among the Dutch in the province on the question of education. Of the German heads of families and adult males who signed the ship lists, only one-fifth failed to sign for themselves. With the added incentives of the New World, many of the arrivals came to value learning for themselves and more especially for their children. Some others, particularly among the more restrictive sects, felt that education was dangerous and led to pride and wickedness. As in other aspects of the Pennsylvania Dutch experience, it is extremely difficult to generalize for the group as a whole.

Those among the Dutch who favored education were interested in practical and moral aspects of schooling, in preparing the children for the requirements of everyday life, as well as in religious precepts for life after death. In the few short weeks of winter schooling, often reluctant pupils learned to read, write, and cipher. Reading selections ordinarily were chosen from scriptural passages, for the essential purpose of education was to be able to read the Bible. Literacy constituted a positive value in America and most Germans aspired to be able to write, at least to sign their names when document or contract demanded it. Even those Dutchmen regarded as slow-witted by their neighbors could figure prices and accounts rather accurately. By reputation, at least, they rarely accepted a bad bargain.

Some literate parents provided early education at home, and many young people managed quite well with that home training and no other schooling. In the immigrant families, in the tradition of family Bible readings and devotions, the family sat around the kitchen table after the evening meal. Father read aloud from the Scriptures for the edification of all, and each child was expected to do the same when called upon. This was especially important in light of their Protestant status and a reverence for the vernacular Bible, available to all in a language they understood.

In rare instances successful Dutch parents, often in urban centers such as Germantown, imitated their English-speaking neighbors and hired a traveling pedagogue to tutor their children. The traveling tutor was less common in Pennsylvania than in the colonies to the south, where the social and economic system centered about the plantation. In the Dutch country a few wandering souls, doubling as hired hands and as tutors, moved from one locale to another. But Muhlenberg, who was greatly saddened by the lack of schools, did not consider them men of good reputation. "When those who had been half-baked schoolmasters in Germany come here, they usually go far out in the country and set themselves up as preachers. . . . Others profess to be schoolmasters and try to earn their passage-money by teaching school, whereas they ought to go to school themselves first." Yet some qualified Germans were not hired, he said, "as tutors and preceptors because there are enough . . . from Scotland and Ireland . . . employed in such positions."[22]

Twenty-five years later the Coetus of the Reformed Church in Pennsylvania (a regional assembly of ecclesiastical officials) still complained of "a lack of teachers for the church schools." In consequence, German church leaders had to hire "English schoolmasters, most of whom are imported Irishmen."[23] Michael Schlatter, scholar and pastor, and founder of the Coetus, served as tutor to the ten-year-old daughter of Isaac Norris. That was an exceptional case, though, for Mary Norris learned German from Schlatter after she learned French by living with a French-speaking family in Philadelphia, then polished her French by advanced study under Peter Fontaine.[24]

There was also formal schooling in organized classes. Often the schoolhouse stood near the church building. Many times the Sunday preacher was also the weekday schoolmaster, although occasionally professional schoolteachers were not clergymen. They held another occupation at the same time, often farming, to improve their financial status.[25]

The first school in Germantown opened in 1702, paid for by tuition and contributions. Francis Daniel Pastorius, formerly a teacher in the Friends School in Philadelphia, now taught at Germantown until 1718. During a portion of that time, he conducted daytime classes for neighborhood children and evening sessions for persons who worked during the day. Anthony Benezet taught for a time at the Germantown school, as did Wolfgang Leitzel and a Moravian theological student identified only as Döling. Hilarius Becker also served at schools in Germantown in the 1750s and 1760s, including some time in the German Charity School founded under the auspices of the Society for the Propagation of the Gospel.[26]

Of all the teachers in the independent German schools of the province, none was more diligent in his work, more devoted in service, nor greater in local prominence than was Christopher Dock, Mennonite schoolmaster. He taught for at least five decades of the eighteenth century, first in Europe, then in schools from Germantown to Salford. He is best known as the Skippack schoolmaster and as a kindly teacher in an age of petty school tyrants. Moreover, he wrote the first American treatise on pedagogy.

Dock's influence led his students to appreciate an education and to value its results. As an incentive to his pupils, he gave small rewards of his own creation. By his novel approach, this man sought to accomplish by words of kindness and approbation what most of his fellows insisted could be driven home only with a birch rod. At Skippack, where Dock began to teach the year of his arrival from Germany in 1718, the Mennonite school was built seven years before the meetinghouse. Simple in its construction and its furniture, the German schoolhouse allowed full communication between the teacher and his pupils.

For a ten-year period, the schoolmaster abandoned teaching, concentrating on farming newly acquired land. He resumed teaching in 1738, serving schools at Skippack and Salford concurrently. Thus he spent Monday, Wednesday, and Friday at one school and Tuesdays, Thursdays, and Saturdays at the other, an arrangement he continued for most of his career. Four times he taught the summer months at Germantown, probably before 1749, conducting sessions there while his Skippack and Salford schools were in summer recess.[27]

Christopher Dock felt a divine call to teach. He took his work seriously. He specifically stood *in loco parentis*; indeed when the parents failed to provide a proper example, this innovator insisted the teacher must counteract parental neglect. Education at the hands of Christopher Dock was scripturally based and aimed at the best interests of the children. He felt that morality and character building were prime purposes of schooling, but he objected to increasing state control. Although he taught in schools that charged tuition, he insisted children should not be denied an education for lack of funds. Moreover, he sustained an interest in his pupils many years after their classroom days and endeavored to follow their progress and achievements twenty or thirty years after they had sat in his classes.

Dock attempted to inculcate learning in his students in nonschool hours by telling them Bible stories during their lunch hour and requiring them to prepare work at home for the next day's classes. Above all he attempted to challenge and inspire the young, and he deprecated the beating or slapping of pupils, then a common practice. He encouraged his students at Skippack and Salford to correspond with children from the distant school as a means of furthering the lessons he taught, and Dock himself served as postman, carrying the letters as he traveled to the other school on alternate days. His students also read excerpts from Sauer's newspaper in the classroom as well as the usual selections from the Bible.[28]

Had not Christopher Sauer so admired Dock's methods as schoolmaster, it is likely we would know little more about the Skippack schoolmaster than we know of most of his contemporaries. Through Dielman Kolb, a mutual friend, the Germantown printer asked Dock to set down the rules for school management. Christopher Dock agreed to do that but insisted the treatise be withheld from publication until after his death, lest he be guilty of overt pride and desire for fame. Sauer observed that request until very nearly the end of Dock's life. When he did publish it, the schoolmaster obviously had only a few months to live. So successful was the publication that a second edition was immediately required, and German schoolmasters throughout America were urged to emulate the novel but successful ideas of the old master. Sauer concluded his preface with this observation: "One sees almost everywhere how much more zeal is used to teach the children conformity to the world and to other useless things rather than useful endeavors that lead to salvation."[29] He hoped Dock's principles might help reverse that trend.

Christopher Dock wrote the *Schul-Ordnung* (*A Simple and Thoroughly Prepared School Management*) in recognition of "the duties contained in this calling" of schoolmaster, and considering "the spoiled state of youth, and the many offenses of this world whereby youth is spoiled and is made to stumble by its elders." This Pennsylvania Dutch teacher relates the proper order of things in school from enrollment of the children and the beginning of the schoolday, to grading, disciplining, and the ways by which to stop chattering in the schoolroom. He taught love and respect and had little time for thrashing the disobedient child. At Skippack, Salford, and Germantown, this modest teacher created an atmosphere of harmony and love most conducive to learning. He consciously used the students' own natural enthusiasm to lead them to a desire to learn and to continue in pursuit of learning for the rest of their lives.

Above all he demonstrated by his own example the values he thought important. He did not just exhort the children to be thankful and , pious—he prayed aloud with them. His own joy in achievement was a model far more convincing than the loudest shouts and most profane threats of willow-wielding teachers elsewhere in America. He wrote hymns for the pupils to sing and poems for them to recite. He made them ABC books with his own pen. The especially gifted and the students who earned his praise for their diligence and their accomplishments he rewarded with illuminated Fraktur commendations, which they took home to cherish.[30]

Unfortunately for American education, the advanced ideas of Christopher Dock were generally forgotten. Later editions appeared in the nineteenth century for use in German schools of Ohio and Pennsylvania, but no English translation was available until more than a century after Dock's death. Over the years Americans have listened more intently to Froebel, Pestalozzi, or Montessori, while ignoring similarly valuable concepts in Dock. Appropriately enough, excerpts from Dock's *School Management* do appear in a recent documentary history of educational ideas, under the heading "Toward a More Humane Conception of the Child."[31]

Certainly in the eighteenth as in the seventeenth century, one of the chief goals of education was religious awareness. As early as the sixteenth century, Menno Simons had insisted that responsible parents who cared for their children would ensure that they were trained to read and write. Education in the Dutch country emphasized little else than reading and writing, except by teachers like Christopher Dock. Basic education was important for those persons preparing for leadership in colonial and early national churches. A majority of American religious groups now insisted upon a trained, educated, and consecrated clergy. Except among those sects opposed to education, the value and advisability of local schools was accepted early by most of the Pennsylvania German community.

Many individuals in the Dutch country distrusted education, finding it too frivolous and too expensive. Raised in a tradition which deprecated the sins of vanity and pride, these people saw in schooling the promotion of vanity and superiority. If leaders insisted upon education, the ordinary folk would limit it to fundamentals in reading, writing, and arithmetic. Literature, unless it be Scripture or selections from religious writings, seemed misleading, an invitation to sin and vice.

These same people retained their stereotype of the teacher as an austere and monastic bachelor type, who was avid in his discipline. Both minister and teacher (often the same person) were subject to community admonitions, which were both direct and public. The teacher had neither the status nor the pay that his European German counterpart had had. Benjamin Franklin noted that his Dutch neighbors delighted in making demands upon clergymen and others placed in authority. This tendency was augmented by practical observations that children might more sensibly be engaged in field work which brought a return, rather than wasting their time on silly books and thus escaping the normal exertions of life. Quite simply, they placed little trust in schooling which seemed to bring no visible practical results.

One legitimate concern among those who opposed schooling, or who were at least wary of it, was the danger that the school would be used as a vehicle for subversion. In Pennsylvania in the mideighteenth century, this became the specific policy of the Proprietary government and of many English cultural leaders in the province. The policy of Anglifying the Dutch was promoted both officially and unofficially. English language schools, first optional, then later required, served as a means of weaning the German element away from their language and culture. Many of the migrants feared and destested this infringement upon their ways and customs.

Specifically, the educational proposal was to initiate schools for German-speaking Pennsylvania youths under the aegis of England's Society for the Propagation of the Gospel in Foreign Parts. Charitable donations from wealthy Englishmen would pay for buildings and teachers, all under close supervision of religious and provincial authorities. Classes taught in English would properly prepare these young people, gradually displacing German customs and values. A Royal donation set the tone, presumably improving the chances of employing American teachers with the proper perspective.[32]

To their chagrin, Dutchmen perceived the Reverend Michael Schlatter, who was one of their own, though recently arrived, in the vanguard of this subversive educational movement. Schlatter's testimony, when he endorsed the idea of English schools in letters to Thomas Penn, was so derogatory as to be scarcely credible.

I Must assure you, Honoured Sir, that the Large body of Germans that inhabite your territorie are in danger of growing Savage, if there are not some Wise Methods taken to reclaim them. . . . They must in Such a Situation, by becoming bad men, become also very bad and troublesome Subjects, of which we have seen Fatal instances alredy.[33]

Now Schlatter perceived tendencies in German history to "Rebellion and Revolt," due, no doubt, to the hot tempers and revolutionary actions of such people. He felt sure that schools would restrict the spirit of revolt. He presumed some hope still remained for the Pennsylvania Dutch, "who at present can scarcely be called Men."[34]

Schlatter carried his message to England and the European continent in 1751, where he raised the goodly sum of twelve thousand pounds "for the benefit of the American churches." On his return he brought six young ministers to America with him to aid in the work. The vigor of his appeal and the extreme arguments he used to justify the charity-school scheme aroused many objections to his plans.[35] Others of the German community, particularly established elements who had been in Pennsylvania a full generation or two, made public their differing views.

For the Schwenkfelders and Mennonites, Christopher Schultz provided the leadership in drawing up a response to the outrageous Schlatter charges. A petition to Governor Robert Hunter Morris attempted to set the record straight. The petitioners stopped short of calling Michael Schlatter a liar, but were content to let scripture do that for them.

Some Spirit, we will not determine what Name to give him (v. Reg. 22:21–22) accused us very publickly both here and in England, of a secret Conspirace against our King and Government, which is no small Matter to charge a Body of People with. . . . A very hard Charge indeed to a Number of People against which no such Accusation can be aledged with Justice.[36]

In 1754 and in 1756 Schlatter was also disowned on the charity-school issue by Lutheran and Reformed leaders in America, although his suggestions still carried much weight with Thomas

Penn. The Proprietor himself tied Michael Schlatter to the promotion, "I hope on the arrival of Mr. Schlatter with his Letters from the Classes, you will be soon forming the Schools." In almost the same breath, Penn indicated his chief concern was for the security of the province. Education was more or less an incidental matter. He could even wish that "endeavours of the Dutch and German Ministers will be exerted to make those People every Day more sensible of the Advantages they reap by being in an English Government, which they could not have under the absolute Government of the French." Education in the use of the English language seemed one way to ensure loyal conduct in the province. Thomas Penn proposed to reinforce that value: "I shall endeavor to get a general Act passed here for the Colonies to oblige the Germans to make their Wills and take Bonds, &c. in English."[37]

Thus gradually the initial proposal took form in America as "The Charitable Scheme to Educate the Poor Germans." Many Germans were impressed with the advantages of a school offering classes in both German and English, especially if it cost them little. Had they initially understood that the charity-school plan was really an arm of the Anglican Society for the Propagation of the Gospel, the Pennsylvania Dutch would have been even more reluctant. William Smith's vigorous support of the project did not diminish his denunciations of the Pennsylvania Germans, so its attractiveness lessened.

Basically, the plan Smith proposed would operate under six trustees-general and a superintendent. It would provide six or more schools, each with five to eight local assistant trustees, all constituting the "Society for Propagating the Knowledge of God among the Germans." They were directed to employ teachers who "understand the English and high Dutch, with Mathematics, Geography, Drawing, History, Ethics [and] the Constitutions and interests of the Colonies." In order to obtain the best results, they desired men trained in the New World. Instructors were to give to "Protestant Youth of all Denominations" a basic education, by teaching "both the English and German languages; likewise in Writing, Keeping of common Accounts, Singing of Psalms and the true Principles of the holy Protestant Religion."[38]

William Smith of the Academy of Philadelphia, general propagandist for the school proposals, wrote *A Brief History of the Rise and Progress of the Charitable Scheme* for the trustees, and had twenty-three hundred copies printed for a wide distribution. He offered students from his academy to serve as teachers and reiterated the importance of teaching English to the German-speaking students, "giving them an Opportunity of learning English, by speaking of which they may expect to rise to Places of Profit and Honor in the Country." They would thus directly understand trade and legal proceedings and "know what is doing in the Country around them." In short, the Pennsylvania Dutch might "judge and act entirely for themselves, without being obligated to take Things upon the Word of others, whose Interest it may be to deceive and mislead them."[39]

Early proposals envisaged as many as twenty-five schools throughout the German districts of the province. More than twenty thousand pounds was raised in England, Holland, and Pennsylvania to finance the educational project. Local trustees were immediately appointed for five locations—Lancaster, New Providence-Skippack, Reading, Easton, and New Hanover. Ideas and suggestions from general and local trustees received consideration. William Parsons, leading assistant trustee at Easton, recommended the education of girls as well as boys, for Dutch mothers teaching preschool children at home could jeopardize the entire plan. Education of poor females was incorporated into the aims of the program but was implemented at only one location, New Providence (Trappe), "where a few girls were taught reading and sewing" by the wife of Charles C. Raboteau, the charity-school teacher there. That experiment was short-lived.

The entire charity-school proposal was calculated to draw Pennsylvania Germans to its support, since they were reluctant to spend their own money on schools. With money available from other sources eighteen communities petitioned for schools to be established in their areas. German petitioners of various faiths in the new town of Easton asked for a school, promising to build the schoolhouse and pay "a pious sober English School Master"; indeed they promised to exceed the financial requirements of the Charitable School Act. Workers and donors pledged labor, goods, and cash to ensure its success.[40]

Only a dozen schools opened under this school project. Several of them survived a few years, 1753 to 1760, whereas others had a very short existence. Financial problems plagued them all, for within a decade both interest and principal of the original trust had been expended and at least two schools, at Lebanon and Germantown, had to resort to lotteries to raise operating capital. Indian incursions and the threat of further attacks hampered the operation of several charity schools on the frontier and forced closing of at least two of them.

Greatest objection to the charity-school scheme emanated from the German settlement itself. Many perceived it to be a pernicious means of eliminating the German language and custom in Pennsylvania by forcing their youth to learn English. A vigorous, influential critic of the program was Christopher Sauer, Sr. While Schlatter and Muhlenberg led Church Germans in an initial approval of the scheme, Sauer excoriated its proponents as well as its officers. The trustees-general (Governor James Hamilton, Chief Justice William Allen, Provincial Secretary Richard Peters, Benjamin Franklin, Conrad Weiser, and William Smith) were to him political appointees who care "little about religion, nor do they care for the cultivation of the minds of the Germans, except that they should form the militia and defend their properties."[41]

The Germantown printer elaborated many other complaints against the school program he felt was a conspiracy to Anglicize the Pennsylvania Dutch. He criticized Weiser, token German trustee, and denounced Schlatter, the Superintendent, as a malevolent falsifier and betrayer of traditional values. As for educating poor, ignorant Germans, Sauer and other naturalized immigrants pointed to a high level of literacy within their group. A recent assessment by Alan Tully, using social science techniques, appears to invalidate the "ignorant German" theory.[42]

Sauer charged the English acted not from true benevolence but from fear of an unlikely alliance between German and French in the New World. He printed that charge in his *Pensylvanische Berichte* of 1754 and reiterated it in a well-publicized letter to "A Friend" in autumn 1755. As if to verify these charges, William

Smith in November, 1756, replaced Schlatter as Superintendent of the schools and recommended both missions and the charity schools to the Bishop of Oxford as a means of preventing "disaffected Germans" from joining a "French German" colony at the edge of Pennsylvania settlement.

On the emotional issue of subverting German forms by a forced conversion to use of English, Penn had made his position clear and was joined by the trustees-general in mid-1755, when they officially spoke of "the great design for promoting the English tongue among the Germans." William Smith said as much, but more forcibly, fifteen months later, "In short, till we can succeed in making our Germans speak English and become good Protestants, I doubt we shall never have a firm hold on them."[43]

The chief defect of the school proposal and major cause of its failure was the simple discrepancy between a theoretical proposal and its actual performance. Try as they might, the trustees were unable to develop English-German schools, although the proposition had quite clearly stated that "the Youth will be instructed in both the English and German languages." Bilingual teachers were simply not available and the device of a segregated English school and a German school in the same building proved essentially unworkable. Perhaps it was too much to hope in those days that financially stable elements of the population would provide a free education for poor children. "If ye original Intention of ye Society was that ye Children of English parents should receive ye Benefit of ye Charity freely, and that ye poor Germans should pay for it," complained a Quaker trustee of one abortive school attempt, "then the School at Easton is upon a Right Establishment at present, otherwise it is not."[44]

Indian raids and the unsettled frontier caused two of the schools, at Easton and Cordous, to close. The organized body of German and Dutch Reformed pastors, the Coetus of Pennsylvania, recognized the imminent danger, "Schools ... in very many places suffer great loss through these troublesome times and the great misfortunes of war." But dangerous as that situation was, it was a problem caused by outside factors. The greater threat, as judged by the Coetus, was an internal one. Initially they had "a very good and favorable opinion of this praise-worthy undertaking." They resolved to thank the trustees, and sought to determine "how many schoolteachers and in what places they are needed." But just two years later, following the resignation of Michael Schlatter as superintendent, the Coetus drew a far different picture: "Now with regard to the schools we can do but little to promote them, since the Directors try to erect nothing but English schools, and care nothing for the German language." Their conclusion was inevitable, "Hence, now as before, the Germans themselves ought to look out for their schools in which their children may be instructed in German."[45]

This novel and original school experiment, though it failed, did produce some positive, if temporary, results. Five years after the scheme was initiated, eight schools accommodated 440 male students, nearly two-thirds of them Pennsylvania Dutch. The English and German school at Germantown has continued as Germantown Academy. The summary report for that year emphasized that 600 students had been provided for annually, and a peak enrollment of 750 had been attained before Indian attacks made frontier schooling impossible.

Of course the free schools provided for only minute percentages of students educated in colonial Pennsylvania, where private and parochial schools continued to serve the vast majority. By 1761, war costs and taxes took their toll in the province, and the Coetus noted the total lack of contributions from England since 1759. "Regarding the free schools, we can hardly say anything, because the entire matter has been taken out of our hands. In General, we can say that there are still three schools of which we know; two of them are all English and one half German."[46] Three years later, no funds remained and financial support from England, including royal contributions, ceased entirely. The free school existed no longer. After a few years, the trustees paid remaining moneys to the College of Philadelphia for use in its charity school. No further accounting was made.[47]

Although both the Society for the Instruction of poor Germans and most of its Pennsylvania Dutch critics agreed that the school project had failed, it had pointed out educational needs. Particularly in the field of language study, offerings in contemporary foreign language and literature helped to bestow upon the College of Philadelphia (later University of Pennsylvania) clear leadership among American colleges. Some new teachers were recruited as a result of the school project. David James Dove, a Germantown English-school teacher, turned satirist in the decade before the American Revolution. Samuel Magaw, later vice provost of the University of Pennsylvania, was another. In a way, William Smith's Doctor of Divinity degree from the University of Oxford celebrated his leadership in the school scheme. His citation noted his achievements as "Trustee for the Free Schools, lately erected, among the vast Body of his Majesty's German Subjects . . . by an honorable Society in London; in order to instruct the children of the said Germans, in the English tongue and the Principles of Protestantism, and defeat the wicked Designs of the French and Papish Emissaries that swarm among them."[48]

The value of, and necessity for, free public schools was emphasized through this movement, even though it did finally collapse. As an integral part of the school project, a competing German press was established in Philadelphia, answering vigorous attacks by the elder Sauer. Profits from the new German press were earmarked for the free schools. Records do not clearly indicate how much, if any, money was so provided, but the intention was clear.

Partly as a response to evolving political patterns of the 1760s and partly as a defense of the German language and values threatened by the charity-school plan, German citizens of Philadelphia and Germantown organized a German Society (Teutschen Geselschaft) in 1764. Their rules and regulations directly stated their need for organization. In succeeding years they attempted to protect their ethnic interests. Johann Heinrich Keppele, one of the few Dutch elected to the Provincial Assembly at the time, was chosen the first president of the society, and other prominent German leaders became members.[49]

Another example of the pride of the Pennsylvania Dutch was their effort to initiate their own Free German School (Freischule) in Philadelphia, in conjunction with the parochial school of St. Michael's and Zion's Lutheran Church. They called their organization "The American Society for the Propagation of Christianity and Useful Knowledge among the Germans in America," obviously harking back to the English Society which had floundered a decade before. Henry M. Muhlenberg had supported the earlier attempt in face of criticisms but now opposed the efforts of the American Germans.

Largely through the efforts of Johann Christoph Kunze, pastor at St. Michael's and Zion Church, the society was organized, funds raised, and a teacher obtained for the experimental school known as Kunze's *Deutsches Seminarium*. Since the first teacher did not remain, Dominie Kunze assumed the German teaching duties himself, while John Gartley served as English teacher. Other teachers remained briefly. Many persons in the local German community became involved in the school and in its various projects. Henry Muhlenberg and Henry Helmuth used their ministerial standing to help Kunze raise money. Christopher Ludwick, a leading baker in Philadelphia and later Washington's Baker-General for the Continental forces, donated the bricks and supervised the construction of a bakeoven which was attached to the school building.[50]

The school survived only from 1773 to 1777, when the British occupied Philadelphia and seized the school building, which ended this educational institution (*welches dieser Anstalt ein Ende machte*). It was later reestablished as a part of the University of Pennsylvania under the name of "The German Institute." The Reverends Johann Christoph Kunze and Caspar Weyberg were named members of the University Board of Trustees. Under the newly adopted charter faculty members could not serve as trustees, so Kunze resigned the latter post to continue as professor of Oriental and German Languages for five years longer.[51]

When a free public elementary school system was mandated by law in 1834–1835, Pennsylvania Germans George Wolf and Joseph Ritner from opposite ends of the state took the lead in establishing and implementing the program, although not without political struggles. In both eighteenth and nineteenth centuries, educators and political figures assumed that free schools and private schools could coexist. A great many schools and seminaries, some to evolve into denominational colleges, were established in Pennsylvania and surrounding states in this century and a half. Numerous schools of this type associated themselves with the Pennsylvania German Reformed and Lutheran Churches or church personnel, as had the charity-school movement. Moravians, Mennonites, and Brethren also looked to their own educational needs. Church-directed elementary schools of the colonial period assumed the burden of teaching pupils, particularly where they preferred to maintain the integrity of their own language. So also in the midnineteenth century, the great surge to found colleges and schools of higher learning came in the form of church-related institutions, some of which were Pennsylvania Dutch in origin.

CHAPTER VIII

Partners in the War for Independence

No ASSESSMENT OF THE POLITICAL AND MILITARY STRUGGLE WHICH was the American Revolution can thoroughly examine all the facets and pressures of the period. Issues of the time were many and complex and have often been oversimplified in retrospect. It was a war in which only a minority of the citizens took active part but a conflict which aroused strong emotions nonetheless. The population split, with more Patriots than Loyalists, but as many as 40 percent remained neutral (or waited to discern an advantage). We have become aware of the difficulty (if not impossibility) of writing an impartial history of the American War for Independence. It tends to be either empire history or a study of American values. This is not surprising, since historians have often lauded their own national institutions.

Time and sophistication have not resolved these conflicts in historical judgment, though we may now be less intolerant of differences. While the Revolution continued, both participants and bystanders tended to condemn persons who failed to agree with them. It was a civil war within the British imperial system, but it was also a war for national independence.

The German element in late Colonial Pennsylvania found their ranks split in much the same way the general population did. As their dialect differed from county to county (with some relation to their previous German situation) so the response of Pietists and Church Germans, printers and plowmen, tavernkeepers and pastors never remotely approached consensus. Still, discernible patterns did emerge along certain religious, ethnic, social, and occupational lines. Only the Scots-Irish, for example, exceeded the Church German congregations in their zeal for the Patriot cause. They had become thoroughly

Pennsylvanian; their homeland lay here, at their feet. But with all other Pennsylvanians in 1775, these American Germans had to choose among very difficult options.

In the most awkward position of all, caught between the fires, as it were, stood Pennsylvania's pietist pacifist groups, English and Welsh Quakers, and the German and Swiss Mennonites, Amish, and Brethren alike. In many ways they understood the aims and goals, as well as the complaints, of both sides in the war. Many of the Pennsylvania Dutch had joined the Quakers in the New World to escape both forced military service and the devastation of recurring wars. In such a situation, those who refused to fight on either side were naturally condemned by both, although more extensively criticized by the Patriots in Pennsylvania, who were most numerous in the state. In addition, the non-English pacifists were attacked as ungrateful interlopers or as outsiders who had taken advantage of an English system but who had refused to be Anglified. Now, it seemed, at the time of the empire's greatest American need they stood apart with casual unconcern.

External criticism was not the only adverse reaction heaped upon the objectors. Many of their fellows who were Church Germans took no pacifist stand but flocked to the Patriot side in great numbers. In doing so, they often violently criticized their countrymen in the province who refused to defend the new life, the social and economic opportunities that Pennsylvania had offered. Many of the Pennsylvania Dutch, especially among the farming elements, busied themselves with hand to the plow and face toward the furrow, attempting to ignore policy problems and the war.

Many young men had taken passage as redemptioners or worked long years as indentured servants to escape the repeated wars and threats of wars in Europe. To them it seemed an unkind fate indeed to submit now to the same kind of pressures in America. In addition, they were now older, settled, and less flexible. Adamantly they stated their case as Mennonites and Dunkers, affirming their right to abstain from warfare.

We find no Freedom in giving, or doing, or assisting in any Thing by which Men's Lives are destroyed or hurt. . . . and we would be letting [the Assembly] know that we are thankful as above mentioned and that we are not at Liberty in Conscience to take up arms to Conquer our Enemies.[1]

Most Mennonites simply adjusted to the patterns of Pennsylvania living and withstood verbal barbs and assorted harassment visited upon them by neighbors and officials in the state during the war. Since most of them were rural, they still had to face the local problem of the destination of their grain, meat, and produce. That was regarded as an individual matter, not subject to religious discipline. Some swallowed their objections to inflated provincial and continental currency, whereas others held out for hard (British) cash. Occasionally the problem was solved for them by requisition, confiscation, or simple theft of their goods.

Brethren and Adventists had problems very similar to those of the Mennonites and Amish. For the most part they attempted to find solutions within a pacifist framework while continuing to reside and to participate as normally as possible in nonhostile and nonmilitary aspects of provincial life.

On the whole, the decade before the Revolution found the Pennsylvania Dutch in mood and situation very little different from their English neighbors. They complained vigorously about additional taxes imposed after 1763, much preferring the earlier British neglect. Publishers of German newspapers joined other editors in decrying the Stamp Act. They suspended and resumed publication upon passage and repeal of the act.

Merchants of all backgrounds generally complained of interference with their prerogatives and their trade as a result of the new imperial policies. The Dutch also experimented with bay leaves and with tea herbs as substitutes for English tea after the passage of new tea duty regulations in the 1770s, to avoid tax payments to the monopoly company designated by the British. German merchants and shippers were free to smuggle in duty-free goods as did other Americans.

In the wake of the anti-import decisions of the First Continental Congress and its resultant attempts to foster home industries, Pennsylvania tried printing innovations. "As printing types are now being made to a considerable degree of perfection by an ingenious artist in Germantown, it is recommended to the printers to use such types in preference to any which they may hereafter import."[2] Jacob Bay, "a German who resided in Germantown," was the worker in the Sauer Print Shop who cast type to order for local printing, an example followed shortly by another town businessman, Justus Fox.

Many otherwise calm and peaceable Pennsylvania Dutch farmers roused themselves heatedly in defense of their new possessions. A few among them spoke of liberty and freedom, and gradually even German churchmen spoke glowingly of "republican virtues." But the call of the land, the realization of opportunity in America, and the chance at stable guarantees concerned virtually everyone. They had been willing to risk the casualty rates of transatlantic passage, endure the years of indenture, and face Indian threats on the frontier to qualify for ownership of that land. Now they would certainly not stand by casually and lose their land again.

Pennsylvania was their only home. William Penn had invited landless, penniless German workers and farmers to come share in the new experiment. Pennsylvania had sheltered them while allowing them to retain customs and values characteristic of their own life-style. Questions basic to the Revolution revolved about the issue of loyalty and thus imposed harsh limitations. The choice of the great majority of Pennsylvania Germans was resolved by their close association with provincial opportunities. They chose to be loyal to Pennsylvania and thus loyal to the United Colonies (later United States) of which Pennsylvania was a part, and they decried the lack of spirit among individuals and colonies who did not share that view.

In contrast to pietist Germans in Pennsylvania, who found themselves again at a disadvantage (as when an illegal minority in the German homeland), Lutheran and Reformed elements rallied to the defense of the province. They took up arms against the royal troops. Owen S. Ireland has recently seen this action by Church Germans as a part of a general Calvinist domination of politics in the state during the war.[3] But it is difficult to fit Pennsylvania's German Lutherans, Moravians, and Schwenkfelders into a strict Calvinist/Anti-Calvinist distinction. A vigorous Pennsylvania suspicion of Massachusetts and Connecticut Yankees existed. "Ethnicity and religion are valuable explanatory variables for the analysis" of this period, the same author suggests elsewhere.[4] Surely that convincing premise deserves our attention. But in this key province, the Lutheran and Reformed Pennsylvania Dutch were linked in so many localities in Union Churches despite theological, doctrinal differences that they acted in concert rather than contending against one another.

What repelled the Dutch of Pennsylvania from early support of the British was the vigor of General Thomas Gage's response in Massachusetts against citizens who had gathered some reserves of powder and shot. Without questioning the propriety of concealed war supplies, German-Americans could only abhor use of royal troops against ordinary citizens. There were still some survivors in the New World who had witnessed seizures and forced dispossession by imperial dragoons in the Old. Practically all those of German background in America had heard the stories and tales of heartless actions and citizen deaths.

British attack was bad enough but worse followed ("Was aber das ärgste ist") in Gage's proclamation of June 12, restricting normal operation of English law in Massachusetts. American and homeland Englishmen had firmly insisted that English legal guarantees protected those living under the system. Arbitrary imposition of military law was not allowed. Pennsylvania German Lutheran and Reformed clergy vigorously denounced Gage and his resort to coercion. They not only voiced those opinions to their people and associates within the province but also circulated their ideas. Pamphlets printed in Philadelphia presumed to influence "Freunde und Landsleute" in New York and North Carolina.[5] In fact they also circulated in Pennsylvania and found their way into neighboring German settlements. Church Germans thus early declared for the Patriots.

The early violence of the British clearly called for resistance and response in kind. If that meant war in defense of home, family, and church, then war it must be. Certainly many of these Pennsylvanians lacked military experience, and were hardly professional in their conduct under arms. Great numbers of them owned rifles, which had at times fed families and protected farm buildings. A few men had even served briefly in militia units of the 1750s. Central to this development is the fact that Church Germans were not pacifists. Virtually all the German Lutheran and Reformed pastors supported the Patriot side. A very few joined Tory sympathizers, and some remained neutral. Both denominations regularly instructed church members in their duties to the state and their fellowmen. From among the limited number of Lutheran and Reformed pastors in America, several, like Abraham Blumer and Philip Jacob Michael, became chaplains in the militia or the army; at least one became a line officer.[6]

Church members from virtually every German congregation volunteered for service either in the regular Continental Army forces or as militia troops called up in local emergencies. Both officers and enlisted men came from that source, although the vast majority of Pennsylvania Dutch volunteers were enlisted personnel.[7] The German church found itself in a generally difficult position, noting just after the skirmishes at Lexington and Concord, "We live in precarious times, the like of which, so far as we know, has never been seen in America." But they also concluded, "The Lord Knows what he has in store for us."[8]

Among the most renowned German families in the Colonies was the Muhlenberg clan. All of the members of the family were exposed to the war to some degree. Henry Melchior Muhlenberg, *pater familias,* decided to remain neutral, although his heart went out to the Continental soldiers as he observed their wretched condition, when they marched by his farm. But he saw the powerful British government lose its sense of judgment, responding violently to the earnest pleadings of the provincial leaders. His three sons served as Lutheran pastors in New York, Pennsylvania, and Virginia when the war broke out. Of the three—Henry Ernest, Frederick, and Peter—only the first still served his Pennsylvania church when the Revolution ended.

Frederick Augustus Conrad Muhlenberg found his feelings for the empire shaken in the late summer of 1775, when British warships sent naval gunfire into the city of New York. His wife and two children joined the fifteen hundred refugees from the city. Cathy and the children went on to her parents' home in

Philadelphia for safety. Frederick Muhlenberg remained in New York, but his mind was now made up. He would cast his lot with the American cause.[9]

In Virginia, where he had ministered to the congregation at Woodstock since 1772, John Peter Gabriel Muhlenberg observed with great concern the early rumblings of what was coming. In June, 1774, Peter Muhlenberg served as chairman of a meeting of Woodstock freeholders to consider the proper course of action in the wake of the retaliatory closing of the port of Boston. He was at the convention in Williamsburg as delegate when Patrick Henry issued his "liberty or death" statement. After he was elected chairman of the Committee of Correspondence and Safety for Dunmore County, his role as active supporter of the Revolution was determined. He spent the next eight years on the Patriot side.

His brother Frederick advised him against such political activity, but Peter had already made up his mind. Peter Muhlenberg who had contemplated service as a chaplain with the Virginia troops, now responded to a different call. Of Virginia's additional troops for the Continental line, the Eighth Virginia Regiment was to be recruited from the German population of the Shenandoah Valley. Most of these settlers had migrated south from Pennsylvania. The second week in January, the Virginia Convention appointed Peter Muhlenberg to be colonel commanding this new regiment.

The following Sunday, Muhlenberg preached his farewell sermon at Woodstock, an occurrence which has been so often described that fact and fiction can hardly be separated. He undoubtedly told his congregation of his decision to enter army service, and he explained his action in biblical terms: "There is a time to preach and a time to pray, but those times had passed away; there was also a time to fight and that time had now come."[10] Pastor Muhlenberg then surprised his people by flinging open his clerical robe to reveal the uniform of a Continental Army officer underneath; at least that is the most dramatic version of the event. Other accounts have him in military garb for the whole service, or insist that he preached in his clerical robes, but put on his colonel's uniform before reappearing to the view of his congregation. Three hundred men of the neighborhood volunteered to join Muhlenberg's Eighth Regiment. The basic facts are clear enough. Colonel Muhlenberg had accepted his commission a week before his farewell sermon, whose climax contained the "time to pray, time to fight" statement. Colonel Muhlenberg served during the war with the Eighth Virginia Regiment to win commendations and praise from General Washington and others in command. Even his father saw the logic of Peter's decision and wrote privately, "the young people are right in fighting for their God-given native liberty."[11]

The decision Peter Muhlenberg made was a critical one for him, since he remained in secular employment even after the end of the war. When Frederick, his brother, made a similar decision to leave the ministry, he entered civil government affairs rather than the military. His flight from New York, as British units moved in to occupy the city and island land nearby, convinced him he could not remain a Loyalist.

Another of the Pennsylvania Dutch who chose early to support the Patriot cause was Christopher Ludwick, who had discovered that Philadelphia, modern town that it was, had no bakery to speak of. In the fifteen years before the outbreak of the American Revolution, Ludwick built a substantial business, supplying leading families of the town. Many of these had baked their own bread but were happy to depend upon an enterprising baker for their supply.[12] He found time for other activities, serving as initial secretary for the German Society of Philadelphia and attending to other charitable causes as well.

As a moderate Whig, he followed closely the political events of the early 1770s and in May, 1774, was elected to the Philadelphia Committee of Correspondence. He served on committees looking forward to independence. Ludwick helped establish a manufacturing operation in Philadelphia, which supplied woolen cloth to the Continental Army until closed by the British occupation of the city. He also secured gunpowder and saltpeter, needed by the Continental Army to supplement its meager ammunition supply. Although past the age of fifty, Christopher Ludwick joined special military forces intent upon relief of General Washington in New York.

Born in Hesse-Darmstadt, he spoke the dialect of the Hessian soldiers who served with the British forces in America. When the Continental Congress determined to encourage Hessian desertions, the Pennsylvania baker was one of the first men sent behind British lines. Posing as a deserter, he carried out spy activities against the British and propagandized the Hessians on the great advantages of settling in Pennsylvania.[13] One account had Ludwick as country baker, reconnoitering British and Hessian deployment in Trenton and improving Continental chances in the dangerous night crossing of the Delaware River and the subsequent American victory at Trenton.

In the fall of 1776, Christopher Ludwick responded to a Pennsylvania Council of Safety inquiry about supplies. "Mr. Ludwig recommends a pound of flour per week per man to be allowed the army."[14] Six months later, the Congress appointed him "superintendent of Bakers and director of baking, in the grand army of the United States." As Baker General of the Continental army, he had to approve and license all its bakers. After Washington had properly congratulated him, Ludwick joined the army at Morristown, New Jersey. That summer, Washington encouraged him "to continue baking as fast as you can, because two other divisions ... will want Bread." Preparing for military operations of late 1777, Ludwick had auxiliary ovens built at Skippack and experienced the harsh winters of 1777–78 at Valley Forge and 1778–79 in New Jersey.[15]

Except for the antiwar sects, a high percentage of the Pennsylvania Dutch saw military service either as militia in local matters or in the Continental army. Many of the first generation immigrants had involuntarily served in military units in Germany and thus had some experience. Others felt that, compared to loss of their land, a short military term was the lesser disadvantage. Moreover as they had heard the old tales of forced service back in the German homeland, a fight to defend home and family seemed vastly more logical than warfare for the aggrandizement of a petty local prince.

Early in the war, when enthusiasm ran high, even young men of the educational institutions of Philadelphia held military muster. Thus, Jacob Mordecai could remember many years later "Michael Leib's company of German school boys in Cherry Alley ... at the Lutheran Church,"[16] with military uniforms quite like those of the company from the Academy of Philadelphia, of nankeen cloth but with a blue facing.

People in Philadelphia kept abreast of the news emanating from the State House in June and July of 1776. The decision to break entirely from Great Britain came July 2 and was followed by the adoption of the formal draft on the fourth. The elder Muhlenberg expressed his mixed emotions, "Today the Continental Congress openly declared the united provinces of North America to be free and *independent* states." He judged "some thoughtful and far-seeing *melancholici* to be down in the mouth," while it led others to "exult and shout with joy."[17] Henrich Miller's *Pennsylvanischer Staatsbote* was first to carry news of the adoption of the Declaration of Independence. The *Staatsbote* also printed the first version of the text in a language other than English, under the heading, *Eine Erklärung durch die Repräsentanten der Vereinigten Staaten von America.*[18]

Clearly the political figures who had gathered in Philadelphia for the continuation of the Second Continental Congress had struck a responsive chord among many citizens of the new nation and the state. But the decision was not easy for many, particularly among older citizens. Henry Muhlenberg had twice taken the special oath of loyalty to the king of England, required of all the Germans in Pennsylvania, on debarkation and when naturalized. He felt the pressure. "Robbed of my fromer protection, old and cast aside, unwilling to change my oath of allegiance, nor yet to be a sacrifice to *Anarchie* at the hands of an angry mob," he decided to move back to Trappe. He foresaw "the flames of war spreading farther over the united North American provinces during the coming year," and eventually he signed a Pennsylvania loyalty oath.[19]

Many of Muhlenberg's neighbors did organize military units in the vicinity. Through Trappe passed "a company of men from Reading, a hundred strong, on the march to the province of Jersey. Most of them were settlers and young men born in this country and recently enlisted with others to form an army of observation in Jersey."[20] Soldiers camped "here in Providence." Numerous individuals billeted at the two inns in town. Two weeks later a company of riflemen filed through Trappe. "Most of them are native youngsters from in and around Reading who learned bush fighting like that of the Indians." In August parts of two battalions of Pennsylvania Dutch troops also marched by, led by Colonel Henry Grubb and Colonel John Potts. "I was asked to give them a word of admonition in English and German in Augustus Church, for they were on the march to the camp in Jersey."[21]

Often, as in the militia companies from Pennsylvania, the rifle companies wore buckskin as a distinctive uniform of their own, "outer shirts shaggy, almost like the pictures of ... sylvan spirits of ancient times." They fought Indian-style, armed with rifles and tomahawks. The riflemen's "peculiar form of dress, much like that of the savage Indians," identified them even though "most are enlisted as native-born men of English and German extraction." Part of the difficulty encountered by the civil militia was that of recurring short-term calls, for it was required "time after time to take its place along with others in the breach." They were not always ready, and the interrupted training proved a handicap at times.[22]

Although not forced into service, Church Germans chose to fight for the patriot cause. Peggy Kunze, daughter of Henry M. Muhlenberg and wife of the school director, hinted at some local pressure: "Our Milishe are all going towards New York, the Yagers [riflemen] are most all gone. Next Sunday we shall have very few men in our Church, all my neabors are gone. ... The men must go, or be taken to gail, or tard and fetheard."[23] Officers and men who were Pennsylvania Dutch served with Continental forces in all campaigns and virtually every skirmish, but in many cases their presence was noted only as units of soldiers from the Dutch country. General George Washington recognized the value of minority personnel and chose his bodyguard troops from present Berks, Montgomery, and Lebanon Counties. Escorting the commander from Newburgh, New York, to Mount Vernon at war's end was a Guard of Honor composed entirely of Pennsylvania Germans.[24]

Great numbers of refugees fled from Philadelphia and Muhlenberg's home and church served as "hospital" for civilians

and soldiers. A newly promoted brigadier general was Peter
Muhlenberg's brigade major, Francis Swaine, a neighbor from
Trappe. Both actively recruited additional soldiers from Penn-
sylvania and Virginia.

In August General William Howe landed a British army in
the Chesapeake and news of the arrival reached southeastern
Pennsylvania only days before the British troops. General Muhlenberg settled his brigade on the Brandywine Creek as part
of Nathaniel Greene's division, waiting for the impending
British attack. When the battle was joined, British experience
and superior manpower brought victory to Howe, Knyphausen,
and Cornwallis. Muhlenberg's Brigade stood off the main charge
for several hours. The Americans, forced to retreat and then
withdraw, remained a fighting force; they had certainly not
disgraced themselves.[25]

When it became apparent that British occupation of Philadelphia was near, Christopher Ludwick moved all his baking
operations out of Philadelphia. Facilities at Skippack proved
entirely insufficient, so bakeovens were hastily built. Even so,
the British destroyed four thousand barrels of flour he had
on hand as they moved on Philadelphia. The Skippack oven
provided bread for the Continental troops as the British occupied the city in September and made further supplies available
to patriot forces to and from Germantown. In the crucial
engagement in and around the streets of the original German
settlement in Pennsylvania, Washington's forces came within
final grasp of victory, but smoke and mist produced confusion
and uncertainty, so defeat resulted when success seemed so
near. The Germantown and Brandywine battles demonstrated
the resilience of the Continental army, but left the British in
unchallenged possession of Philadelphia, chief city of the
United States. American forces were subject to the worst kind
of conditions in the winter encampment at Valley Forge, fifteen
miles west of the city.[26]

The Continental army's forty-five hundred veterans of hap-
pier campaigns dug in for a miserable winter of cold and snow,
of shortages, deprivation, and complaints. Washington and his
headquarters' staff occupied old farm and mill buildings near
the center of the encampment. Baker General Ludwick erected

new sets of ovens throughout the encampment but settled his main efforts in new ovens at the house of Colonel William Dewees. Ludwick kept a small supply of flour at Valley Forge, but his main storage was at Reading. With many others in the patriot cause, Ludwick spent his own money on supplies, and even sold a house in order to realize more ready cash.[27]

General Peter Muhlenberg at Valley Forge was much concerned about the danger of a British raid against Trappe. He feared for his parents' safety; yet both his father and mother refused to move. Later in the winter two of the sisters heard a raid was in the offing. Angry Hessians supposedly organized to hang the elder Muhlenberg, but nothing came of it. Late that winter, a band of Oneida Indians stopped overnight near the Muhlenberg farm, on the move to join the Continental Army at Valley Forge. The Indian leaders requested that no one sell brandy to the men. After a few cheerful "Yo-hah's" of approval, the Oneidas left early the next morning.

The Continental army reached the lowest ebb of morale and endurance in the Valley Forge camp. The soldiers knew that British winter quarters in Philadelphia were both warm and secure. The chilling, precarious, debilitating situation of the American troops at the skeleton winter encampment was demoralizing. The Continentals entered winter quarters a ragtag collection of disappointed men. Thanks to the assistance of the Prussian drillmaster, the "Baron" Friederich Wilhelm von Steuben, they emerged in spring a disciplined and trained army. Moreover, when Lafayette made a difficult but urgent withdrawal over the Schuylkill river with bridges in a most dilapidated condition, his rear guard was protected and the detachment saved by those seventy Oneida Indians who had passed the time of day with the Muhlenbergs.[28]

Just before the British occupation of Philadelphia, an action with symbolic overtones occurred. Officials in Philadelphia acted to save the State House tower bell from confiscation and probable destruction by the British. In celebration of the fiftieth anniversary of the Charter of Privileges of 1701, provincial officials had ordered the bell in 1751. It proved defective and was recast in Philadelphia, again with the legend from Leviticus, "Proclaim Liberty throughout the Land, Unto all the

Inhabitants thereof." Its motto had taken on additional significance when the free United States government was proclaimed
in Philadelphia, and the safety of the bell became a matter of
patriot pride.

In one of the best-kept open secrets of the war, the bell
was removed from the belltower, loaded on the hay wagon
of a Pennsylvania Dutch farmer, perhaps Frederick Leaser
or John Jacob Mickley, and covered with hay for concealment
on its route to the hinterland. The Congress itself then withdrew to security in the inland town of Lancaster, and a short
time later moved to York, another forty miles to the west.

Rumors circulated concerning the location of the bell. Sir
William Howe's men collected all bells and other brass, bronze,
and copper items to be melted down and recast as cannon for
use of His Majesty's Forces. Only when it was safe to return
the bell, after the end of the British occupation in late spring,
1778, was the hiding place revealed. It had been hauled northward while the government moved west and rested safely in
the basement of Zion German Reformed Church, Allentown,
Pennsylvania, a mere fifty miles from the center of British
operations in the Quaker city.[29]

Howe hoped to make it possible for many leading citizens
in Philadelphia to espouse the loyalist cause. Howe's drive into
the city and the embarrassment of the rebel government was
eminently successful. His effect upon the population of the chief
city was also embarrassing, for many prominent citizens were
active Tories. Others who had straddled the fence, now convinced of British victory, openly declared for the crown.

Two sons of Christopher Sauer, Jr., spoke up clearly in the
British interest. In fact, Christopher III became the semi-
official printer of the king's occupation government. There were
other Germans of the same mind, especially those whose
scruples against fighting emanated from religious principles.
Many others like the elder Sauer or the youngest of the Muhlenberg brothers, Henry Ernest, tried so hard to be neutral that
they offended both sides. Both were compromised by their
situation. The younger Muhlenberg's stay in Philadelphia led
to rumors that his father secretly supported the British, but
Henry Melchior Muhlenberg, at the Trappe, was able to dis-

prove the charges. Less fortunate, the elder Sauer, who had not disciplined his Tory sons, was arrested May 24, 1778, as the British departed from the city. In retaliation for his sons' use of a press confiscated from Henrich Miller, the patriot army leaders seized the Sauer house and printing establishment and sold all items, effects, and real estate at the convenience of the State of Pennsylvania.[30]

The general attitude of most of the Pennsylvania Dutch may be seen in the activities of a John Peter Muhlenberg or a Christopher Ludwick. With them lay the sympathies of vast numbers of the Germanic population, as occasionally expressed in one of the folk rhymes then current:

> Kleine Georgel, Kaiser, Koenig,
> Ist fer Gott un uns zu wennich.[31]

Most of the Pennsylvania Germans opposed the Tories and their allies.

Pennsylvania Dutch inhabitants most specifically disliked the use of Hessian mercenaries. Pennsylvanians who had migrated from the Germanies or from Switzerland earlier fully understood the machinations of homeland politics which made pawns of a helpless population. Men found themselves sold as a commodity, as mercenary soldiers whose activities (and very lives) were utilized toward political and military ends which were of absolutely no concern to them.[32]

German mercenary troops from Waldeck, Hesse, or Brunswick commented favorably on the climate and topography of the New World and sometimes discussed events they had witnessed. Some noted the dedication of American troops they faced, whereas others were critical of the population. In Philadelphia, one soldier reported, "I have never seen so many foolish people as here," though few were as uncomplimentary as Lieutenant Andreas Wiederholt:

Most inhabitants of German descent are of the lowest class and are the dregs of that nation. They want to imitate the hospitality and candor of the others, but they remain raw and unrefined German peasants. They are steeped in the American idea of Liberty but know nothing of what liberty really is, and are therefore worse than all others and almost unbearable. But here and there one finds honest and upright Germans.[33]

German cousins in Pennsylvania were wont to compare life and opportunities in America with conditions in the Germanies. They first detested mercenaries but then felt sad for them.[34]

The Pennsylvania Germans arrived at a New World solution; they conspired to subvert the Hessians and other mercenary troops, aiming their propaganda efforts particularly at those who had been captured.[35] In 1776, Christopher Ludwick, in charge of German prisoners, was delighted with the first eight Hessians sent to him.

Let us take them to Philadelphia and there show them our fine German churches. Let them see how our tradesmen eat good beef, drink out of silver cups every day, and ride out in chairs every afternoon; and then let us send them back to their countrymen, and they will all soon run away and settle in our city and be as good whigs as any of us.[36]

But release of Hessian prisoners should be coupled with general prisoner exchange, lest it "carry the marks of design and occasion precautions to be taken to prevent the ends we have in view."[37] Many years later Jacob Mordecai recalled, "Deserters came to us by pairs and dozens."[38]

Word spread that the contracts with the rulers of the German states who supplied troops to the British, called for extra payment in case of battle wounds or death in the war. Criticism of the system became more widespread in the United States, which led to more elaborate plans to agitate Hessian and other German mercenary soldiers, who were usually segregated from the English prisoners. The greatest number of them were sent to prisoner camps in Pennsylvania or Virginia.[39] There the citizens plied them with accounts of local advantages and told of achievements of other Germans who had migrated earlier. Camps located in or near Lancaster, York, Reading, and Easton, in areas of high German population, produced many escapes. The state population increased by many hundreds as the way to freedom became apparent.[40]

Both sides attempted to recruit volunteers from among their prisoners. Enlistment of Hessians into the Continental army was not only allowed, but encouraged. Those who enlisted might remain in the United States after their term of service was up. In addition, Christopher Ludwick had asked concessions from the Continental Congress for those "Hessians and Waldekish Prisoners of War" who would agree to voluntary work assignment, to be assigned as "journeymen and labourers ... to discreet and humane ... masters and Employers" for the duration of their detention. Prompt return of the prisoners in case of exchange must, however, also be guaranteed. Pennsylvania tried the plan, and Hessian shoemakers were employed at Lancaster making shoes for the province.[41]

Some few among the Dutch sided with the British during the Revolution and their fate was to lose all property and standing. William Nelson states broadly that the Low Dutch and Germans tended to support the Revolution in areas "where they were already anglicized," but that they sympathized with the Tories "where they had kept their language and separate outlook."[42] How thoroughly that applied to Lutheran and Reformed Germans may be questioned, although some who had established themselves in commerce and society ceased to sympathize with fellow German immigrants.

Vigorously patriot was the almost mythical Reverend John Wesley Gilbert Nevelling, who preached in German in parishes in the Amwell Valley of West Jersey, converted his property to cash, and then loaned it to the Continental Congress. He was also reputed to have served as chaplain with the Continental forces, thus inviting British prosecution, though documents to support those claims are still lacking.[43]

One of the most celebrated incidents of the war occurred at the Battle of Monmouth in June, 1778, where "Molly Pitcher" was said to have replaced her dead husband in artillery action. But her husband had not been killed at all. In fact, the woman who helped in battle was Mary Ludwig Hays, whose father, a Palatine migrant, farmed near Trenton. She had worked as a servant girl near Carlisle, then followed her soldier husband to New Jersey with the Pennsylvania forces. She did carry water from a nearby well to the relief of the fighting troops and earned her name of "Molly Pitcher." But at the end of the war, she accompanied her husband back to Carlisle, after he had recovered from his war wounds.[44]

Among other important German names of the war period, which have been forgotten by later generations, is that of Doctor Bodo Otto. That Pennsylvania Dutchman, senior surgeon at Reading, lent his knowledge to save many lives of Continental soldiers and Hessian prisoners. He was one of the leading medical personalities of the era; yet few notices of him have survived into the twentieth century.[45]

General Peter Muhlenberg found the winter of 1780–81 almost unbelievably bad for military activities in Virginia. In the preceding twelve months he raised troops in his adopted state for the fighting farther south. In the autumn of 1780, when Virginia was threatened by British military action, he found the situation deplorable. Field units simply had insufficient manpower and few arms, little clothing or food, and almost no transportation. Baron Steuben in Virginia was outraged to find Muhlenberg charged with military campaign responsibilities under such conditions. The drillmaster stated sadly, "The Men under general Muhlenberg, I found in a most Destrist Situation so intirely Destitute of Cloathing that it was impossible to get them to march."[46]

Only slightly later, in January, 1781, other Germans, while stationed in New Jersey, participated in the mutiny of the Pennsylvania line. They did make it quite clear they had no "ideas of turning Arnolds (as they express it)" according to General Anthony Wayne, but they were outraged by the continuing lack of pay.[47]

At that very same time the British put unusual pressure on Muhlenberg and his motley assortment of Virginia last defenders. They sent General Benedict Arnold with sixteen hundred British regulars to raid Jamestown, Westover, and Richmond. He did it so successfully that Steuben called for two hundred volunteers to defend the state capitol, but only half of the arrivals were armed. They failed to harass the enemy as ordered, but marched off in the opposite direction. Thereupon Muhlenberg was called into action again to oppose Arnold and confine him to the seacoast. In light of the general hatred and fear which Arnold's presence aroused, Governor Thomas Jefferson issued orders to "undertake to seize and bring off this greatest of traitors." He handed the job to the Shenandoah County German militia. General Peter Muhlenberg prepared a trap and tried to lure General Arnold into it, but it failed when Arnold would not leave Portsmouth. In the process Muhlenberg with a number of his men, "was in the Enemies Lines [and] cut off their Pickett."[48] The Virginia forces never again had that good an opportunity. Muhlenberg received a letter of commendation from General Von Steuben.

In May and June, 1781, General Peter Muhlenberg advocated an early strike against Generals Earl Charles Cornwallis and Arnold. In October, then, Muhlenberg and his fellow German General Weeden, with their brigades, stood high in the order of battle drawn up by recently arrived General George Washington. While Alexander Hamilton led the assault on Redoubt Number Ten of the Yorktown defenses, the senior commander in the field, in charge of the column that took the redoubt, was General Peter Muhlenberg, although historical literature has rarely recognized his presence.[49]

In regard to the economic aspects of the war, the significance of the Pennsylvania Dutch becomes increasingly clear. The Pennsylvania farm country in which the Dutch were preponderant was the breadbasket of the nation. While the fortunes of war ebbed and flowed, the farmers continued their steady efforts to produce enough wheat and corn to meet the military and civilian demands, never entirely successfully. They placed more lands under cultivation in an effort to increase production, and then were outraged when the runaway inflation of Continental currency robbed them of much of the real value their crops should have brought.

Thomas Anbury spoke of those difficulties midway through the war. "We do not so readily procure necessaries from the country people . . . having only Congress money to pay them for their commodities."[50] Many of the Pennsylvania Dutch farmers sold goods for hard British cash. That was especially true while the occupation of Philadelphia continued and while vigorous competition for supplies prevailed. Some drove their wagons of supplies past the encampment at Valley Forge to sell to the

English in the city. In Trappe, on the edge of the farm area which supplied both Americans and British, Henry M. Muhlenberg noted that the high costs of farming and the absence of so many ablebodied field workers resulted in a short supply of farm products and contributed to "the dearness of things."[51]

Several leading Pennsylvania Germans held positions of economic responsibility with the new governments. David Rittenhouse and Michael Hillegas served in the last Assembly under the Charter of 1701. Both were named to a committee to determine supplies and rations for the Pennsylvania troops, and both were appointed to the Pennsylvania Committee of Public Safety. State officials chose Michael Hillegas treasurer of Pennsylvania, an office he held until in October, 1776, when he was also appointed treasurer of the Continental Congress.

After two months' service as both state and national treasurer, Hillegas was ordered away from Philadelphia by Congress. In December David Rittenhouse was appointed treasurer of Pennsylvania in place of Hillegas. Both continued their respective service for the duration of the war and throughout most of the decade of the 1780s as well.[52]

Presiding as treasurer of Pennsylvania Rittenhouse became the focal point of legal action in the celebrated war-prize case of the sloop *Active,* a case which demonstrates the sectional hostility which existed during the war. The Pennsylvania ship *Convention* and the privateer *Gerard* captured the British sloop *Active,* but not until four Connecticut seamen who had been impressed into Royal Navy duty, mutinied on the *Active* and gained control of her. When the *Active* was brought into Philadelphia as prize vessel, Pennsylvania courts awarded four quarter-claims, one-fourth to Gideon Olmstead and his Connecticut associates, one-fourth to each of the two vessels which captured the *Active,* and one-quarter to the state of Pennsylvania. Over eleven thousand pounds was placed in the hands of David Rittenhouse as treasurer, but only against strenuous challenge by Connecticut claimants.

Pending final settlement, Rittenhouse invested the money and attempted unsuccessfully several times to deliver the securities and accumulated interest to the State of Pennsylvania, which was unwilling to receive it while Connecticut claims were still pending. The Continental Congress, acting as admiralty court, ordered the full claim paid to the Connecticut seamen. Then it became known that Benedict Arnold as military commandant of Philadelphia had bought into the Connecticut seamen's claim and used pressure to validate the appeal. Regional jealousies made Pennsylvania unwilling to honor the claim or to accede to Congress' judgment; injection of Arnold in the case made them adamant in their refusal. The judgment remained unpaid for thirty years.[53]

Little of the fighting of the Revolutionary War occurred in Pennsylvania and, except for Brandywine, Germantown and British-occupied Philadelphia, few cases of direct war-caused damage resulted. True, the forces under General Howe burned a dozen or so of the finest country homes in the outskirts of the city, as much to punish patriots as for a defensive line. The Continental army encampment at Valley Forge also produced some raids against neighboring farms, even though General Washington specifically outlawed such depredations. War inflation, on the other hand, cost millions of dollars which the frugal Dutch farmer spent years of subsequent peacetime energy to repay.

Pennsylvania Dutch had responded first to Washington's call. Companies of riflemen from Berks, York, Lancaster, and Northampton Counties had joined him at Cambridge, Massachusetts. They were the scourge of the British, "shirt-tail men with their cursed twisted guns—the most fatal widow-orphan-makers in the world."[54] Military hospitals at Skippack, Trappe, Ephrata, Reading, Bethlehem, Lancaster, Easton, and Allentown served soldiers and units from Continental and state militia forces throughout the war. Yet it was the technology of the Dutch settlers of Pennsylvania which gave the American cause not only the Pennsylvania rifle but also the Conestoga wagon, the greatest freight carrier the Continental army ever found.[55]

Arthur Graeff has used this metaphor to explain the war:

In one sense the Revolution was a war between ships and wagons, and wagons won . . . Pennsylvania provided the motive force which gave the American armies their superiority of mobility. . . . The many furnaces, forges and slitting mills which formed along the Schuylkill River and its tributaries, forged the cannon and the cannon balls, as well as tires for wagon wheels, barrels for guns and all sorts of digging tools. Gun powder manufacture required the ingredient of sulphur and saltpetre . . . furnished by York County[56]

Peace brought a return to more normal conditions. Many who had actively served in the patriot cause received land bounties at the end of the hostilities. That gave them some opportunity to compete with civilians who had remained home to enjoy the financial returns of the war economy. Others failed to recover cash they had forwarded to be used by Congress.[57]

The postwar period with its deflationary monetary policies caused added hardship. Hundreds of those who held government obligations but had only a meagre income at the moment sold their government paper at fifteen cents on the dollar. When they saw the speculators paid off dollar for dollar they complained loudly. Even stranger was the unfriendly treatment accorded German Mennonites and Brethren who had been neutral during the war. They were handled as though they had been disloyal, at the very same time Pennsylvania welcomed back Tories of English background, who had been so vigorously engaged on the Tory side that they had had to flee the state for their own safety. Beginning in 1792, some of the offended Mennonites left for Ontario.[58]

In the War for American Independence, the Pennsylvania Dutch made their major contribution, asking little else than the opportunity to express themselves in action. Some among them refused to choose sides. Others would have preferred not to make a choice, but circumstances forced them to do so.

CHAPTER IX

Folk Art and Formal Art: Dutch Arts and Crafts

THE URGE TO CREATE LASTING THINGS OF VALUE, BEAUTY, AND utility is innate in mankind. It surfaces in the works and achievements of both simple and sophisticated societies. This includes not only fine arts—painting, sculpture, music, and poetry—but also casual, decorated, handcrafted items for ordinary chores and daily use. Driven by the drudgery and limitations of everyday life, many of the Pennsylvania Dutch, with no notion of creating great masterpieces, painted, scratched, carved, cast, or sewed designs in and upon basic materials. Some of the ideas and patterns originated in the river valleys or wooded mountainsides of Germany and Switzerland. Other aspects of their art reflected their experiences in Pennsylvania. Though only a few of these regional artists achieved national prominence in the arts, most did gain temporary recognition in their own locality.

Pennsylvania German art is essentially folk art, although a half-dozen professional painters competed successfully enough among the growing number of artists and illustrators of their time. Folk art relates directly to folk culture, and their creations are an outgrowth of their religious sentiments. Thus any attempt to explain their folk art without reference to religious and cultural values can only fail or become pedantic. In short, folk art is one of the cultural forms of the Pennsylvania Dutch, expressing the life and spirit of this more or less homogeneous segment of early American society. As folk art it is indigenous to the community and expressive of its spirit and its ideals rather than those of individuals.

Folk art permits individualism in style. One artist may stress

158

flowers, another birds, or some special calligraphic or geometric motif. For final clarity of the symbolism of this folk art, it must also be related directly to the local literary tradition and thoroughly founded in religious values.[1]

In this way, lives of toil, hardship, and sorrow were relieved by bright-hued paints on the red barns and blue gates, by striking color contrasts of patchwork quilts, and by word pictures of the delights to come. Such designs remained the basis for innumerable intriguing and inventive children's games. They learned moral lessons from scriptural parables summarized in cast-iron stoveplates. Superstitions survived in the semimagical hidden hex signs which challenged and confused spirits of evil intention.

Furnaces and forges abounded in the Dutch country from colonial times. When the ironworkers tapped the melt and ran the molten iron through channels of sand to form pigs of raw iron, they showed little originality. When they made small finished products—hinges, locks and keyhole fixtures, and other hardware—they developed new shapes and designs both utilitarian and decorative. Yet the really creative ironwork derived from efforts of the furnace- and forge-men who cast the great heavy stoveplates for the sides of the six- and eight-sided stoves which jutted through the back of the fireplace wall into the next room, providing an effective space heater. The stoveplates often depicted Biblical stories. Through very delicate sand-casting methods figures of persons in the tale, and modest background design, were included. The whole was based upon legend or scriptural reference. From Adam and Eve to the prodigal son, from the sons of Abraham to the visions of Paul—these scenes appeared as religious lessons in iron for impressionable youngsters, just as the carvings and statuary of gigantic cathedrals had served as Bibles in stone in the cities of their European ancesors. These were veritable "Bibles in iron."[2]

Many of the enterprising furnaces developed comparable stylized Pennsylvania Dutch motifs in bird and flower, as created by pen and brush in other media. The name of the furnace was often incorporated into the design in an early example of artistic advertising. Certainly the men who produced stoveplates were not great artists; yet their work clearly illustrates the urge toward beauty as well as utility. Blacksmiths whose shops served as social centers for men of town and country ordinarily hammered out prosaic items such as horseshoes, chain links, and wagon fixtures. But on special jobs—harness metalpieces, hasps, or fasteners on dower chests or bible boxes—the smiths indulged in more creative styles.

On the whole the Dutch and their English neighbors agreed on values and methods; even many of their mannerisms were similar. Above all they adopted the same frontier philosophy, "Make do, or do without." Each in turn, from wooden rakes to tombstone carvings, showed the value of combining practical, basic designs with the simplicity of folk art. Although not originally intended as a compliment, the appellation "Dutch Yankees" indicates rather clearly what their values were.

For generations the farm laborers of German states and Swiss cantons had fashioned many simple wooden tools and artifacts for their own daily use. They did the same in America. Baking paddles, grain flails, wagon slats, eating utensils, and game boards—all of these were created almost by second nature as the Pennsylvania German worked with knife in hand, while he discussed planting times and harvest when he was closed in by winter weather.

Most men had had experience with the carving bench they called *schnitzelbank*, with its all-purpose clamp to hold the items they fashioned. Some never really mastered the process, but virtually all manner of creative construction, from buckets and pails to doughboards and sideboards, might be cut and smoothed on that marvelous machine.

Primitive artistic tendencies also appeared in the symmetry of the local garden plots. Devoted to the soil and agrarian values as they were, the Pennsylvania Dutch paid special attention to their plantings. Herbs and condiments grew in neat patches, divided to keep each growth separate from other, often similar, specimens. Each housewife managed to find time and space for added color in the form of tulips, lilies, or other small flowers. Here also, the tendency toward symmetry appeared as an unconscious development rather than a deliberate attempt to "be artistic."[3]

One very specialized form of folk art associated in America

only with the Pennsylvania Dutch has been called "Fraktur." Illuminations on manuscript pages, especially capital letters of Gothic style with a break in each major letter and combined with calligraphic embellishments, constitute this art form in its broadest sense. Fraktur letters and illuminated writings occurred on birth and baptismal certificates, *Vorschriften* ("writing specimens"), and as initial chapter or paragraph letters in books. Religious broadsides were framed in decorated borders, and house blessings or labyrinths in Fraktur style graced otherwise plain walls. Watercolor scenes or portraits also contained elements of Fraktur.

Basically, Fraktur consists of pen and ink drawings or lettering, embellished with bright colors which contrast sharply with proximate colors. Since the life-style of the Pennsylvania Germans emphasized plainness and simplicity in most things, their occasional use of vivid color, as in the bright blue milk-base paint on furniture indoors or Conestoga wagons outdoors, stood in stark contrast. So also is the use of surprisingly ornate line and vivid color of the Fraktur an unanticipated delight.[4]

An art form in itself, Fraktur combines two elements almost in equal balance: script and design. In some part these decorated forms, certificates or letters, originated in Europe, where various Swiss, German, or Alsatian French primitive examples have been found. But in force, color, and extensive decoration, the Pennsylvania Dutch illuminated writing is a more sophisticated achievement than similar remaining items from the Rhineland or neighboring areas.[5]

The *Taufscheine* ("birth and baptismal certificates") were important as documentary evidence. The earliest certificates produced in America were entirely handwritten and illuminated. Before the end of the eighteenth century, partially printed forms were in common use. Each of the artists who produced such certificates developed a style of his own and emphasized particular motifs. Donald Shelley has identified no less than twenty-one persons who produced handwritten certificates, and a total of 160 and more who were Fraktur illuminators of all types. As recently as 1972, Monroe Fabian first identified the person previously known only as the "Easton Bible artist"; he was John Spangenberg.[6]

In addition, New Year wishes, occasional letters, religious mottoes, and scriptural verses were included in the vast array of Fraktur. Christopher Dock undoubtedly contributed to the value of Fraktur as keepsakes when he presented his own as classroom rewards to certain pupils he taught before the American Revolution. In his forty-three years of teaching, Dock may well have distributed hundreds of these school rewards, but unlike the professional itinerant Fraktur artist, the Skippack schoolmaster rarely, if ever, signed them. On the *Taufschein* the name of the child is prominently displayed, but Dock's school awards omitted the name of the honored pupil. He may have prepared numerous copies of the Fraktur beforehand, or possibly the recipient was not chosen until the day he received the award. Dock included birds, tulips, hearts, and human faces along with geometric designs and stippling.[7] Later, the use of marriage, birth, and baptismal certificates printed in English replaced manuscript items in German. An art form had died.

The period of great popularity of these Fraktur items spanned the years from 1750 to 1850, although some artists continued nearly to the end of the nineteenth century. Although many people assume that Fraktur was limited to the eighteenth century, its period of greatest popularity ran from 1785 to 1835.

Although some Fraktur has appeared in New York, Maryland, New Jersey, and Virginia, it is indigenous to the Pennsylvania German settlement. So highly prized were these Frakturs that they were preserved by recipients and their descendants for generations. Most often tucked into the capacious family Bible, sometimes framed, they were also applied inside the lids of dower chests or occasionally attached to other pieces of furniture.[8]

Many of the same designs which appear consistently in Fraktur, especially the *dullaboona* ("tulip") and the *distelfink* ("goldfinch"), also may be seen in ornamentation on the cast-iron stoveplates or in other craft products. It is difficult to know in which medium these designs first were used. Scenes on stoveplates, where direct, simple art was literally scriptural, told moral stories or illustrated biblical events.[9]

More traditional (i.e., more symbolic) art forms were applied on glass and pottery. Artists experimented on both with forms akin to the motifs found in Fraktur. One man came to symbolize glass manufacture, not only in the Dutch country, but beyond. Heinrich Wilhelm Stiegel, self-styled "Baron," and occasionally "von Stiegel," was a Rhinelander who came to Philadelphia in the great migration of 1750. He spent some time in England, where he observed English glass-production methods and learned the language, both advantageous attainments.

Yet Stiegel was really a traditional figure in folk art. Only a couple of years after his arrival, this young man married into the Huber family, which owned a Lancaster iron-furnace enterprise.[10] For a decade, Henry Stiegel made no glass at all, only iron. His stoveplates tended to the standard literal Calvinist picture stories of biblical verse, although late in the decade he experimented with symbolic flowers and trees.

Then, three times in the decade of the 1760s, Stiegel tried unsuccessfully to establish a financially viable glasshouse, to produce American glass products that could compete with those of English or European manufacture. The failure of his ventures stemmed from no defect in the products or from lack of imaginative planning, for he attempted to exploit the local market and at one time he employed a hundred glassmakers. He failed, rather, because British tax policies penalized colonial glass production. Try as he might, he could not meet the price of transatlantic glass which entered free, whereas his American glass was taxed. Stiegel solved the matter bluntly; he deliberately ignored the tax laws to dramatize his situation. He made, advertised, and sold *American* glass without charging tax or paying any to the local British authorities. Both seller and purchaser protested the glass tax as surely as their Boston cousins did the tax on tea.

He made high quality glassware with enameled motifs, or with designs etched into the glass. Finches, doves, roosters, parrots, and peacocks appeared on his pieces, as did lilies, tulips, and violets. Some designs carried an inscription, most did not. Stiegel glass appeared in six opaque colors and black and white.[11]

The first American glasshouse to add lead to the blown glass was Stiegel's Manheim Glass Works which produced the finest colonial flint glass. Stiegel brought specialized workers from Europe, but together they made an authentic American glass. His Pennsylvania products sold rapidly from shelf stock in

Boston and in Baltimore. Stiegel glassware was an international success; agents in fifteen towns and cities distributed it. But essentially Stiegel failed as a business man, for he responded to setbacks with more frantic glass production. In his monomania for glassmaking, bills went unpaid and friends regretted their investments. At the collapse of his enterprise, his stores from Baltimore and Hagerstown to New York and Boston were closed. As might be expected, Stiegel ended in bankruptcy and in jail. Yet he had made, in "Stiegel glass," an excellent and distinctly American product.[12]

Other contributions to American glass were made by the Wistar family and later by the Stangers in Salem and Glassboro, New Jersey. Caspar Wistar arrived in Philadelphia from Germany in 1717 and first produced brass buttons which sold well in the Quaker City. Seven Stanger brothers worked briefly for Richard Wistar before erecting their own establishment in 1781. All these persons were from the Pennsylvania Dutch community. Yet for all the color added to American glass by the New Jersey production, the rich symbolic design of Stiegel's Pennsylvania glass was absent.[13] Of all these German producers, the works at Wistarberg in South Jersey survived longest by adapting to an American market.

Pottery as a form of folk art went through several stages. Earliest was the unglazed earthenware pottery. Examples predating 1750 included hearts, violets, and grasses incised in the rough forms. At least one tile cake mold and numerous plain roof tiles from that period have survived.

The second stage, which was longest and most productive, was that of glazed pottery, utilitarian pieces of plain design, which often served as gift or memento pieces. Slipware and sgrafitto forms carried slightly raised or incised lines on moderately glazed earthenware pottery. Pelicans, the double eagle, and other birds existed alone or in conjunction with flowers. Both the *Schimmelreiter* and General Washington appeared on white chargers. Other pieces were decorated with betrothed couples and men in military apparel. Sometimes an inscription ran around the rim of the plate or jug, but often no legend at all accompanied the incised or raised image. George Hübner of Perkiomen and Johannes Neesz of Tylersport reproduced on pottery many scenes or stories from folklore, scripture, or rural life. Some themes were distinctly American.[14]

The third phase of Pennsylvania German pottery was a high-glaze production in the last half of the nineteenth century, centered in the valleys of Pennsylvania, Maryland, and Virginia. It featured much more lifelike creatures, dogs, lions, and men (as well as angels) but contained no symbolic or stylized characterizations. Dutch pottery in this late transitional phase now competed in a wider market.

One of the most highly developed of craft skills in colonial America was the art of the pewterer, with an occasional fine silversmith also in evidence. Whereas the market for pewter was extensive, silver was but seldom used in the Dutch country. Numerous craftsmen were of Swiss, Palatine, or Moravian origins. Only a few pewterers have been fully identified, although others worked here also. At least five, whose pieces have survived, are known by name. Among them, William Will of Philadelphia was an outstanding American producer. Other artists in pewter included at least two generations of Höran or Hera family, and Johann Christopher Heyne of Lancaster.[15]

Of the American pewterers of German background, Heyne may well be the most interesting in his clearly noticeable shift from a style directly European to one showing English influence. William Will, a second generation American, was a more prolific craftsman. His father worked in New York prior to William's departure for Philadelphia. Since the pewterers did have individual marks to identify their products, it is far easier to recognize the work of each one. William Will used the lamb and dove in his early touchmark but later adopted the federal eagle.[16] Although extensive production followed, the late-eighteenth-century pewterers represented the high point in that Dutch art. Recognition came to some, but no other matched William Will in fame.

Carved wood pieces ranged from realistic children's toys to butter molds, stylized in design but utilitarian in purpose. At market, butter in competitive sale was identified by the design pressed into each pound- or two-pound block. Each family had their own distinctive design, flowers, acorns, hearts, and stars among them. It was the brand of a particular producer, instantly known by buyer and seller alike.[17]

Closely related craft and folk-art production was also apparent in the wooden furniture of the period. Cupboards, bedsteads, sideboards, and dry sinks all had carvings or designs related to the Dutch folk culture. Dower chests and bible boxes were carved and painted in the lily, tulip, and bird motifs.

Of all the furniture of the period, perhaps the finest combination of functional and artistic forms was the tall clock. Among the many occupations of the elder Christopher Sauer was that of clockmaking. He learned the trade from Christopher Witt, astronomer, clockmaker, and philosopher of Germantown. Although some craftsmen bought clockworks from England to be placed inside a cabinet made locally, most of the Dutch, like Sauer, fashioned both works and cabinet.[18] Pennsylvania clock craftsmen of the eighteenth century were preponderantly of German origin.

The most famous of all the Pennsylvania clockmakers was David Rittenhouse, who made a total of about seventy-five tall clocks, and whose brother Benjamin added perhaps forty to that total. Able mathematicians as well, they combined excellent time pieces and plain clock cases. In a number of his clocks David Rittenhouse also put an almanac into the clock works. It was he who provided astronomical calculations, length of days, and rising and setting times of the sun for James Humphrey's *Universal Almanack* in the 1770s. The publisher was careful to acknowledge the contribution of Rittenhouse, which also served to advertise the authenticity of the information in his almanac. As had his father, grandfather, and great-grandfather before him, David Rittenhouse spoke Holland Dutch and English, but in daily transactions with rural neighbors, he used High-German or the Pennsylvania version of that language.[19]

Many other local clockmakers of the German community contributed their knowledge, skills, and efforts in the manufacture of clocks in southeastern Pennsylvania. Each local community boasted of its clockmaker, like the Hageys of Trappe or the Schlotterers of Schwenksville, and many others whose names have been forgotten. Few of them gained recognition beyond their immediate locality.

Pennsylvania clock cases were oiled or varnished to show the wood grain but were rarely painted. Ornamentation in scroll-work, finials, and decorative features around the dial of the clock took the form of acorns, birds, or flowers, in a style not unrelated to other types of folk art. In short, the Pennsylvania clock is a part of folk art. The clock appeared in much of the Fraktur of the area. The central design in "clock Fraktur" was surrounded by sayings concerning time. Cast-off pieces of polished clock case wood often served as children's blocks.

The Fraktur principle in folk art appears in the decoration of clock dials. A moon was an inevitable feature painted on the white enameled clock face, for the relation of astrology and seasonal changes was considered important in the farm country. To this were added the forms dominant in Fraktur art, flowers and finches among others. Stars appeared in profusion, with five, six, or seven points, each type purported to have a special significance. Stars and circles recur regularly.[20]

The formal art of America in the century and a half between 1710 and 1860 emerged from cautious and primitive self-portraiture to the assurances of manifest destiny and the exuberance of expansion, both transcontinental and transpacific. In provincial America, portraiture depicted subjects in contemporary costume. American painters endorsed a kind of democracy by replicating not only its heroes, but its "least citizens" as well. When local handicraft production was challenged by the mechanical processes of a new industrial age, the artist often caught the clash on canvas and board. The art historian Oliver Larkin insists that art and life are interconnected components of a distinctive American civilization.[21]

In the process whereby artists reflected and interpreted American values in their art, the professionals of Pennsylvania of German origin have been almost completely overlooked. Yet the Dutchman did participate, and his art reflects his own American locality. Still, only a half-dozen *Deitsch* painters became sufficiently recognized to be noted nationally in their time. This is a small number indeed compared to the tally of significant artists of Irish, Scottish, French, and English origin. The fact is that the folk art of the Pennsylvania Dutch has come to be celebrated as part of our national achievement, to the detriment of these formal professional artists. We have indeed honored some German painters in America, for example, Leutze, Bierstadt, Bodmer, or Wimar, but they emerged from a later German tradition. Of the early non-English artists, only the Swedes Gustavus and John Hesselius have been properly recognized.

Young John Meng of Germantown painted a few portraits in the early 1750s. His father John Christopher Meng objected to his son's painting and sent the young man to sea. The son never returned, presumably lost in the Caribbean. Young Meng emphasized plainness and concentrated upon the character of the subject. His backgrounds, while not aggressive, do include details related to the interests of the central figure. In the longevity lottery of life, John Meng was surely shortchanged, for when he died in 1754, he was only twenty years old.[22]

Other German painters in colonial America included John Jacob Müller, secretary to Count Nicholas von Zinzendorf, and the Reverend George Michael Weiss, who sent portraits of Indians which he had painted at Goshenhoppen to Holland as early as 1740.[23] In 1754, John Valentine Haidt, a mature artist and goldsmith, former child prodigy, and court painter in Berlin, arrived in Bethlehem, Pennsylvania. Trained in art centers of Italy and Germany, Haidt found himself drawn to pietism in religion and art. A friend of von Zinzendorf in Germany, he later joined the count in the New World. Dark colors and a universally somber mood dominate the fifty or more portraits he painted, which for years have graced the walls of the Moravian Archives. Simplicity was the hallmark of Haidt's style. Little known outside the Moravian community, he probably had more formal training than any other artist in early America.[24]

The one Pennsylvania German who did achieve prominence in his time, who has retained (or regained) his proper place among nineteenth-century portraitists, was Jacob Eichholtz of Lancaster. Born in the year of independence, he descended from German immigrants, among whom were several active patriots, as Jacob himself liked to recall. A friend of Gilbert Stuart and Thomas Sully, Eichholtz experimented at times by employing styles those artists used, but he remained "a self-taught painter from the 'back country.'"[25]

After a brief fling at Franklin College, Jacob Eichholtz was early apprenticed to a tin and coppersmith. "It was a wretched contrast [to] a picture maker," the artist later recalled. He observed the works of others and took instructions variously from a tavern-sign painter, from Stuart, and from Sully. His work has been compared with that of Ralph Earl in New England; yet Eichholtz' style is distinctly different. He painted in Philadelphia, Baltimore, and Pittsburgh as well as Lancaster, but "he remained in spirit the artist of Lancaster and the Pennsylvania Germans."[26]

The American world was now facing inland, producing new state capitals, new politics, and new portraiture. While far from primitive, a simpler style spoke for a plainer, less ornate America. Eichholtz joined Ezra Ames of Albany and Chester Harding of Massachusetts in simplifying portraits.

Eichholtz, the craftsman-painter, for a while spent part of each workday practicing painting and tinsmithing. But by 1808, he had decided on art, set up a shop in his hometown and advertised for customers. Between then and 1842, this Dutchman painted nearly a thousand portraits and perhaps forty or fifty scenes, sketches, or landscapes. An early commission required a likeness of William Pitt for a sign to be hung at an inn in Lancaster.[27] Eichholtz painted some figures of national importance, such as Thaddeus Stevens, James Buchanan, Alexander James Dallas, and Nicholas Biddle, the latter several times. He did not paint the sweetness or beauty in women, but he caught something of his subject's personality. Especially well interpreted were his portraits of elderly people. Even at the height of his success, Eichholtz remained at the service of fellow citizens who elected him to the Lancaster City Council, and who were elated when he agreed to embellish the fire company's new hose vehicle. His portraits of Mathias Musser, John George Hoff, and George Bomberger reveal more of Eichholtz the artist than do his commissions of more famous personalities.[28]

What Eichholtz did for Lancaster, Lewis Miller in his own folksy way accomplished for the town of York and York County. This Pennsylvania painter comes close to bridging the gap between formal art and folk art. In his lifetime, between 1796 and 1882, he sketched and described the world of ordinary people, from solemn moments to caricature, and delineated

famous personalities who visited his town. He claimed to have
visited every town and village of York County and had lived
in the big cities of Lancaster, Baltimore, Marietta, and Columbia.
He also sailed from New York with two friends on a grand
tour of Europe. This carpenter and part-time artist visited "all
the chief towns and cities of Germany, Switzerland, Austria,
Bohemia, France, Italy, and Poland." He and Henry Herzog
spent most of their time in the Rhineland-Baden-Württemberg
area of Germany.[29]

"Loui" Miller not only found a choice street corner to watch
the Confederate soldiers occupy York in 1863, but he recorded
his impressions artistically. He saw the Grand Army Review in
Washington, D.C., in 1865. In New York, he was especially
enchanted with Central Park. He pictured children's pranks
as well as funerals and has left us his impressions of the railroad
and the telegraph.

For all his parochial subjects and local (if not inside) jokes,
Lewis Miller was cosmopolitan in his interests and highly
nationalistic in his promotion of the America he knew. His
art embraced many variations even to the inclusion of Fraktur
designs as borders for many of his sketches. The real value of
Lewis Miller's works continues to be their vitality. Donald
Shelley, executive director of the Henry Ford Museum, calls
them "stenographic pictorial sketches plus written commentary,"
a genre which amounts to visual recording of history before film
or photographic plate. He was as much the reporter artist as
Winslow Homer or Alfred Waud, two of his Civil War contemporaries.

A true artist, he experimented with perspective and distribution of figures in his scenes, although he rarely took the poetic
license of inaccurate historical placement. He shows us special
moments of everyday life, and was long remembered with great
sentiment by his neighbors.[30]

It is appropriate that Pennsylvania Dutch enthusiasts for
American expansion in a territorial sense should also be leaders
among artists who drew the nation's attention toward new
regions and new resources. A scientist, a topographer, and a
doctor, each of the three Kern brothers of Philadelphia, also
served as early artist-publicists for the mountainous west in the

1840s. Richard, Benjamin, and Edward Kern descended from Rhineland migrants to Pennsylvania, and the brothers carried the same enthusiasm for new opportunities as had their grandparents and great-grandparents in earlier times.[31]

Benjamin, the physician, made some modest attempts in the line of art, but Richard and Edward were professional artists in Philadelphia who opted for the West as a place conducive to their artistic inclinations. They produced salable commodities, as America thirsted for scenes and descriptions of the West. Ned Kern found his opportunity in John C. Frémont's exploration of the great American West. He was hired as "illustrator" for the third Frémont expedition. While other members of the party cursed river obstacles or gaped at the castellated hills and shied away from the precipitous mountain ravines, Ned Kern measured, sketched, and captured the countryside in pictures. As any artist-reporter his techniques were sharpened to key his sketches to particular features or striking landmarks, and Kern's fame rests upon line drawings with descriptive notes.

This young vagabond summed up his impressions in color rather than in verbal form. A youthful romantic who had been brought into contact with awesome extremes of nature, he was "glad to be away from 'civilization and brandy,'" as he put it.[32] On the fourth Frémont expedition, all three Kern brothers joined as scientific observers, topographers, and artists. Benjamin practiced sufficient medicine to charm the Indians into trading mules to the Frémont forces, albeit reluctantly.

While the panorama of the new West dumbfounded some observers, caused others to express themselves in gigantic extravaganzas of word pictures or painted ones (e.g., those of Samuel Clemens and Albert Bierstadt), the Kerns reduced the West to sketchbook size. In cryptic miniature they mapped, sketched, and described their visual experiences. Indian portraits worthy of a Catlin or Henry Bird King, and splashes of color that would complement George Caleb Bingham, show insight into the curious and unexpected frivolities in this new land.[33]

Richard and Edward Kern learned their basic techniques in a Quaker City ripe with the art of Thomas Birch, Thomas Cole, and Thomas Sully, all of whom they knew. Jacob Eichholtz learned from Sully, then produced a true Pennsylvania Dutch portraiture. Similarly the Kerns' contribution was a new vision, an early western American art form, created by Pennsylvania Dutchmen. Americans before the Civil War, avidly interested in western phenomena almost to a point of national orgy, saw reproductions of the scenes pictorially described by Ned or Richard Kern, often with not even a faint idea who had produced the originals. The line drawings and pen sketches of these artist-reporters were lithographed for book illustrations in the ante-bellum explosion of books on the West.[34]

Thomas U. Walter, descendant of a redemptioner, was Pennsylvania's foremost architect in the nineteenth century. He designed early Girard College buildings, the fortresslike Moyamensing Prison, and Philadelphia City Hall, crowned by the statue of William Penn. His vision of classical regularity in architecture has left a national impression, for in 1851, President Millard Fillmore appointed Walter the Capitol architect. He planned the East Front and House and Senate Wings of the Capitol. To honor his forbears, the architect compiled a family genealogy that was a work of art in itself.[35]

Formal art among the Pennsylvania Dutch remained an expression of a very few artists. Among the much more common folk-art forms was the sometimes bizarre gravestone art. Recurring motifs and themes of death and skulls were added to the more usual tulips, roses, and birds of Fraktur or other forms of popular art. Virtually none of the tombstone carvers is known by name, but the work of several of them can be distinguished by recurring shapes and by peculiarities of design. Occasionally small bits of verse were also chiseled into the stone, but for the most part only the name, or just initials and vital data, were lettered. Any other incising was in the form of flowers or the sun or moon. In the space available, the craftsman shaped legible sized letters, breaking a word whenever he ran out of space, then commenced the next line with any letters left over from the previous word. Stylized creations were added after the lettering was completed.[36]

Music was a favorite means of expression among the Dutch, who produced both folk music and formal music with equal enthusiasm. In repetitive or drudging manual work, the Germans of Pennsylvania were in the habit of singing worksongs from the old country.

When officials provided them little entertainment, people simply furnished their own, often inventing it as they went. In this way unaccompanied singing of folksongs took rhythmic and melodic form, easy to follow and with solid, repeated beat. Verse tumbled after verse in improvised and almost interminable musical stories. Many of the folksongs were direct importations from Swabia or Württemberg, although life in Pennsylvania produced additional songs and legends. Borrowings or adaptations from English or Welsh around them, and occasionally from Indian lore, further separated Pennsylvania folk tradition from the old country.

In many ways the link between music of the Dutch community and other developing aspects of folk life was the organ builder, who was also the organist or composer as well. Johann Klemm, who had been employed by Gustavus Hesselius, the painter, became one of the first organ builders of the province. A graduate of the University at Leipzig, he met Count Zinzendorf at Herrnhut, and by 1750 had severed his ties with the German homeland to become involved in the Moravian experiment at Bethlehem. Klemm built organs in Bethlehem, Philadelphia, and New York, returning whenever possible to Bethlehem or Nazareth. He trained David Tannenberger who taught Jacob Frying, and so the pattern developed. Klemm and Tannenberger set up a business of organ building in Nazareth about 1760, where Klemm's student became the most renowned organmaker of all Pennsylvania. Tannenberger then constructed organs from Philadelphia to Nazareth to Lancaster and at Lititz, where he set up a factory. In 1790, Tannenberger's organ in Zion Lutheran Church in Philadelphia was acclaimed the finest instrument in the state.[37]

One whose musical talents as organist had brought him to America was Gottlieb Mittelberger. He felt that his musical efforts were wasted among the lowbrows of Philadelphia and Providence (Trappe). Fortunately the experience of George Neisser and John Jacob Diffenbach proved less distracting, and the province supported a dozen or more organ and piano builders in colonial and early national times. One Krause and his family along the Perkiomen and John Ziegler in Skippack carried the musical tradition from the early national period well into the mid-nineteenth century.[38]

Choral music was also extremely important, particularly in religious communities. Beissel at Ephrata trained a choral ensemble to lead the musical portions of worship in his community. His print shop also made hymnbooks with musical scores. Tunes of German composers were used, but some words and music were original.[39]

The most surprising development was the extensive use of portable musical instruments, a musical tradition that has disappeared from our national memory. Homemade drums, primitive strings, and bark flute-whistles might have seemed appropriate for a backwoods society. Later Americans could not believe that a sophisticated musical development had existed earlier, though in fact it had. A string quartet pleasantly entertained Doctor Alexander Hamilton on his *Itinerarium* through Philadelphia in 1744. Sir William Johnson's guests listened to Handel compositions on the New York frontier in the years of the French and Indian War. Thus instrumental music in secular and religious life was not surprising in mid-eighteenth-century Bethlehem.[40]

According to tradition, Franklin told his wife of the fine instrumental music he heard at Bethlehem. He mentioned flute, oboe, French horn, and trumpet among instruments played in 1756.[41] In fact at this Moravian outpost, the trombone choirs or quartets aroused the greatest acclamation. The Moravians, moderate as they were in most things, seemed extremists where music was concerned. One brass player was queried by a visiting pastor whether he would use the same instrument he had used for secular tunes on Saturday, in the Sabbath service to follow. The young man responded in question form, "Will you also pray with the some mouth tomorrow, with which you are now eating sausages?" Bethlehem supported a fifteen-piece orchestra in the midst of the War for Independence.

The efforts of John Antes at secular musical composition were lost until reconstructed by musicologists within the last thirty years. His father had been an officer confidant of General Washington. Antes, trained in Bethlehem, made violins and other musical instruments in America and was a watchmaker briefly in Germany. In Egypt, as missionary for the Moravian Church, he encountered court resistance to his mission, whereupon he turned to musical composition. Influenced by his contemporaries Joseph Haydn and G. F. Handel, John Antes composed trios in suite and sonata style, utilizing unison passages to underscore his melodic themes. Not until the 1960s were the John Antes Trios recorded commercially by Columbia Records.[42]

The most prolific composers of the Moravian community were those who composed arias, anthems, and chorales on religious themes. Along with John Antes, the group comprised Johannes Herbst, John Frederick Peter, David Michael, and Edward Leinbach. Antes' "Lovliest Immanuel" and "Go, Congregation Go!," Michael's "Hearken!" "Stay Close to Jesus Christ," and Leinbach's "Hosanna" demonstrate the versatility of this group of composers writing within the limits of religious congregational music. More than ten thousand original compositions are located in the Moravian Archives today.[43]

This was, after all, the century of Isaac Watts, premier American hymnodist of New England. Church figures in the German religious community of Pennsylvania were no less active than the New England divines. Hymns, psalms, and other musical expressions of religious conviction offered these pilgrims opportunities to express their emotions. Many isolated rural churches had no organ nor other musical instruments, nor had they any competent performers. Among others who shunned instruments as worldly influences were many who sang *a cappella*. Alternation of hymn verses gave rise to the *Vorsinger*. He set the pitch and the tempo. In addition, for parishioners who could not read, he gave the words of each line, which the congregation repeated.

By the same token, music was to many of the Pennsylvania Dutch not to be associated only with religion. This social communication at festive occasions had no religious connotation whatever. The country fiddlers or *Geikenspielers* performed at country fairs, cornhuskings, barnraisings, and other entertainments, to great popular acclaim. Most of these country fiddlers were self-taught practitioners of a musical folk art which emphasized agility, speed, and duration, rather than musical quality.

Among the gentler arts of the Pennsylvania Dutch was poetry. In a way, this is unusual, for poetic expression is ordinarily reserved for an elite, formal language. In no way does the *Deitsch Sproch* fit this description. It was not even a single dialect, but a mixture of several brought to America in the eighteenth century, with an overgenerous infusion of English words and equivalents. German word order held out most tenaciously against English encroachment.

Isolated from the sources of High German, which they listened to in church services, they made no effort to make their own speech conform to *Hoch Deutsch*. Poetry in the earliest years of the settlement in Pennsylvania was written by its leaders, and poetic forms were essentially religious, usually in the form of verses for hymns. Johannes Kelpius or Francis Daniel Pastorius wrote much of the early poetry that has survived. Pastorius departed from strictly religious motifs. Such early poetry was written in scholarly High German, of course.[44] Later the early mystical poetry mingled with popular Fraktur verses or dialect versions in the newspapers of the day.

In the nineteenth century, the earlier spiritual love theme transmuted into a dream of democratic brotherhood. This coincided with the efforts of the Dutch population toward political independence. It was also spurred by the federal and republican politics of the early nation. Some maintain that it climaxed in the Jacksonian era of equality of participation, though Henrich Miller had already written in this spirit in his *Staatsbote* of 1777.[45]

The great epoch of popular poets and authors of the *Pennsylfawnisch Deitsch* tradition occurred between 1830 and 1945. By then ties with a formal German language had disappeared. The now isolated Pennsylvania Dutchman set down in written form the same dialect he used in speech. Consequently, the most disconcerting variation in spelling exists. Each author simply made the English letters correspond to his *Deitsch* sounds. For example, the word *schee* (*schön* in High German) means beautiful, but appears variously in written *Deitsch* as *schey, shay, schaa,* and *schai.* To this day, there is no universally accepted standard orthography for the sounds thus represented.

One specialist in the problem of spoken-written language

of this era divided the last period into "Language Conscious," "Local Color," and "Folk Conscious" stages to the middle 1940s. This spans folksy poetry from "Loui" Miller in the 1830s, through Henry Harbaugh in Civil War times, to local favorites John Birmelin, William Troxell, Preston Barba, or Russell Gilbert in the twentieth century.[46]

In many cases the effort to translate old or new English poetry into *Deitsch* has produced most charming results. William Shakespeare and Billy Rose have undergone marvelous translations.

One classification of folk literature is the sayings and beliefs of the Pennsylvania Germans, including those of superstition or *hexerei*. Edwin M. Fogel assembled common *Sprochwarte* fifty years ago in his *Beliefs and Superstitions of the Pennsylvania Germans*.[47] Aphorisms or maxims which fit a particular occasion were immensely popular. Some continue to use words totally archaic in *Hoch Deutsch* as the locally oft repeated "G'schenkte gaul, gook net ins maul" (You don't look a gift horse in the mouth).

This is a folk culture of extensive proportions, much of which has survived into the twentieth century. With the advent of mass media, radio, and television, the dialect language has tended to be used more sparingly, and cultural differences are gradually disappearing, although Pennsylvania Germans in some areas have clung tenaciously to their values and forms nonetheless.

CHAPTER X

Party and Politics
Among the Pennsylvania Dutch

AFTER THE NATION EMERGED FROM THE TRAUMA OF THE WAR for Independence, it attempted to operate a national government on confederation principles, although partisan politics at the state level divided the Pennsylvania Germans. Most continued as small farmers, although many had expanded their operations in the tight-commodity easy-money days of the war. Postwar monetary contraction caught those who had overexpanded in wartime and in the uncertain period which followed. Small farmers supposedly favored the Confederation limits on central authority, whereas merchants, bankers, and entrepreneurs advocated greater controls under a more powerful central government. That may well hold for the Pennsylvania Dutch as for the nation, but a study of individual cases reveals many exceptions and contradictions to such general assumptions.

Many Dutchmen gained land rights for their wartime service, or staked claims to larger and better farms farther north or west. They owed their new standing at least partially to the Confederation government and to the state Constitution of 1776. State and national governments both eased requirements for land acquisition.[1] Still, it is not clear that the entire agrarian element embraced the state Constitutional or Radical faction in their politics. Indeed the so-called Republican party, led by banker Robert Morris, gained extensive support in Northampton County, where Pennsylvania German small farmers abounded. In 1787, Pennsylvania was really the only state with two organized political parties, which had been functioning for twenty years. Because of later connotations, the party designations of the postwar decade are misleading. The Constitutional (Radical)

178

party favored the state Constitution and the Confederation system, hence they opposed a new federal Constitution in 1787. Morris' Republicans on the other hand (not in any sense Jeffersonian Democratic-Republicans) were really *Federal* Republicans. They vigorously supported the Constitution of 1787. The concept of an aristocratic party versus an agrarian party is considerably exaggerated, since both parties had support from farm followers.[2]

The Pennsylvania Dutch, one-third of the state's population, failed to exercise the political force they might have had as an ethnic or occupational bloc. So disparate a group as Pennsylvania's Germans simply could not be organized into a cohesive force. Each made his choice as an individual. Agrarian interests backed the Constitutional party, whose mercantile and professional leadership included William Will, David Rittenhouse, and Frederick Kuhl along with non-German Charles Pettit and William Irvine. Other conservative Dutchmen favored stability by voting for state and local Republican candidates. Frederick A. C. Muhlenberg and Frederick Antes were among the leadership of the latter party. The common conviction that the best government governed least led others to avoid any participation.[3]

In 1784, Dutch votes contributed to a victory for the State Constitutionalists in a critical Assembly election at the expense of Robert Morris' Federal Republicans. As a result, David Rittenhouse felt reinforced in his position as state treasurer, which he held under the Constitution of 1776, and took firm fiscal steps in several cases. The financial decisions of Rittenhouse were not enthusiastically received by his fellow Germans, still wary of any economic regulations, even by one of their own.[4]

The Pennsylvania Germans restricted their politics to the local level, allowing others to fight the battles of national importance. Deliberations over the proposed new federal Constitution may be illustrative of it. Not a single Pennsylvania German sat in the state delegation to the Constitutional Convention at Philadelphia in the summer of 1787. Rather, they acted in the state convention to ratify the new federal document.[5]

Attempts to explain post–Revolutionary American history in terms of class struggle are unconvincing when applied to the Pennsylvania Germans. They were much too individualistic to be summed up in one general theory. Some Dutch small farmers were conservative and some were radical, whereas some of their wealthiest merchants, who theoretically should have been strong supporters of central government, actually led the move to retain the weaker Articles of Confederation.[6]

David Rittenhouse would gladly have joined those voting against the Constitution, for he considered the Articles of Confederation quite sufficient. But Philadelphia voters produced a landslide victory for ratification despite the fame of State Constitutionalists like Rittenhouse and Charles Pettit. As candidate for presidential elector, Rittenhouse was defeated, and the new majority even questioned his actions as state treasurer.[7] Popular feeling at Easton and Chambersburg, and in Northumberland County, all Pennsylvania Dutch strongholds, celebrated the triumph of the Constitution.

The rout of the old Constitutionalists, or Radical party, was completed when the Assembly scrapped the Constitution of 1776 in favor of a more moderate Constitution of 1790, which set some limits on popular controls. Those who had lost power continued to see pernicious results, such as an upper house of legislature where "the better born may be separated from the common countrymen."[8] After nine decades of a unicameral legislature, Pennsylvania accepted the more ordinary two-house system.

Changes occurred everywhere. Pennsylvania's Republican party easily and silently became its Federalist party. The Constitutional party (erstwhile Radicals) joined forces with Jeffersonians and other states'-righters to form the Anti-Federalist coalition. Perhaps designations are not significant, but some former Constitutionalists, now Anti-Federalists, swallowed hard when the opposition party emerged as Jeffersonian Democrat-Republicans by 1798 or 1800. Still, it took some courage to criticize the Federalist power emerging under Washington in the 1790s, for vituperation rapidly followed, as the American political system warmed up.

In the new national government, Frederick A. C. Muhlenberg, Michael Hillegas, Michael Leib, and Peter Muhlenberg all emerged as Pennsylvania Dutch leaders of the Federalists. Frederick Muhlenberg consolidated his position and attracted further voter support by his enthusiasm for the federal Constitution after 1787. Overwhelmingly chosen to represent Montgomery County in the Federal House of Representatives of 1789, he was immediately voted first Speaker of the House by the other representatives. Frederick Muhlenberg had more solid political support from his fellow Dutchmen than any other government figure up to that time.

Yet the Speaker of the House never fully mustered the political strength of his supporters, due perhaps to a lack of imagination or a nonmagnetic personality. He pointed up the importance of the German vote, which was recognized when Anti-Federalists included his name in their ticket of endorsed candidates for the national House in 1788. Indeed after some maneuvering, the Federalists followed suit and three names, all German (F. A. C. Muhlenberg, Daniel Hiester, and Peter Muhlenberg), were included in both tickets. It epitomized the dilemma of the Dutch country: interests sometimes competed and sometimes merged. The brothers Muhlenberg were both elected to the House.

Frederick, a true Federalist in his support of the Constitution, was resolved at all costs to defend the rights of man. Peter, a true Anti-federalist in his support of the rights of man, was resolved at all costs to defend the Constitution. . . . The two Muhlenbergs were political balance wheels. They both felt the need of a strong central government, and at the same time they recognized the rights of man. . . . The Muhlenbergs in politics were not crusaders. At the same time they had no phobias. They were plain good men, who took each day as it came [and] passed judgment on policies as they arose.[9]

Frederick Muhlenberg transmitted official notice of Pennsylvania's adoption of the Constitution. Peter Muhlenberg, as vice president of Pennsylvania, marched in the forefront of the celebration which was the "Federal Procession" in Philadelphia. In the Federalist administration, Frederick Muhlenberg exercised some strength in the Congress, Michael Hillegas was appointed treasurer of the United States, and Peter Muhlenberg was relegated to the back benches. Michael Leib attempted to revive opposition to the Federalists, with some success.[10]

From 1790, the national government resided in nearby Philadelphia, its shortcomings apparent, with leaders whose concerns often differed from those of the people. Frederick Muhlenberg spoke for the Pennsylvania congressional delegation (except William Maclay) when he asked in May, 1790, "Shall we vote for a bill giving the temporary residence, ten years, to Philadelphia and the permanent residence [of the federal capital] to the Potomac?"[11] That was the basis for eventual settlement. It raised little joy among the Pennsylvanians who preferred to have the government in Philadelphia where they could observe it, and who objected to the prestige it gave the Virginians. Muhlenberg political fortunes rose and fell as the decade unfolded. Frederick immediately returned to the House though Peter failed to get reelected; later he was chosen Senator from Pennsylvania. He served two days, then resigned to accept a position with the Customs at the Port of Philadelphia. Frederick staunchly stood with Federalist leadership and fell with them as the decade expired.[12]

The influence of the Pennsylvania Dutch voters remained strong, although they split as to party. Grudging tribute to that strength was a recurring tendecy of the 1790s to include the prominent German names (Muhlenberg and Hiester) on both slates of nominees. Rarely does practical politics allow candidates to "reside in both houses," as it were. But in the last decade of the eighteenth century neither party was willing to chance the loss of those German votes attracted by German candidates. Pennsylvania citizens from non-German backgrounds claimed candidates were proposed not on their qualifications for office but "because they were German." To such objectors, the goal of the Pennsylvania Dutch stood stripped of any disguise: "They would monopolize State politics and appropriate all the 'loaves and fishes' to themselves."[13]

Among the first of the Anti-Federalist societies to organize was Pennsylvania's "German Republican Society," one of about ten which arose in 1793 and 1794, to honor republican virtues and advance popular politics. They opposed excise taxes, further centralization of government, and overt or covert Anglophile activities by the American government. Some claimed to be nonpartisan, which they managed no better than the so-called nonpartisan newspapers of their day. Persons who greeted Edmund Genêt most cordially upon his arrival later appeared as members of newly organized Democratic Societies. The German Republican Society stood in opposition to the excise, Jay's Treaty, and other government measures. Peter Muhlenberg, Michael Leib, and Henry Kammerer were active organizers, and the latter became president of the society. The three major goals were to further interest in representative government and in the German language and to achieve greater political participation. Leib was secretary of both the German Republican Society and the Pennsylvania Democratic Society. David Rittenhouse avoided close ties because of apparent conflicts with his government position as director of the mint.[14]

Many citizens of the commonwealth were willing to concede the Dutch to be energetic and effective farmers, but few welcomed their new activity in local, state, and national politics. At the most four men of Pennsylvania's eleven in the House of Representatives were of German background, and they were not all of the same political faction. Only one senator in the first dozen years of federal government was Pennsylvania German, and after two days of service he stepped down in favor of George Logan.

The Federalist era produced a vigorous antiforeign mood, a xenophobia quite alien to the early harmony in a government of men who had all been born under other flags. Contradictory or not, the mood grew. Scots-Irish armed resistance to federal excise on liquor first brought Federal proclamations, then militia units into western Pennsylvania.[15] The German Republican Society of Philadelphia early protested the use of force, though Pennsylvania Dutch men were included in military units sent west.

The Jay Treaty of 1795 occasioned vigorous debate as Jeffersonian critics assailed unnecessary concessions to Britain, while defenders of the treaty spoke darkly of the threat of Jacobin wiles. The specter of the French Revolution had spread as far as America. Returned Tories seemed now more trustworthy than did the loyal opposition, especially if an opponent had been born on non-English soil or continued to speak a foreign language. Albert Gallatin was finally refused his seat in the United States Senate because of technicalities concerning his birth and the date of his naturalization. A Federalist majority in the

Pennsylvania Assembly expelled members representing four western counties. Withal, Frederick A. C. Muhlenberg found it more and more difficult to justify the actions of the Federalist party, especially since he preferred to think of himself as non-partisan. A commonwealth newspaper described him as "not entirely immersed in party views."[16]

The climax of the antipathy toward foreigners came during the administration of John Adams, who remained firmly convinced of the duplicity of France. Thus after a half-dozen years of growing xenophobia, Adams' Congress passed the Alien Friends Act, the Sedition Act, a new naturalization law with longer time requirements, and a revenue measure to provide finances in case of war against France. Joseph Heister in the House voted against each in turn, though few joined him in opposition. In the state assembly, the Federalist majority translated the 1798 federal excise on slaves and property, to a property tax with assessments based on the number of windows and doors, and the size and construction of dwelling houses throughout the state. It would place the burden of taxes on those who could pay.[17]

President Adams intended to enforce these laws. It was the "Window Tax" that promoted trouble in Pennsylvania Dutch country, just as the tax on whiskey had aroused Scots-Irish resistance. When the Dutch heard that assessors would be counting the window panes (not just the whole window), trouble erupted. Poor citizens could afford multiple small panes in a window sash; only the wealthy had large window glass. The new impost smacked of the hearth tax some had experienced in Europe. Surely the 1798 levy deliberately increased the tax on Germans as the Stamp Act had done more than thirty years earlier.

Jacob Fries, Federalist, veteran of the American Revolution, and sometime auctioneer, was one of the Pennsylvania militiamen dispatched to put down the Whiskey Rebellion. He called for resistance so assessors could not view the houses, even if housewives had to pour kettles of hot water on the tax men. John Jacob Eyermann, a young German preacher and an alien arrived from the Rhineland just a few years earlier, discussed the inequities of the tax in Saturday evening tavern forays.

Others took up the cry, but Fries was the accepted leader. Eyermann became quite explicit. If his house (although he had no property) were visited by the assessor, Eyermann would take his pistol (also theoretical) and shoot the tax man, or at least he would beat him about the ears with his Hebrew books (which the preacher did possess). He encouraged others to resist an unfair tax.

Word spread rapidly and in several weeks, federal marshals arrested the Reverend J. J. Eyermann while he preached a funeral sermon. The charges were sedition and refusal to pay the tax. The preacher, along with some twenty others, was taken to the Sun Tavern in Bethlehem for pretrial imprisonment. Soon Captain Fries, in his 1780 uniform, led a band of armed men to the jail, where they rushed the marshal and freed the prisoners. Although Eyermann had opposed the jailbreak, he fled to New York when freed. President Adams ordered "the insurgents" to disperse within a week.

Fries and his cohorts, when they sobered up, submitted to the authorities and allowed their properties to be assessed. Eyermann was detained in New York on a federal warrant. When it seemed all had settled down, the Adams government called on Governor Mifflin to send militia troops to put down the rebellion. Several dozen suspects were rounded up amid charges that General William MacPherson's troops used "unnecessary severity."[18]

Militiamen then marched from Allentown to Reading, where they seized Jacob Schneider, Anti-Federalist editor of the German language *Readinger Adler* and outspoken critic of the Alien and Sedition Acts. Schneider was dragged to the market house and given a flogging. William Duane printed an account of the military action in his *Philadelphia Aurora*. Next day, when he would not reveal the name of his informant, he was strong-armed by men led by the son of Chief Justice Thomas McKean. Then Duane published an account of the beating he received.[19]

Jacob Fries, John Jacob Eyermann, and twenty-eight other defendants were brought to trial between April and October, 1799. Alexander James Dallas, leading Republican lawyer, and William Lewis, prominent Federalist, jointly served as defense counsel in a very hostile court. Convictions, fines, and jail terms resulted for the accused. Jacob Fries, adjudged guilty of treason, was sentenced to be hanged. Disclosures of a prejudicial juror brought a retrial in April, 1800, with the same results. So intemperate were the presiding judges, Samuel Chase among them, that defense attorneys withdrew for their own professional safety, leaving Fries without counsel. One of his lawyers, Alexander James Dallas, was himself born in Jamaica, so his arguments might well be discounted. Eyermann and several others also stood trial without defense attorneys.[20] When John Adams was apprised of the details, at the urgent suggestions of Dallas and Lewis, he pardoned Fries and commuted the longer sentences. The incidents greatly embarrassed the Pennsylvania Dutch by impugning their loyalty. The Reverend J. J. Eyermann was refused access to his former congregation, indeed, he was denied his status as a minister. He settled in Berks County as a farmer and virtually disappeared there.

Politically the damage had been done. Republican newspapers printed the embarrassing details, accompanied by new charges of government repression. So fearful was the administration that they not only struck at opposition groups in western Pennsylvania but repressed their own in Federalist Bucks and Northampton Counties, As the Federalists floundered, Michael Leib, Alexander James Dallas, and other Republican leaders moved to consolidate their advantage. Many Pennsylvania Dutch in Bucks, Northampton, Berks, Northumberland, and Montgomery Counties had supported the Federalist party. Now the legislation of 1798, the Fries case, and the lack of objectivity in the trials brought serious political reconsiderations. Peter Muhlenberg fought the sedition laws and acted "to defend our rights and to remove our grievances," wrote one citizen, who continued, "He is the Moses of the German Israelites . . . who will lead the people out of the house of Bondage."[21] German counties had been gradually swinging to the Republicans since 1796, as local elections of Jonas Hartzell, Balzar Gehr, Peter Muhlenberg, Peter Frailey, Nathaniel Boileau, and Frederick Conrad indicated.

But a great deal more than that had changed. With the exception of federal officeholders Albert Gallatin and Alexander James Dallas (neither Pennsylvania Dutch), the political concerns of the commonwealth swung to the state level. It is mere coincidence, a political illusion as it were, that loss of the national capital in 1800 produced a loss of interest among Pennsylvanians in national affairs. Pennsylvanians had shown that republican government worked. Victorious Republicans of the Keystone State concentrated on matters within their own boundaries.[22]

The Republicans then split into factions. McKean and Dallas led the elite of the party against a popular faction which claimed to be the real Democratic Republican movement. Ethnic voting patterns firmed up after the Whiskey Uprising and the Fries affair. The Federalists were defeated, which John Adams attributed to the German vote.[23]

When Governor Thomas McKean wrote an intemperate letter insisting that "men of talent," that is, the more aristocratic element, serve in state office, he also condemned the opposite, "those clodpoles (or if they please clodhoppers)" who challenged the elite. Michael Leib's popular faction offered a Northumberland County Dutchman, Speaker of the Assembly Simon Snyder, as their candidate, who acknowledged he was a *schollahupsa* ("clodhopper"). Snyder, who was the son of a poor immigrant farmer and had been a tanner's apprentice, miller, and storekeeper, was a marvelous choice. From his vantage point as justice of the peace, he became a county leader for the Democratic Republicans in the Adams years and represented his county in the state assembly. The 1805 election brought up issues of social class and economic advantage in a way Pennsylvania had not previously experienced, and produced "the first common citizen and the first person of German descent to campaign seriously for the governorship."[24]

Simon Snyder lost the 1805 gubernatorial election to McKean by five thousand votes out of more than eighty thousand cast, but the Democratic Republicans were on the move. McKean would not prove acceptable to even the more conservative wing much longer. In his attempts to retain power, he catered more and more to Federalist remnants and warned of the radicalism of the Gallatin-Duane-Snyder opposition, whom he accused of promoting "equal distribution of property."[25]

Jeffersonians, on the other hand, decried rank and privilege among the Federalists. Although enclaves of Federalist Germans remained in Bucks, Montgomery, and Northampton Counties, the bulk of Pennsylvania Dutch flocked to the Democratic-Republican standard. Some were converted from Federalist principles by the ill-advised measures against the Fries Rebellion, but others were pleased that the Democratic Republicans ran German candidates. As a result, Pennsylvania German governors were elected.

The triennial gubernatorial election and the quadrennial presidential election coincided in Pennsylvania in 1808. Supporters of Simon Snyder and of James Madison had an opportunity to consolidate their strengths. Snyder destroyed the hopes of the resurgent Federalists, crushing their candidate by nearly thirty thousand votes, with forty thousand more Pennsylvanians voting than in 1805. Madison electors in Pennsylvania were swept to victory along with Snyder. Keystone State electoral votes provided Madison's margin over antiwar Federalist Rufus King. A recent assessment of the Pennsylvania political scene spells out the new mood.

The election of 1808 signified that the common people of Pennsylvania had abandoned their deferential attitude towards the rich and wellborn, and had themselves assumed the task of governing. The unprecedented turnout at the polls suggested that they looked upon Snyder as representative of themselves and proclaimed that they need no longer rely on an elite political aristocracy to serve their interests.[26]

Federalists continued to blame their defeats on "the German vote" as they had in 1800.

Adept as a commoner in politics, Snyder acknowledged a joke then current. His young sons, thrilled at the victory, asked their mother, "Are we governors, too?" She replied directly, "Nay, chust me and Pop." In general, Snyder succeeded in turning the forces of the state from local to national issues. Giving vent to his regional sense of humor in the halls of Congress, mid-Pennsylvania Representative George Kremer, bored by excessive Latin and Greek quotations in a speech by John Randolph, counterattacked sharply with extended remarks in Pennsylvania Dutch.[27]

Pennsylvania duly supported the Madison government in 1812, providing more Congressional votes for war against Great Britain than any other state. Keystone State units fought the enemy at Baltimore, in Canada, and on Lake Erie. They particularly assisted by building the Great Lakes fleet for Oliver Hazard Perry. Three Pennsylvania Dutch militia companies from Germantown entered service, as did units from German counties, but they did not philosophize greatly on the war or its merits. After New Orleans, Snyder was able to state:

> During the late war the soil of this commonwealth was never trodden by a hostile foot, yet it had at one time the greater number of militia and volunteers in the service of the United States than were at any other time in the field from any other state in the union.[28]

"Organization Democrats" provided an experiment gradually received with favor on the national scene, when they chose their 1817 candidate for governor in a nominating convention. This so-called Pennsylvania Plan operated more democratically than had the nominating caucus. Another victory for the popular forces was the removal of the state capital to Harrisburg (after a decade in Lancaster) and away from influences in Philadelphia. In the new capital city a wide-open game of rough and tumble politics ensued, "the game without rules," with no holds barred and few promises sacred. With one exception, the governors during that era were Pennsylvania Dutch, as were several of the losing candidates.

In the transition between the Jeffersonian and Jacksonian style of government, political figures in Pennsylvania found choices difficult. This period in United States history up to 1824 is often called "Era of Good Feelings." Doubtful enough as a national premise, an assumption of political unanimity carried no validity at all on the state level. Party positions shifted continually, old alliances ruptured, and new coalitions of strange bedfellows cautiously formed, adjusted, and hardened.

Pennsylvania was little different from other states, but suffered complications as a result of strictly local factors. The ethnic division of Pennsylvania into Pennsylvania Dutch, Scots-Irish, and English continued from Colonial times. Some other ethnics and "foreigners," that is, settlers from other states, gradually arrived. Populous, politically strong southern counties sometimes opposed numerous but sparsely settled Northern counties of the state.[29] In politics English and Scots-Irish groups tended to judge rationally and compromise effectively. The Dutch, whatever their party or faction, tended to stand on tradition. They did participate but they accepted change slowly and with ill grace. They rarely and reluctantly ran for state or national office; yet the occasional *Landsmann* candidate attracted great numbers of the Pennsylvania Dutch vote. Their voting record was astonishing and shows that they used their right to vote more actively than did other ethnic groups. In an election in which a German-sounding candidate competed with any other on the ballot, *Deitsch Friendschaft* usually supported its own, whereas other groups voted less as a bloc.[30]

Pennsylvania Germans commonly sat in the governor's chair, whereas state appointive offices were filled with Scots-Irish. County, state, and national elective offices (other than governor) were contested mainly by English and Scots-Irish personalities. Reasons for this almost firm division of duties and offices are not entirely clear, but the pattern is consistent. The Dutch, except in local matters in their own area, tended to be rather ineffective in practical politics. German governors who held that office almost continually between 1817 and 1832 seemed occupied with local matters. Typical was the three-way political struggle of 1829. Calhoun Democrats nominated George Wolf and Anti-Masons chose Joseph Ritner, while John A. Schulze, incumbent old-ticket Democrat, hesitated in his decision to contest the governorship. All three were German, yet none firmly controlled his own organization.[31]

Once in office, many of the German governors attempted to remain above politics or to effect a nonpartisan program and consequently lost what earlier influence they had. Pennsylvania pressure in Washington, D.C., in the Jackson years was nearly nonexistent; Pennsylvania's governors refused to play the partisan game.[32] Only Simon Snyder, of all the German governors, succeeded in correlating his politics with national issues, and he retired in 1817. That year, one partisan boasted, "If all the GERMANS and IRISH were hoisted out of the state, there would be enough AMERICAN Democrats left to make a governor of Mr. Findlay."[33] Hiester campaigners countered the cartloads of Findlay literature printed in German with the charge that a victorious Findlay might be approached by Dutchmen only "by means of an interpreter." With most German counties voting for Hiester and most Scots-Irish for Findlay, the latter won by a mere seven thousand votes.

Other early Pennsylvania German governors were of little political note; even those who took Governor Joseph Hiester's reform politics seriously often referred to him as "the Old German Grey." His successor, John Andrew Melchior Schulze, sometime preacher, merchant, and state senator, was best known as Henry Muhlenberg's grandson. At his nomination, one speaker praised Schulze for his "democratic principles, firmness, talents and integrity"; another called him not just unrepresentative but completely unknown, "a total stranger to the people of Pennsylvania."[34] Complaints followed. "Who, in God's name, is John A. Schulze?" many asked. The nominating convention asserted that their candidate was a "philosophical Statesman," but a fellow state senator said he had not been aware of it until the convention had placed this label on him. No intellectual, Schulze proved to be frugal, stubborn, and independent. Said one observer, "He was a bred-in-the-bone Pennsylvania German."[35]

In the first half of the nineteenth century, suffrage—in a democratic extension of political franchise—was extended to all free white male citizens regardless of how much property they owned. But for many individual Pennsylvania German citizens, the joys of political democracy were greatly diminished by a near-fatal misunderstanding of legal technicalities. Many of these farmers had settled new lands as authorized by land patents and land warrants, between 1750 and 1800. The land patents were only land rights to locate and settle otherwise unclaimed land, to survey it, and to obtain a legal deed vesting full right in the settler-owner. In their great hunger for land, numerous German claimants who held legal land patents failed to realize that only by recorded deeds was the land ownership finally completed. Thus between 1805 and 1845, land speculators and lawyers familiarized themselves with county land records and found numerous holdings where deeds had never been issued. Under one pretext or another, often simply filing for deeds where none had been issued, they acquired legal title and forced the rightful Dutch owners off the land. That some of these land sharks had been Tories (or of Tory families) in the American Revolution did not ease the irritation in the least.

Rights to political democracy had a hollow sound when presumably legal and proper land development was denied by deed technicalities. To many Pennsylvania Dutchmen, a legal patent was an official paper; he simply did not understand that it was only the start of the process. That even the landless could now vote was small consolation to those who lost their lands.[36]

After1828, two new parties emerged, the Anti-Masons and the Whigs. Pennsylvania Whigs supported the Bank of the United States and welcomed Anti-Jackson Democrats. The Anti-Masonic party, a mixture of Pennsylvania Dutch and Scots-Irish agrarians, stood opposed to privilege and exclusivity. The Anti-Mason party was a force in the Keystone State several years before its major impact on the national scene.

Jackson dumped his Pennsylvania backers in favor of the Van Buren New York Democracy. Yet so great was the Jackson mystique among the voters, especially in the Pennsylvania Dutch sections, and so appealing was his popular, antiwealth program, that havoc ensued in party circles. Governor George Wolf first defended the bank, but then, caught in a squeeze involving the state's internal improvements, endorsed Jackson's bank veto. Pet banks were so ill-thought of in the Keystone State that one of them, the Girard Bank, voluntarily returned federal deposits to ease the pressure. Citizens blamed economic hard times on the Jackson government; yet the personal popularity of Andrew Jackson rose. Political broadsides in German continued to place both credit and blame upon the almost mythical Jackson. One long-suffering wife explained her husband's actions in post–Civil War Pennsylvania by saying: "But Mister, don't get offended at anything he says; he is a good man, if he is old and still votes for Jackson. . . . He can't get Old Hickory out of his head."[37]

The greatest achievement of George Wolf as governor was a measure independent of the Jackson program. In the face of many adverse forces in the state, Wolf advocated free public schools in every annual message. In April, 1834, he signed a bill creating a tax-supported public education system. Factory owners, parochial school advocates, and the Pennsylvania Dutch community joined in vigorous denunciation of waste, extravagance, and unnecessary taxes. Many Dutch feared public schools would end both private schools and instruction in German. To their chagrin, German voters found they could not trust one of their own.

It was an unusual milestone for Pennsylvania to achieve parity in free schools with more advanced states under the governorship of a Pennsylvania Dutchman. That Democratic leader foresaw democratic values in the public school measure which his popular followers missed. Some said Wolf might give his legislature "such an admonition as a German farmer would give his son when embarking on a new business."[38] State officials reiterated that the new schools were not intended to replace German schools, nor would they force use of English on the population.

In the end, Wolf's schools and other financial issues cost him the 1835 election. It would have been his third term and feelings ran high against three terms for any governor. Limited as were his powers, George Wolf had used them effectively. Sentiment favored additional limits. Joseph Ritner, a Berks County German, won over split Democratic opposition. Ritner appealed to the small voter, calling for tax relief and more effective democracy. He opposed secret societies, political intrigue, and usurpation of governmental power. His Anti-Masonic party platform invited Whig and Bank Democrat support, opposing Amos Ellmacher's attempts to keep the Anti-Masons exclusive. Ellmacher carried some weight since he had been the Anti-Mason candidate for vice president of the United States in 1832.

Ritner's appeal may be measured by his hand-at-the-plow portrait. He pointed out that the Panic of 1837, which occurred during his term, had its origins in Jacksonian economic measures, not his own. To his credit, Governor Ritner actively supported the infant public schools, despite opposition to the measure among his backers. Also during his term, a new Constitution of Pennsylvania limited powers of the governor and judges, among other reforms. But the Constitution of 1838 corrected its 1790 predecessor by assuring the franchise to "white freemen."[39] The Pennsylvania German took his voting responsibilities seriously. As one visitor from Europe noted,

> When three generations have sat on their own free hearthstone, and voted for I know not how many presidents, senators, deputies, and countless other officials, it is no wonder that the great-grandson at last stands as upright and unbending as a pine tree.[40]

A new Constitution and choice of governor were placed on the same ballot in 1838. Voters approved the Constitution with a bare twelve hundred vote plurality of nearly a quarter-million votes cast. Eastern counties, the center of Dutch voting strength, were generally opposed. Joseph Ritner lost to David R. Porter for governor, but the legislature was so split that legislative deadlock and eventually street demonstrations ensued. Some feared that Ritner might seize power despite the small but clear majority Porter held. When mob demonstrations in Harrisburg rose to new heights, Governor Ritner, defeated but not yet superseded, called for federal troops from Carlisle, in case of trouble. No force was dispatched. He then ordered out the state militia, armed with buckshot, to keep the peace. Porter adherents looked upon this as an effort to prevent his inauguration, so many of them also descended on Harrisburg in great numbers. In the end it all died down, no militia shots were fired, and no obstacles prevented a legal and orderly succession. The Anti-Masons were discredited in the "Buckshot War" and soon disappeared as a political entity.[41]

In 1844, the strategic importance of Pennsylvania Dutch candidates surfaced again. National and state executive elections once more coincided. Henry A. Muhlenberg, another of Henry Melchior's grandsons, endorsed party harmony when named first United States Minister to Austria, but then got the Democratic gubernatorial nomination, shouldering aside Francis Rahn Shunk, also from the village of Trappe. Two months before the election, Muhlenberg died. Van Buren and Buchanan forces in the party combined to nominate Shunk at the last moment. The Whigs had their own German candidate, Joseph Markle, and the results were predictably close. Shunk defeated Markle by less than 4,500 votes of over three hundred thousand cast.

Nativist propaganda had burgeoned, especially in Philadelphia in 1844. Riots and some deaths ensued, but they had no bearing on the choice of governor.[42]

Governor Francis Shunk, a typical self-made man of this era, rose in politics despite his ordinary attributes. Pennsylvania received special recognition when Polk named James Buchanan to be secretary of state, but otherwise the state received little national patronage. Shunk, on the other hand, concentrated state patronage favors among his friends. The return of prosperity scotched Whig predictions of disaster, and Shunk rolled to an easy reelection in 1847. Emanuel Reigart, a native American candidate from the solidly Dutch Lancaster County, polled a mere eleven thousand votes, a mere 4 percent of the total. The issue of slavery held the interest of many Pennsylvanians, and the state legislature expressed antislavery sentiments.

Slavery itself affected Pennsylvania very little. Governor Shunk's chief claim to fame over the years was his astonishing resignation from the governor's post as a result of ill-health, a most unusual move. An officeholder of that importance simply died on the job. Once again, Shunk showed his contempt for convention and resigned, though he died shortly afterward.

With him, for all practical purposes, ended the run of Pennsylvania German governors. From Simon Snyder to Francis Shunk, the German governors had stood for fiscal responsibility, internal improvements, and industrial beginnings, but none of these at the expense of farming. The commonwealth had benefited from the National Road which ran from Cumberland, Maryland, to Wheeling, Virginia, and beyond. Travelers and freighters brought cash, news, and a spirit of progress to the inns, way stations, and counties of southwestern Pennsylvania. A few of the Dutch "went west" on the National Road to take advantage of the new trade opportunities.

On the National Road were to be seen the high-wheeled canvas-covered freight carriers known as the Conestoga wagons. Annually thousands of these efficient carriers, most of them drawn by teams of Conestoga horses, with Conestoga team bells of Swiss German origin on their harnesses, wheeled along the cartway of the finest road through the mountains. Urging the teams on, and delivering goods rapidly in consequence, were the drivers whose profanity matched the acrid blue-white smoke from their Conestoga cigars. "Stogies," veritable trademark of the Conestoga teamsters, were made of scraps and low-grade tobacco leaf from Pennsylvania and Maryland farms. The heavy freight carriers delivered raw materials, food, and finished products to market.[43]

Pennsylvania Dutch farmers from the interior counties had discovered the trade advantages in Baltimore years before. Trails and rough roads were improved and gradually implemented by turnpike companies. They celebrated economic opportunity in verse.

> Nooch Baltimore geht unser Fuhr
> Mit dem bedeckte Waage;
> Der Turnpike zeicht uns die Geschpurer
> Die Gäul sin gut beschlaage.
> Ein guter Schluck! Glück zu der Reisz![44]

> Our trade goes down to Baltimore
> By covered wagon;
> The turnpike spurs us onward,
> The horses are well shod.
> Down the hatch! Good fortune on the journey!

The journey did not lack in adventure. Just west of Baltimore lay Cumberland, Maryland, the eastern terminus of the National Road.

In competition with the roads and turnpikes, the Pennsylvania State Works envisaged construction of a network of canals to serve the relatively flat territory and the easy grades of the valleys and broad river bottoms of eastern Pennsylvania. David Rittenhouse completed a detailed engineer's map of elevations and obstacles along Lehigh and Schuylkill Rivers as potential links between the Delaware and the Susquehanna, "to keep trade within the province." He lived to see portions of both Delaware and Schuylkill Canal and of the Susquehanna and Schuylkill Canal constructed. Eventually a master plan called for canal service between Philadelphia and Pittsburgh, to rival the Erie Canal. The Union Canal east of the Susquehanna joined the main line of the State Works west of the Susquehanna River, and on to Pittsburgh. Canal links to the upper reaches of

Chesapeake Bay failed to materialize. The main line of the Pennsylvania Canal depended upon inclined railways to haul canal barges over the mountains, so the canal scheme never really succeeded. Steamboats never worked on the shallow Susquehanna, either.[45]

More promising in time was the steam railroad. Maryland interests had a fifteen-year advantage, but the 1846 Charter of the Pennsylvania Railroad Company soon entered an effective challenge. The Philadelphia and Columbia Railroad west of the broad rivers now joined a western road to Pittsburgh. In 1860, on the eve of a greater rivalry, the Baltimore-Philadelphia trade fight continued. Pennsylvania Dutchmen worked in railway construction crews, even as they had assisted turnpike building and the construction of Schuylkill Navigation Canal, Lehigh Coal and Navigation Canal, and the narrow Union Canal. Dutch conductors, stationmasters, and yard gangs shared in the sweat and profit of the newly discovered best solution to the state's transportation needs. In an apologetic tone, the nineteenth-century Pennsylvania German housewife spoke of her husband, "Oh, he's off with the railroad."[46]

Between 1808 and 1848, a majority of German governors presided over the economic, social, and political change of four decades. They were literally "of the people," though they didn't hesitate to tangle with their constituents. Essentially they saw things in a state framework, a not uncommon vantage point for their era. The governor's chair proved a political deadend. When the state constitution allowed strong gubernatorial powers (to 1838) the state refused to elect strong men, but chose the German governors instead. After 1838 the situation did not basically alter. No governor of Pennsylvania has subsequently served in a national cabinet, much less become chief executive or vice president. Only one Keystone State governor before 1838 (Findlay) was later elected senator, and only three have entered the Senate since that date. Pennsylvania Dutch governors are not present even on that small list. One respected historian has pithily summarized the plight of the governors: "The majority were never heard from again."[47] It seems a logical deduction that the surest way to kill off a man politically is to elect him governor of the Commonwealth of Pennsylvania.

CHAPTER XI

Pennsylvania's Dutchmen on the National Scene

THOUGH THE PENNSYLVANIA DUTCH WERE USUALLY RELUCTANT to leave the farm homestead, some of them participated in the westward expansion. These Dutch started moving into frontier valleys of Maryland, Virginia, and North Carolina as early as the 1750s.

Daniel Boone himself, born of English parents between Pottsgrove and Reading, left the company of his Pennsylvania Dutch neighbors and trudged off to Kentucky, where his Pennsylvania-made rifle became famous as the "Kentucky rifle." In the next generation, Robert T. Potts, who was of English and German ancestry and a native of Montgomery County, took part in the exploration of the Missouri River system. He was one of the first Americans to see the wonders of the Yellowstone region. At the insistence of Indians, Potts engaged in individual combat with a bull buffalo. Later he raised cattle commercially, but was lost at sea with his shipment of cattle in a pioneering attempt to transport animals directly from New Orleans to the eastern port cities.[1]

Matthias Young left his Bucks County Dutch homestead to venture westward on the National Road and beyond. He recorded his astonishment at the score of Pawnee leaders (including Petalesharo) that Major Benjamin O'Fallon was bringing to Washington for treaty negotiations. Young established business links between eastern Pennsylvania and developing areas of Ohio and Indiana. These people rejected the sedentary habits of their neighbors and ventured toward the near western horizons.[2]

Despite their provincialism, the German element in Pennsylvania were concerned about local issues and read widely on

198

sectional and national issues. Moreover many of these agrarian or lower-middle-class Americans of German background had definite opinions on sectional issues. They abhorred slavery, feudal remnants, or any other system of economic and institutional subjugation of men. In the early nineteenth century they regarded cotton as an interloper, challenging their own production of woolen and linen cloth, although they eventually came to use cotton themselves for its versatility.

On the other hand, the Pennsylvania Dutch felt a great affinity for the American West. When they considered the vast distances, almost endless frontier, and later, massive agricultural production of the new West, these men and women, pioneers in their own way, felt an almost mystical awe. Like Hector St. John de Crevecoeur who called the American West the "Garden of the World," they were thrilled by the western regions, though they left it to a Lewis Evans or Nathaniel Ames to describe.[3]

Pennsylvanians recognized increased opportunities of cheap land and open space. Those who had not yet established family and farm on the Lehigh or Swatara were drawn toward the frontier, and when free homestead land became available in the 1860s, still more moved westward. The Pennsylvania Dutch Conestoga wagon, with minor changes, became the prairie schooner. The size of the wagon wheels tended to stabilize as they were adapted to the western plains. Most important, the same size wheel front and back (contrasted to the Conestoga wagon's smaller front wheels) made them interchangeable and therefore of greater utility. The familiar blue body and bleached canvas top were retained west of the Mississippi. Many wagons simply remained unpainted as the initial coat faded. The covered wagon has become one of the basic symbols of westward expansion, the great wheels gearing the movement of goods and families into the plains and mountain west. The large, high-sided boatlike bodies floated across rivers where no ford existed. The "gedeckte Waage" of the Pennsylvania Dutch came a long way from the freighting of vegetables into Baltimore to the John Ford motion picture epics of the midtwentieth century.[4]

The fur trade drew Daniel Boone and others onto the high plains for buffalo hides, and wool, but the greatest fur attraction was the beaver of the Rocky Mountains. Peter Weiser worked for early fur entrepreneur Manuel Lisa. Jacob Fowler, Jacob Leese, Henry Boller, and a handful of other Dutch descendants also engaged in the fur business. In addition to those specifically from the Dutch country, another dozen or two men born in Virginia's western valleys, or East Tennessee or Kentucky, derived from German families who had originally settled in Pennsylvania. The names of Isaac Slover, Ewing Young, William Wolfskill, Caleb Greenwood, and George Nidever are also associated with the West.[5]

Those Pennsylvania Dutchmen who were engaged in the fur trade were explorers and pioneers as well. Peter Weiser, descended from a well-known family of Colonial Pennsylvania, volunteered from army duty at Kaskaskia to serve with Meriwether Lewis and William Clark, explorers of the Louisiana territory. Weiser, particularly adept at Indian trading, negotiated for food and horses at several stages of the journey. Injured more than once, he kept a weather eye open for the best beaver streams. The Wiser River was named for him, and the town of Wiser, Idaho, commemorates "Jacob [sic] Wiser, a German trapper." His death at the hands of Blackfeet Indians in 1810 cut short the promising career of one of the first mountain men.[6]

The Kern brothers, Edward, Richard, and Benjamin, were Pennsylvania Dutch explorers of the Great Southwest. John C. Frémont hired them as specialists in his fourth expedition after Edward Kern had so ably assisted him in the third expedition. The three Philadelphians adjusted to the demanding life on the frontier, though Benjamin complained of routine chores which interfered with his medical responsibilities. Richard Kern inscribed his name on Morro Rock, near Zuni, New Mexico, and copied Spanish names dating back to 1606. Dick relieved the monotony of snowbound mountain days by playing his flute. The two elder brothers, Benjamin and Richard, died in Indian attacks, one in 1849, the other in 1853.

Twenty-three-year-old Edward Kern, most adaptable of the brothers, commanded Fort Sutter, California, in the Mexican War. "Little did I think when sitting at home ... that I would be ... a military character, a rale Commandante [sic] of a Fort, with power to do as I pleased and shoot people if they do not obey me."[7] His natural good humor led his companions to consider Ned Kern an asset in perilous times. From a peak in the Rockies, Kern uttered, "Blicke zum Himmel!" Initially he admired the Indians as "picturesque unsophisticated children of nature," but recurring encounters led him to denounce them as scavengers and thieves. He attempted to relieve the distress of the disoriented, eventually cannibalistic Donner Party, which prompted George McKinstry's warning to Ned, "Look out for those man-eating women."[8] Kern County and the Kern River of south central California honor this Pennsylvania Dutchman's efforts on behalf of his beloved United States.

One man's success entailed another man's disaster. The short-lived and much elaborated Bear Flag Revolt of June 14, 1846, took Mexican prisoners at Sonoma, including General Mariano Vallejo. The interpreter for the prisoners, Jacob Leese, was an erstwhile fur trapper, Pennsylvania Dutch mountain man, and cattleman; he was also General Vallejo's son-in-law and thus was mistakenly incarcerated with the Mexicans. Edward Kern had custody of the prisoners, including Leese, at Fort Sutter. Leese complained of his status, his health, and the inhospitable surroundings of Fort Sutter jail. He was soon released with the others.[9]

The Mexican War of 1846–48 proved to be as unpopular in Pennsylvania as among New Englanders, yet numerous young men volunteered to serve. Keystone State contingents included Pennsylvania Dutchmen recruited from Philadelphia to Mauch Chunk and from York to Pittsburgh. New England objections that the war served proslavery ambitions of the South found a sympathetic ear in the Dutch country, where many also continued to oppose war as a matter of principle. In the state's biographical listing of soldier veterans of the Mexican War, German names from Klatz and Kline through Kuhns and Kutz flow uninterrupted for four pages, while Litzingers, Grussenmeyers, and Schnitzbergers are included in the roll which begins with Abel and ends with Zimmerman. Some Dutch served, but the community remained cold to the war. In what seems a contradiction, however, Pennsylvania voted enthusiastically for the Whig presidential candidate Zachary Taylor, in 1848, largely on his achievements in the Mexican War.[10]

In the development of the West, mining played a major role. It offered rewards to the relatively few successful prospectors. Those fortunes in gold, silver, or copper (even though limited to a minute percentage of miners engaged) attracted thousands of adventurers. So did the California Gold Rush. John Sutter, Swiss idealist on whose land gold was first discovered, and whose socioeconomic experiment of "New Helvetia" was shattered in consequence, spoke German as his original language. It is easy to imagine John Sutter and Ned Kern conversing in dialect German. However, the majority of Pennsylvania Dutch in California, those who had come specifically to prospect for gold, never saw the legendary Sutter and had little opportunity to use their dialect in the Golden State. In fact the great variety of types and origins of those who came led few gold seekers to question the backgrounds of those who worked beside them.

Pennsylvanians found the westward journey both exacting and exasperating. They filled journals and diaries with their accounts of routine activity and extraordinary experiences. Two such displaced persons were John A. Markle and Isaac Wistar, whose writings illustrate the challenges they encountered. The former crossed "the Majestic Ohio, the Mudy [sic] Mississippi and the Snaggy Missouri," and stopped at New Fort Kearney, which "would not want more than 10 men with Shotguns to . . . blow it to thunder." This Pennsylvania Dutchman tried to converse with the "friendly, manly, noble looking Sioux warriors . . . but all I could coax out of them was a grunt." He reported sighting "the mightly herds of huge Buffaloes, thundering over the Bluffs as if they were chased by a Streak of Lightning," and tasted his first buffalo steaks "in a pace where there was no wood, so we have to cook with Buffalo Chips, as they term them through politeness." His party "passed several old extinct volcanic craters which appeared as if they had belched forth like Etna or Vesuvius" and later rested by "the Truckey River, a beautiful Stream of Cold Clear water." Markle found gold in California. "Some days," he reported, "we have made as much as 30 dollars a piece, but these days are scarce."[11]

Isaac Wistar left his glassmaking relatives to join California gold seekers. Railroad, stagecoach, and steamboat took him to St. Louis, from whence Wistar drove a wagon to the Pacific

Coast. He noted the buffalo and the beaver. He saw that without the assistance of the Sioux Indians, no wagon train could possibly have crossed Pawnee and Cheyenne country in safety. Using rocker and pan, Wistar and his companions found gold in sufficient quantities to pay costs but not enough to keep them in California. The solitary life lacked the excitement that could be found in the settled towns. Moreover, he found the company distracting. "Criminals, deserters, beachcombers and vagabonds soon swarmed from all shores of the Pacific, ... nuisances [to] be stamped out by the shortest process." Adventuring to Oregon and back into the mountains, he stole horses from Indians and finally returned to Philadelphia from San Francisco by water except for the land crossing in Panama.[12]

The development of an Oriental trade also benefited from the active participation of several of the Pennsylvania Dutch. The China trade was hardly a novelty to men of the Keystone State, for regular sailings left Philadelphia for the Orient before 1790. In 1849, Jacob Leese departed from San Francisco with American goods, headed for the China coast and trade opportunities, which had been opened up by the Burlingame China Treaty of 1842. After ten months, Leese returned, sailing through the Golden Gate with "the richest and most valuable cargo of Chinese goods ever brought to this market."[13] Leese had gone a long way from the home of his Dutch parents in Ohio to the Rocky Mountains and the Pacific Ocean, contracting a Spanish marriage along the way.

Relatively few Pennsylvania Germans shared that great spirit of adventure. Yet another who did was Edward Kern, who, after pioneering in the Rocky Mountains, shipped across the Pacific Ocean on two exploratory expeditions in 1853 and 1858. As artist and draftsman aboard the *Vincennes,* then on the *J. Fenimore Cooper,* he mapped the coasts and harbors of Okinawa and Japan under Lieutenants John Rodgers and John Brooke. Brooke and Kern went ashore at Shimoda and Hakodate and made port at the Bay of Sendai, the first Americans to visit there.[14]

Before the initial expedition returned, Dutchman Edward Kern joined John Brooke on exploratory forays into Siberia and Kamchatka, where Kern found the aboriginal Chuckchis

very reminiscent of Indians of the American Southwest. The
surveyors returned to the Orient in 1858 for a second tour on
the *J. Fenimore Cooper*, by way of Hawaii and the islands
of the western Pacific. Only a few weeks into the mission, the
Fenimore Cooper, lashed by a tropical storm, washed ashore
in Hanagawa harbor. The vessel could not be rehabilitated
so the geodetic mission was scratched and the ship sold to
the Japanese.[15]

John Brooke, Edward Kern, and their restive crew, anxious
to return to the states, found themselves in the midst of an
East-West tug-of-war over proper Japanese handling of the
diplomatic mission to the United States. The U. S. S. *Powhatan*
and the Japanese *Kanrin Maru*, a Dutch-built steam and sail
vessel purchased by the emperor's government, would join to
carry American and Japanese personnel to San Francisco. So
it was that Brooke, Kern, and other stranded Yankee sailors
voyaged across the Pacific as advisors on the first Japanese vessel
to make the crossing. The unexpected arrival of the *Kanrin
Maru* at the Golden Gate caused a sensation. The Japanese
toured San Francisco and newsmen interviewed Brooke, Kern,
and the other Americans who traveled on the Japanese vessel.
"Mr. Kern informs us that the Japanese make excellent engi-
neers," ran the account in the *San Francisco Herald*, but they
proved to be poor sailors, "their navigation hither to having
been confined to the coast of their native land."[16]

At a reception for Japanese diplomats and naval personnel
in San Francisco, a final toast honored Edward Kern. In retrospect, it seems appropriate enough, for this Philadelphia Dutchman not only helped open Japan to American trade by the
charts he produced or corrected, but he assisted in uncovering
the rest of the world for the Japanese and celebrated these
events in sketches and paintings.[17]

The decade of American naval and commercial activity in
the Far East saw slavery the main issue at home. To the
Pennsylvania Germans this was an old and fruitless debate.
With very few exceptions, they owned no slaves and looked
askance at the institution. They found merit in Pennsylvanian
David Wilmot's efforts to exclude slavery from the Great Southwest, even though Congress did not.

Pennsylvania Dutch and blacks lived in close contact in the southern tier of counties in the state. They ignored each other in daily affairs. Virtually no Negroes in Pennsylvania worked as farm labor in the area where Dutch farmers predominated. Few Germans sought employment in the cotton mills, whose black workers were "good at cotton." Pennsylvania Dutch held no animosity toward blacks, as many urban workers of the time did. In fact, to some degree, a feeling of sympathetic understanding existed. The poor German on the same rung of the social ladder as the Negro, often made common cause with him. When asked, "Are you happy in this half-German state of Pennsylvania?," a Negro residing in Bethlehem responded, "Yes, sir, col[ore]d people are as white as anybody here, if they behave." He added, "Col[ore]d people like the Germans, there's no deception with them."[18]

Many of the German communities in the Keystone State had no black population at all, and even Bethlehem had only a handful, who found it useful to learn to speak Pennsylvania Dutch. The Dutch, except for some Mennonite leaders, took little active part in defiant Quaker activity. One of the routes of the Underground Railway ran north through the Susquehanna Valley, and Pennsylvania Germans provided assistance there. Church leaders spoke out against the evils of alcohol, slavery, and new fashions in clothing. Descendants of the Dutch element who had migrated south through western valleys were relatively unreceptive to slavery. Lucretia Mott, outspoken Quaker abolitionist, addressed the essentially Dutch student body at Freeland Seminary in 1850, but she said more against tobacco and liquor than she did about slavery.[19]

The congressional Compromise of 1850 seemed eminently acceptable, although the Germans had no sympathy with Fugitive Slave requirements. Even those who experienced no desire to assist the runaway slaves had equally little tendency to recapture them or abet their return to the South as the new laws required. When Pennsylvania's Personal Liberty Law was negated by a federal court decision, the legislature passed the same law but changed the wording which caused the adverse court ruling. Dutchmen found it impossible to support slavery, but they rarely spoke out publicly on the subject. Some religious leaders did produce antislavery tracts in the German language, or published German translations of material initially printed in English. Henry Harbaugh, a German Reformed pastor, had long been an abolitionist and did not hesitate to speak out on the issues.[20]

When fugitive slaves, sheltered by free Negroes at Christiana, in Lancaster County, were sought for return by their Maryland master under the Fugitive Slave Law, resistance turned to riot. The Maryland slaveholder was killed and his son badly wounded in the fracas, which became a cause célèbre. A local backlash followed as Lancaster County farmers deprecated this violent interference in their calm community life. Essentially the Christiana riots settled nothing but only added some fuel to the flames of the slavery issue.

Neither the Dred Scott decision of the Supreme Court nor affairs in Kansas actively concerned the Dutch, although they became the topic of store and tavern arguments across the commonwealth. Both instances appeared to be blatant proslavery assertions which were not received with favor in the Dutch country. James Buchanan, native of Lancaster County though he was, had been elected president of the United States largely because of his silence on the slavery issue. In office, he appeared to surrender to the slavery wing of the Democratic party. Many Dutchmen found it difficult to accept the increasing arrogance of the forces of slavery. The issue drove many German voters into the new Republican party, which was sufficiently "free soil" to satisfy their doubts about slavery and promised jobs and land to solve the nation's ills.

The presidential election of 1860 offered a difficult choice. Breckinridge and Bell, southern and border candidates, received few votes, but a real contest developed between Abraham Lincoln, Republican, and Stephen Douglas, Union Democrat. In the final analysis, helped by vigorous rural Dutch support of Lincoln, the Republicans prevailed. Perhaps they admired Lincoln's humble country style, or his demeanor when visiting Pennsylvania. His vigorous opposition to further extension of slave territory met with their approval. The Lincoln manner was attractive: straightforward talk in words that all could understand. No less appealing were his self-deprecating remarks and his appreciation of low humor and farce. They valued him the same way they had valued Andrew Jackson; Lincoln was their man. They understood him and his purpose to preserve the Union.

In the Dutch counties of Pennsylvania, the results were astounding. As in previous wars, including the struggle for independence, they were for the Union. Some still respected Stephen Douglas, but he died in 1861, having encouraged support for Lincoln in his last months. Others enthusiastically espoused the cause of General George McClellan, especially because they thought he had been spitefully handled by Lincoln. A few stood firmly with Horace Greeley, particularly those who had admired William Lloyd Garrison.

Active fighting in the spring of 1861 intensified the pressures. Unlike Major Robert Anderson, who surrendered Fort Sumter, Lieutenant Adam Slemmer, of Dutch country origin, with his small garrison, held Fort Pickens in Pensacola Harbor so it remained Union throughout the war.

Within the week, President Lincoln's call for seventy-five thousand short-term volunteers brought instant response. Of the so-called "First Defender" regiments to arrive in Washington, D.C., all four were from Pennsylvania. Three of these regiments were recruited in the heart of the Dutch country, at Allentown, Norristown, and Reading, while the additional regiment, from Pottsville, contained numerous Pennsylvania German volunteers. At the core of each was the local militia unit, the Norris Rifles and the Allen Rifles, for example.

The urgency of the situation registered particularly forcibly in the heart of rural German Pennsylvania. It soon became apparent that ninety-day enlistments were insufficient, and the whole volunteer apparatus was implemented by conscription before the war was half finished. Nonetheless, just as the area of the Pennsylvania Dutch had furnished the guard troops for George Washington in the Revolution, so now they provided the nucleus of initial federal response to the attack on Fort Sumter. A few men thus completed their military obligation, but a majority later volunteered for three-year terms.[21]

The German language newspapers throughout the state nearly unanimously supported the Lincoln government. A series of pamphlets appeared, treating slavery, secession, and the causes of war as well as offering explanations of Union activities. When it became apparent that a long war was developing, and a call for a third of a million volunteers followed, one German leader translated the popular response for his particular audience, "Wir kommen Vater Abraham." Harbaugh, in his magazine *The Guardian*, published an article in 1861 on "War and Christianity," in which he endorsed actions by the federal government and pointed out some positive results of war. In 1862, he published a poem in Dutch, "Das Union Arch."[22]

The dilemma of those whose religious scruples against war remained unresolved became even more complicated in the Civil War than in earlier conflicts. The Quakers had provided an impetus for the Abolitionist movement and had engaged in vigorous social action to achieve it. They now found bearing arms quite a different matter. German pietists faced the same conflict of values, with peaceable intentions and the evils of slavery posing a most delicate balance.

Quakers and Mennonites found their American Revolution roles reversed in the Civil War. Earlier Nathaniel Greene and Timothy Matlack had led a fighting Quaker response, while large numbers of Mennonite pietists had refused to engage on either side, Loyalist or patriot. In the Civil War it was the Quakers who generally abstained. Mennonite and other usually pacific Germans joined their Church German associates and joined the fight, concurring with the New England proposition, "War is not the worst of evils."[23]

In a sense both Quakers and Mennonites found themselves in a vast generation gap but with slightly different particulars. Young Quakers chided their back-sliding elders for using wine and tobacco, contrary to the growing fashion of temperance-abstinence movements, and they deprecated the tendency to justify violence, even in a good cause. Young Mennonites, on the other hand, became impatient with the inertia and false tolerance of their elders who objected to slavery but allowed it to continue as a national institution. These young men were also bold enough to inquire how the religious values and guarantees their fathers held dear were to be retained if the nation did not fight to uphold them.

One Pennsylvania Dutchman, who was liberal enough in his Mennonite views that he dispensed local law as justice of the peace, was hurt and shocked to see two of his sons march off as volunteers in the Union army. One son, Charles Hunsicker, summed it up quite simply, "Pop don't understand this war business."[24] Tens of thousands of young men from all parts of the Pennsylvania Dutch community joined the military effort. Some fought to preserve the Union, some to terminate slavery, and others simply for adventure. The service posed an alternative to daily routines of the agricultural community. Pennsylvania sent more men into uniform than did any other state; the number of Pennsylvania German citizens who entered service was disproportionately high.

In that light, it is not surprising that the greatest ideological trauma was felt by transplanted Pennsylvania Germans who had migrated earlier to the interior valleys of Virginia and North Carolina. Their fierce individualism combined with an intense revulsion at the notion of fighting in defense of slavery. Large numbers of draft evaders and conscientious objectors posed grave problems for the manpower-poor Confederate States of America. In addition, these Piedmont farmers, competing as they did with slave-labor agriculture, found it intolerable that plantation owners were exempted from military service if they owned sufficiently large numbers of slaves.[25]

Manpower advantage, which population and continued immigration assured to the Union, placed available males in the South under even greater pressure to serve. Thus a number of Pennsylvanians who had gone south to new farms or rural employment served in Virginia units. Samuel W. Pennypacker later recalled such a case: "A branch of my own family just after the Revolution, went up into the Valley of Virginia, and they have been there ever since. Some of them have reached distinction and all of them were rebels in the War of 1861."[26] Some individuals also left the Keystone State specifically to volunteer for service in the Confederate army, but that number fell far short of the tally of Southerners who continued in the United States Army despite secession. Some Pennsylvania Dutch descendants volunteered for Confederate service, which boasted of General John D. Imboden and Colonel John F. Neff, whose parents were all Dutch.[27]

Of the foreign volunteers in the Civil War, 90 percent served in the Union military; few wore Confederate gray. It was tempting for Southerners to call these Union volunteers "adventurers, the scum and refuse of Europe." Sectional feelings against Yankees had always run high. The Confederate partisan FitzGerald Ross insisted that New Englanders were "making Dutch and Irishmen fight Yankee battles," just as Southerners had fought Yankee battles in the War for Independence.[28]

Since Union army regiments were raised by counties, some tended to be thoroughly Pennsylvania Dutch in composition. However the famed "German Division" under Louis Blenker and later, Franz Sigel, was New York based and composed of relatively recent arrivals. Other units of the Army of the Potomac found fault with foreign-speaking units, and it made little difference whether they spoke High German or Pennsylvania German, for they were just "Dutch" to neighboring regiments.

Rumors spread, complaining of personal habits or idiosyncrasies. These Dutch troops were poor fighters, they were hard to get along with, they were the most vigorous scavengers in a devastating Union army, so the tales ran. The Eleventh Corps had so many Germans and Pennsylvania German units that it drew unfavorable comments as "a German command," particularly while Franz Sigel was corps commander, "The Dutchmen might stack their arms and butcher their cattle and let their excellent bands play, while the real Army of the Potomac took care of the fighting."[29] As fate would have it, General Joseph Hooker's miscalculations at Chancellorsville brought the weight of "Stonewall" Jackson's surprise attack heavily upon the Eleventh Corps after urgent warnings and intelligence sent by Prussian volunteers had been disregarded.[30]

Soldiers who spoke broken English were often regarded as mindless followers. It got so the Dutch told stories about themselves. Union soldiers burned barns in the Shenandoah Valley late in the war on direct orders from Grant. They were pursued by angry Confederates bent on vengeance. Among those they apprehended was "a little dark-eyed Pennsylvania Dutchman," whom they afforded rough treatment. "Vat you fellows vant to do mit me?" "We are going to take you down here and hang you," was their immediate response. The Dutchman, in a resigned tone, said, "Vell, vatever is de rule," which saved him from that punishment.[31]

Late in the war, General Louis Wagner commanded a black regiment raised in Pennsylvania. Dutch soldiers accepted black troops who came in close contact with them. Dutch units of the Ninth Corps, such as Fifty-First Regiment, Pennsylvania Veteran Volunteers, served beside black regiments of the Ninth Corps, "all over rebeldom," under numerous commands. This did not mean the Dutch would lead the postwar fight for Negro rights, but they felt blacks should receive credit for services rendered.[32]

Isaac J. Wistar, fresh from trips to Denver and northern Virginia, helped organize the Seventy-First Regiment, Pennsylvania Volunteers. This unit was familiarly called the "California Regiment," since so many of its officers and enlisted men had traveled in California, many of them in gold-fever days.[33]

Lincoln took notice of the German-American element and their feeling that they were sometimes badly used. At least in offhand remarks he noted that it was time to call in Schimmelfenning for a conference, which was subsequentlly publicized. Or he counteracted the widespread criticism with a public letter to Carl Schurz. Lincoln was a realist. Considering the degree to which Pennsylvania supplied critical material and manpower, he had no intention of alienating the support of German counties in the state.[34]

Whatever the reactions of individual Pennsylvania Dutch soldiers, they found their horizons extended. War service took men who tended to remain close to home and dispatched them to distant points. It was an education for many of them. And war soon came much closer to home.[35]

For two relatively brief periods, the fighting war churned up Pennsylvania soil. Since food, shoes, horses, and supplies constituted major goals of Lee's two invasions, in the fall of 1862 and early summer of 1863, they struck at the heart of Pennsylvania Dutch Country. Astonishingly, by modern standards, civilian deaths were almost nil, though property losses ran high. Casualty lists in both armies were moderate, by

prevailing standards, in that offensive strike at Cashtown and
Chambersburg.

At Antietam when McClellan attempted to seal off with-
drawing Confederate forces backed against the flood-swollen
Potomac, losses to both sides were devastating. As the line of
battle formed, Pennsylvania units, including Hartranft's 51st
and Wistar's 71st, occupied strategic positions. Regular troops
and short-term volunteers assumed a major role in Union
attacks on entrenched Confederate positions. Christian Good,
Henry Meyers, and Davis Hunsicker were three of the many
Pennsylvania Germans among the several thousand deaths at
Antietam Creek.[36]

The real shock of war for Pennsylvania came in Lee's second
invasion in June and July, 1863. Lee was successful in supply
raids, effective in the destruction of strategic buildings, and
daring in the dispatch of cavalry to the very banks of the
Susquehanna River. Local defense units were called up for
limited service but only so long as Lee's forces operated on
Pennsylvania soil. Samuel Pennypacker served in one of those
units. As Confederate forces probed southeastward, they accidentally engaged federal units south of the country town of
Gettysburg. There for three days the tide of battle swept back
and forth across the shallow valleys, from Confederate positions on Seminary Ridge to the Union defensive fishhook
entrenchment along Cemetery Ridge to Culp's Hill. By the
end of the third day, July 3, 1863, Lee's offensive potential
was dulled and Confederate military victory in the war rendered impossible.[37]

One of the many men killed at Gettysburg was Brigadier
General Samuel Kosciusko Zook of Amish descent, who, despite
his pietist ancestry, had had extensive military experience. Zook
first entered federal service with a New York three-month
regiment, then organized and led the 57th New York Volunteers. While brigade commander in the Second Corps at the
Wheatfield on Gettysburg's second day of fighting, he was
mortally wounded.[38]

The experiences of one Adams County German family illustrate the fratricidal nature of the Civil War. The Culp farm just
southeast of Gettysburg town was near the elevation called

Culp's Hill, a pivotal point of the battle. In the decade prior to the war, a younger son had left home to go to Virginia to find work, while an older brother continued on the family farm in Pennsylvania. In the early years of the Civil War, each found himself called to military service, the elder in Union garb, the younger in Confederate gray. As initial fighting occurred while units deployed and dug in, Virginia troops and Pennsylvania troops by chance placed the brothers Culp in the line opposite each other on the approaches to Culp's Hill. The Pennsylvania Culp in Confederate service died, whereas his brother was wounded but eventually recovered. Certainly this family situation was not unique, but it was one of the most dramatic illustrations of families split by the war.

Other Pennsylvania Dutch in Union military service included tens of thousands of enlisted personnel to a few of the highest ranking officers. General John Hartranft, of Schwenkfelder origin, commanded from regiment to army headquarters. General Samuel P. Heintzelman fought "mit Sigel" and handled responsible assignments in corps command. Less fortunate was Captain Edward Kern, who accepted an engineer's commission in John Frémont's unique personal force in Missouri the first summer of the war. When Frémont's actions led Lincoln to disband the units, Kern's commission was revoked in Washington, so he retired to run an art studio in Philadelphia, where he died in 1863.[39]

In all, less than 6 percent of Pennsylvania troops were drafted or were substitutes. In the Dutch counties volunteers far outnumbered draftees. Although some resistance to conscription arose in the state's coal towns as it did in New York City, it seemed to center among the Irish, whereas the German element generally remained silent.[40]

In another area of Civil War experience, Doctor Samuel P. Boyer, a recent graduate of the University of Pennsylvania Medical School, of the family of Daniel Boyer, a country doctor in Reading, joined the navy. He had attempted to set up a practice in Seisholtzville when initially rejected by the navy. On second thought, they commissioned him, and for two years he served as surgeon with the South Atlantic Blockading Squadron, and, for the last year of the war, he was transferred to the North Atlantic Blockading Squadron. He found duty boring, though not without varied cases for him to study, but he would have preferred open sea cruising. "All work and no prize money makes Jack a lazy dog," he wrote.[41]

On the home front as on the battlefield, the Civil War made a lasting impression. From the thoroughly Dutch town of York, one observer described "a nation, from internal resources alone, carrying on . . . the most gigantic war of modern times . . . all this while growing richer and more prosperous."[42]

Vigorous demand for equipment, supplies, and products of Pennsylvania made that state the industrial heart of the Union war effort as well as the nation's leading agricultural producer. Coal and iron yielded rails and cannon. Sharps breech-loading rifles, designed and produced in Philadelphia, changed the very form of infantry warfare. Philadelphia and the towns of the southern Pennsylvania Dutch country formed the center of cotton and woolen ready-made clothing industry and drew thousands of workers from the fields to the factories. In six years the number of wage earners in Pennsylvania increased by 60 percent.[43]

In the wake of battle, professional men dropped their regular employment and family obligations to attend to the needs of wounded and dying soldiers in schools, churches, homes, and barns around about the battlefield. They were occasionally joined by women volunteers who had already assisted by providing bandages, food, and comfort in Ladies' Army Aid Societies. Confederate wounded were also cared for, though occasionally to the accompaniment of a lecture on loyalty to the Union.[44]

Emancipation of the Negro made little practical difference to the Pennsylvania Dutch farmer or laborer, except that competition for factory or industrial jobs increased in towns bordering former slave territory. Just as the Pennsylvania German had silently opposed the slave system, he now silently noted its demise. Occasionally sermons to Lutheran or Reformed congregations alluded to the new order concerning God and man, but few volunteered for Reconstruction efforts in the South, leaving those duties to Quakers or Yankees.

The death of Lincoln, on the other hand, was regarded as

a great tragedy to the nation. Pennsylvania's German newspapers printed detailed accounts of the event and took a harsh line on John Wilkes Booth and a resurgent South. Newspapers in the Keystone state also observed that their own General W. S. Hancock commanded the military District of Washington, D. C., while General John Hartranft, descendent of German pietists, commanded the guard detail and the firing squad for Lincoln's assassination conspirators.[45]

CHAPTER XII

Open Hearth and Kitchen Hearth

IN MANY WAYS THE ERA BETWEEN THE CIVIL WAR AND WORLD War I was a golden age for the Pennsylvania Dutch. It was a grand compromise between the old and the new, the parochial and the cosmopolitan, the serious and the frivolous. It allowed a range of choice to those who would choose but assured a large measure of stability to others.

The Dutch found their particular place in American society and were accepted for their productive worth under the system; yet they were able to retain their dialect, methods of agriculture, and religious practice largely as they saw fit. In the Pennsylvania Dutch counties it was business as usual. Non-German neighbors paid little attention to them, which suited them quite well. Many of the *Deitsch* continued to farm in their isolated valleys, concerned with the outside world only as a cash market or as source of products the local community was unable to produce. Dialect authors and poets began to appear, singing and telling of the homely values of country life.

Those Pennsylvania Dutchmen who had seen the world as a result of manifest destiny, the Civil War, or the revolution in industrial production, further expanded their horizons. Many of them were absorbed into the national scene, and a few never returned to their Pennsylvania origins.

Thus, Adam Slemmer, finally relieved of his desk job with wounded soldiers, commanded the army garrison at Fort Laramie, Wyoming Territory, until his premature death in 1868.[1] Doctor Samuel Boyer, still possessed of the "unmistakeable flavor of the 'Pennsylvania Dutch,'" continued his surgeon's career in the United States Navy on coastal duty in early years of reconstruction. In 1868 he was assigned duty stations in Japan, at Yokohama, Osaka, and Nagasaki. He observed the civil war

216

in Japan and the resurgence of antiforeign sentiment. He was one of the first westerners to visit the inland capital at Kyoto, where he treated the desperately ill Prince of Hizen. Only months after his release from the navy and his announced intention to treat "someone besides sailors," Boyer died.[2]

Others left military service to become leaders in the Keystone State. John Hartranft's prewar law training and his military service combined to ease his way in politics, and he advanced rapidly from auditor general to serve two terms as governor. In addition to his political obligations as governor, he was also chosen national president of the Grand Army of the Republic, a social and political organization of Union army war veterans. Hartranft was the last governor under the Constitution of 1838 and the first under the Constitution of 1873. While the exgeneral ran the state government in Harrisburg, Simon Cameron exercised the strongest political leadership as Republican boss of Pennsylvania from his Senate seat in Washington.

Industrial growth was the most powerful influence in post–Civil War Pennsylvania. Coal, steel, and oil became predominant on the local scene. Among the emerging economic magnates, a few descendants of Pennsylvania Dutch ancestors thoroughly and successfully competed. Wounded and released from service, Isaac J. Wistar submitted suggestions for military reform which were quickly rejected. He then turned to the field of transportation as president of the Union Canal Company, which was being challenged by stiff railroad competition. To resolve that, Wistar negotiated with the Reading Company, then with the Pennsylvania Railroad. He was instrumental in consolidation of rail and canal freight service under one corporate roof and ran the Pennsylvania Canal as one division of the Pennsylvania Railroad System.[3] In Chicago, Charles Yerkes controlled the traction company.

Closer to the people throughout the state was the economic reality of employment, food, and shelter. Workers found themselves in an unfavorable bargaining position, since labor costs were considered the most variable component of competitive production. Great numbers of the Dutch clung to agriculture, though as industry boomed, many of the sons accepted industrial jobs in preference to farming. Others who continued to work marginal farms took jobs in industry as a financial hedge.

With the vast majority of their fellow laborers in American industry, they disliked unions and distrusted organizers of labor associations. Thus many Pennsylvania German plant and factory workers, glad of their jobs, still found the pay insufficient for subsistence. For decades they rejected labor unions as an acceptable solution. Naturally management encouraged that viewpoint.

Although tradition insisted that Philip Ginder accidentally discovered coal in northeast Pennsylvania in 1791, English, Irish, or Welsh coal mines were far more numerous than those run by Pennsylvania Dutch. Still, Hazelton, which grew up around Jacob Drumheller's tavern, was a mining town quite thoroughly Dutch in population. The German Pennsylvania Coal Company was organized by German refugees of 1848, and their company town of Tresckow was commonly called "Dutchtown." Kemmerer, Wentz, and Rothermel were Pennsylvania Dutch coal operators, descendants of Germans who had arrived a century or more earlier. George Markle of Hazelton designed the first coal-breaker building, invented a new mine pump, and with his son John, built the Jeddo-Highland Coal Company into one of the industry's soundest units.

The Mahantongo Valley, first settled by Pennsylvania Dutch migrating from other parts of the state, soon saw the emergence of Shamokin as a coal center. Some Dutch continued as miners and breaker boys, but increasingly they competed with Polish, Lithuanian, and Ukranian workers in addition to the Welsh and Irish. Even styles of work varied. The German miner swung his miner's pick free and easy from the shoulder, while the English or Welsh, experienced in small-seam British mines, chopped with short strokes, keeping the pick in front of him. Pennsylvania Dutch miners also improvised fuses to touch off blasting-powder charges, from hollow wheat straws filled with powder. These fuses were known as "Germans." Although relatively few in number, Dutchmen worked in the mines from initial digs to the twentieth century, and they developed traditions of their own in the process.[4]

As in other matters, the tendency is to think of Pennsylvania Dutch achievement only within the boundaries of the state. In truth, their influence was felt in many distant places. The discovery of silver in Tombstone, Arizona, resulted from the tenacity of Ed Schieffelin, born a Pennsylvania German. He had failed in business in Oregon and prospected unsuccessfully in Nevada, Idaho, Utah, and his adopted Oregon. He touched off the last great silver rush in 1877 when he located rich silver ore in Apache-held southeastern Arizona. The silver soon gave out there, but Tombstone became more famous for Wyatt Earp, Boot Hill, and the *Tombstone Epitaph* than for silver.[5]

Silver mining in Utah tended to compete along lines of national origin. Thus Cornish Jacks worked Cornish owned mines. Irish in Irish Catholic diggings, and John Beck, "the Crazy Dutchman" of the Champion Mines of Eureka, though German-born, offered jobs to Pennsylvania Germans. As a result, one section of Eureka, complete with its own school, was well known as "Dutchtown."[6]

Somehow, though, the symbol of Pennsylvania Dutch acceptance in industry is best epitomized by the development of Bethlehem Steel. Both management and labor sources were drawn from the quiet old Moravian town on the Lehigh River, and surrounding Dutch countryside. The modern steelworks and its parent corporation, so thoroughly associated with the Scottish genius of Andrew Carnegie, had a decided "Dutch accent" in Bethlehem Steel. Thus great numbers of steelworkers, dwelling in the ladderlike row houses on the hills of South Bethlehem, thought and worked in the dialect. How true that was is indicated by the fact that other workers, black or Ukranian or Italian though they might be, found it necessary to gain at least rudimentary competence in *Deitsch*. For many years Pennsylvania Dutch workers predominated at the open hearth.

The Pennsylvania Dutch found a worthwhile change in populist agrarian solutions. That suited their nature better than did industrial unions, for agrarian movements generally proposed loose coalitions or associations of individual farmers. The Pennsylvania State Agricultural society dated from antebellum years, and the state Dairy Association, Poultry Association, and Potato Growers' Association developed soon after the war. More generally accepted than the specialty groups was Oliver Kelley's Grange of the Patrons of Husbandry. Kelley himself canvased

Pennsylvania to organize local units. Although starting slowly, the Grange movement grew rapidly, and Pennsylvania soon became "a strong granger state." In many rural areas of north and east Pennsylvania, the Pomona Grange was both an economic and social center. In many local units, ceremonies, plays, and lectures were conducted in Pennsylvania Dutch.[7]

The Dutch farmers of the state were relatively willing to accept new machinery. Consequently plows, harrows, drills, and binders increased production. The Dutchman was much slower to accept new theories and new organizations. In an open economy where market price was the real determinant, the farmer, dependent on rainfall and weather, distrusted both industry and government. That distrust did not diminish when agricultural scientists condemned the bank barn as a dank, dark incubator of bovine tuberculosis. Yet disease control methods eventually improved milk production. Fruit farms in Pennsylvania felt the keen competition when transcontinental railroads brought cheaper fruit from California. The alternative to poor apple sales was to turn the crop into cider and then meditate over the liquid results. H. J. Heinz turned garden vegetables into a national canned food industry, combining the merits of agriculture, the factory, and commercial profit.[8]

After the Civil War, further pressure was exerted on the schools. Initial public school measures were governed by local option, and almost half the districts which opted against local public schools were in the Pennsylvania German counties. By 1850, of one hundred seventy-seven nonaccepting school districts, those counties contained one hundred forty-one. For some years, parochial schools received state money from the public educational funds.

A series of actions in the 1870s spelled the end for German language schools in the commonwealth. While German, or a corruption, of that language, continued to be the only local language of thousands of citizens, the state slowly but inexorably required English schools. For the most part, it succeeded by taking control of the situation out of local hands. In 1873, the new State Constitution specifically denied any state funds to sectarian schools. Normal Schools as teacher training institutions provided for English language teachers only. Hopes of

Monroe County Dutch that at least one German language Normal School might be sanctioned at Gilbert, where such a private school already existed, were dashed when the Normal School was located at East Stroudsburg. So strong was popular resentment, however, that the change to instruction solely in English was not mandated by the state school code until 1911. Elimination of German language instruction occasioned a split in the Pennsylvania Dutch population. Many intellectual leaders and public officials of Dutch origin insisted on the use of English to prepare students for full participation in American life. The rural segment fought vigorously but unsuccessfully to retain instruction in German. They pointed out that there were many districts of the state where children never heard English spoken until they arrived at the local one-room school; then, instantaneously they were expected to learn in English. Small wonder these children were reluctant to speak up; hence the tendency to label them thick-headed or stupid.[9]

The agrarian age produced strong Populist movements for political action in some parts of the country, but the Pennsylvania Dutch held to one of the two old parties. When progressivism swept upon the scene with its reform program and call for citizen participation, it succeeded best within existing party lines. Thus John Wanamaker carried Pennsylvania Dutch standards into the movement as Republican mayor of Philadelphia.

Descended from both Holland Dutch and Pennsylvania Dutch progenitors, Samuel W. Pennypacker, historian, reluctantly accepted nomination and was elected governor of Pennsylvania, serving from 1903 to 1907. A bond existed between Pennypacker and Theodore Roosevelt, and state voters enthusiastically supported both. President Roosevelt supported Pennypacker's gubernatorial candidacy saying, "Pennypacker's defeat would be a national calamity." Dutch country votes heavily favored both men, and Roosevelt was regarded as a leader-hero much as Lincoln had been.[10]

One of the events around which Roosevelt built his Progressive Republican program was the resolution of the Coal Strike of 1902 in Pennsylvania. He used the politically unorthodox act of recognizing some demands of the union leader, John Mitchell.

Two of the outspoken leaders of industry, George Baer of the Reading Company and John Markle of Jeddo-Highland Coal Company, were of Pennsylvania Dutch background; but so were many of John Mitchell's miners.

At any rate, the call for reform was abroad, and Samuel Pennypacker, though originally chosen as candidate by the Republican machine, now strongly urged reform legislation. When the Assembly did not respond he called the legislators into special session. Child labor laws were passed, the State Police were modernized, and urban civil service was begun. Unfortunately for the historical reputation of Governor Penny-packer, a scandal developed about costs of construction of the new state capitol building. Though he was not involved, and profited not a cent from it, the scandal tarnished his reform program. The press derided the governor as an "ugly little dwarf."[11]

On the status of women and their achievements within the framework of Pennsylvania Dutch society, the Dutchman has been ambivalent. He assumed that a male-dominated social order was proper and that women had special responsibilities only in certain areas which he called *Kinner, Kich un Karrich* ("children, kitchen and church"). Of course the husband ran the farm, operated the mill, and concerned himself generally with economic enterprise.

In Colonial Pennsylvania, he had been greatly distressed by the unusual demands of the women of his English neighbors: "very haughty, they are fond of dress and demand a great deal of attention from men."[12] Englishmen of Pennsylvania made much of their women, cared for them, and did not allow them to work. No wonder Pennsylvania was renowned as "a paradise for women, a purgatory for men, and a hell for horses."[13]

The simple fact was that all colonies in America suffered a scarcity of women. Still, the German male was shocked by the relative independence of women, whose husbands feared to punish them lest it backfire. He found it perfectly normal to judge by the size of farm buildings to see who was the boss in a family. If the barn were larger, then the husband dominated; if the house, then it was the wife. That surely satisfied the male ego, for, of course, the barn was always larger.

Males rarely underestimated the value of a wife's contributions to the family. "As cook, seamstress, nurse, laundress, baker, teacher, cloth maker, and supervisor of household production the woman was indispensable in rural economy." Palatine women were in demand "because of their faithfulness and intelligence."[14]

The Pennsylvania Dutch differed from virtually all their neighbors of British background in that German women helped in harvesting and in strenuous farm work. Near Philadelphia, men working as indentured farm servants were occasionally joined at the height of manpower needs by wives or sisters, who in turn were paid on a per diem basis. Usually childbirth kept them out of the fields for only three weeks. Thus women could earn money for family needs, household items, or even to buy off remaining time on the husband's indenture.[15]

The sight of Pennsylvania Dutch women working in the fields caused repeated comments by travelers. Hector St. John de Crevecoeur noted that "German women ... vie with their husbands and often share with them the most severe toils of the field."[16] Fifty years later, another Frenchman, Michel Chevalier, noted the advantages enjoyed by American women, with but few exceptions. "Only among the Canadian French and Pennsylvania Germans, their women labor at least as much as the men."[17]

The Scots-Irish considered field work for women to be degrading and barbarous. Among them, it provided "an almost absolute clue to status." Women who worked in this manner revealed that their family had a low social standing. Early in the Colonial era, whether on the frontier or not, a Scots-Irishman "who valued his social position [would not] permit field labor for his wife and daughters."[18] Crevecoeur observed that of a dozen immigrant families each of Scots, German, and Irish origins, seven Scots, nine German, and four Irish would succeed. "The Scotch are frugal and laborious, but their wives cannot work so hard as German women [in] the field."[19]

The Pennsylvania Dutch farmer was practical about children, rather than sentimental. "Upon the birth of a son, they exult in the gift of a plowman or waggoner; and upon the birth of a daughter they rejoice in the addition of another spinster or milkmaid to the family."[20] Ordinarily the boys worked in the fields and the girls at house duties, but both girls and boys watched cattle at pasture so they did not invade the food crops. At harvest time, at haying, and in butchering, the entire family joined in the harshest physical work.

Substantial foods and good eating have been hallmarks of the Pennsylvania Dutch culture over the years. Some dishes and types of food preparation were imported from the old country, although variations are numerous, perhaps reflecting the regional and provincial differences in origin of these settlers. Of the food items peculiar to the Dutch, none had retained its unchanged identity longer than the pretzel, which can be found in sixteenth-century paintings by Brueghel and Cranach.

Women were sometimes the butt of jokes or the object of plays and stories, as in Clarence Iobst's *En Quart Millich un en halb Beint Raum*, where Abbie Dauvaspeck, a sloppy housekeeper, is surprised by the unexpected return of her husband who missed his streetcar to work and thinks he is the milkman. In the end, it turns out well, for she only feigned her mistake to make the husband jealous. "When you are married twenty-three years you get so used to each other that you don't have much regard for each other." The rest of the play shows her success, burlesqued by the fact that men acted all parts in the drama.[21]

Women came off less well in Thomas Harter's *Boonastiel* letter, "De Weipsleit in Bolidix" (Women in Politics), wherein Becky Kissinger, "oldt maidel," disrupts the smooth operation of "Demagrawdish bolidix." Harter speared politicians and women with a single effort. In a subsequent comment, *Boonastiel* also observed, "Won der divel gaed fisha far monsleit, don doot are ma weibsmensch si shtroomp-bendel usa far bait" ("When the Devil goes fishing for men, he uses a woman's garter for bait").[22]

John Birmelin's poems treated women variously. Two of his lengthy ballads celebrated the eighteenth-century experiences of Regina Hartmann and Celia Zorndorf. Birmelin repeatedly referred to medical or curative knowledge the old women possessed. Yet he wrote sympathetically of the harassed homelife of "Der Henry Peck, er hockt im Eck, Un hot net viel zu saage" ("that is Henn Peck, who sits in the corner and never has much to say)."[23] Birmelin did not suggest that Dutchmen generally fit that pattern.

The woman in the Pennsylvania Dutch home, who was expected to be subservient to her husband, was much more than the farmer's wife. Busy to the point of daily exhaustion, she was the living example of frugality and duty in action. In the very close Pennsylvania Dutch family units, ties between mother and daughter were particularly intimate. Young ladies of Mennonite and Amish origins were introduced into American fiction by Helen R. Martin, but she produced a caricature. Elsie Singmaster corrected some of the earlier misleading notions, although it remained for Joseph W. Yoder to present Amish ways in a really sympathetic fashion in *Rosanna of the Amish* in 1940.[24]

Traditional European arranged marriages and dowry payments did not continue in America. Although in some early instances a dowry was expected, it soon became obsolete. Opportunities for young persons reduced parental control within a few generations.

In early church functions of the Germans in Pennsylvania, women had no status at all, except that of simple membership. The husband drove the buggy to church, chose the pew they sat in, paid the tithe, or decided how much of it they could pay, and received the approbation of the church community, or its admonitions. Gradually women's social organizations grew, though many improved opportunities in the German church in America are twentieth-century phenomena. The Evangelical and Reformed church (including the former German Reformed) authorized female ordination and countenanced women pastors after 1945.

Certainly the twentieth century has placed additional stress upon the Pennsylvania German woman. She had to adjust as the realities of homelife changed, and she had to mollify the husband who found that his role had changed. Other than dress and religion, most visible reminders of distinctive Pennsylvania culture are those of the kitchen or of woman's handwork. The shoo-fly pie and Dutch needlework are far more familiar items of Americana than are any attributes of male domain among the Dutch.

Over the years a few individual women of the Pennsylvania

Dutch have achieved prominence on the historical scene. In family matters they have always been exceedingly important. But they have been historically anonymous for the most part, and so they remain.

At high and low level, Germans of Pennsylvania participated in the growth of the nation, sustained it in civil war, and joined the industrial surge. Coal miners conversing in Pennsylvania Dutch, a governor who wrote verse in Holland Dutch, German, French, and English, explorers who mused in Dutch from mountaintops, and surgeons who complained that navy fare of pork and beans was too Yankee for Pennsylvania Dutch taste—all these were part of the process. By 1914 all these outlooks faced a major challenge. Suddenly the world was not the same, nor would it ever be again.

CHAPTER XIII

Uncomfortable Minority in
Two World Wars

OVER A PERIOD OF SIX OR SEVEN GENERATIONS, THE PENNSYLVANIA Dutch struck a cultural compromise with their surroundings. They retained their agrarian tradition, language, religion, and at least basic elements of family and social institutions. But they also adopted Anglo institutions in government and political parties, and in the law, as they accepted, though with some misgivings, Scots-Irish or Welsh settlements around them. Though accustomed to autocratic government, the Dutch soon subscribed to the American compromise in democracy and business.

Despite occasional wanderers from their valleys, single family defections, or sporadic migrations of discontented religious splinter groups, the Pennsylvania Germans retained many of their ethnic and clan defenses. As small farmers, they did not experience the ghetto manner of living of other, newer arrivals. In common with nearly all immigrant groups, they tended to stay among their own as much as possible.[1] Occasionally, business, church, or politics interjected some English, Scots-Irish, Italian, or Ukrainian into their midst. A minor percentage of those achieved acceptance in the otherwise tight Dutch community. More often, the *Deitsch* warded off such incursions and guarded their children from the influences of outside groups. Intermarriage with such outsiders was frowned upon unless the partner's acceptability was demonstrated by successful survival in the Dutch area for two or three generations. Parents actively interfered in social relationships of sons and daughters, citing religious differences and cultural incompatibility of other ethnic groups.

This did not mean that a wall of division was successfully

maintained, although the Amish nearly did. Much more common was the cultural adoption of some novelty, particularly where little other choice existed. As already noted, these people found the suffrage and democratic participation so valuable that they exercised their franchise as a jealously guarded right. They set their own criteria for political candidates. They adopted the English vocabulary, subject to *Deitsch* endings and pronunciation, in a language bastardization which made the language experts scream. Just as centuries before the English accepted legal terms essentially Norman French, so Pennsylvania Dutch legal expressions were borrowed directly from the English. An often-repeated example shows his stubborn resistance to forced use of English:

Judge: Ask your client whether he is ready to settle for the damages on that basis.
Lawyer: Hoscht sell verschtanne, John? (Did you understand that, John?)
John: Nee, verdammtsei net! (No, damn it!)
Lawyer: Er hot g'saat, "Bischt du ready for die damages uf sellre bassis ze settle?" (He said, are you ready, etc.)
John: Oh! Ferwas hoscht sell net glei g'saat? (Oh! Why didn't you say that in the first place?)[2]

In initial contacts, many an illiterate German migrant had his names anglicized by the clerk. It proved simpler legally to retain the new spelling. Some others whose literacy had preserved proper spelling, in the nineteenth century deliberately anglicized the name to improve status, gain commercial advantage, or simply to join the Americanizing process. Thus Abraham Grünzweig, with a satisfactory name while on the family farm, became Abraham Greene when he traveled beyond.

Not entirely explainable was the renewal of German pride among the Pennsylvania Germans between 1890 and 1914. It did coincide with renewed interest in genealogy, international emphasis upon Teutonic achievement, and Anglo-Saxon racial claims. Some leaders among the Dutch accepted new racial theories as valid. At the grass-roots level, this minority resented the switch to English schools and other appearances of denigration of the "Dumb Dutch." Two journals that began publication in this period, the *Pennsylvania German*, a literary magazine, and *Penn Germania*, attempted to renew interest and sustain old values. Samuel Pennypacker, a scholar, and Martin Brumbaugh, an educator, both emphasized their pride in German origins while serving in the governor's chair.[3]

Indeed it appeared at last that the waves of vigorous criticism Pennsylvania Dutch had long encountered might well be in process of wearing out. Brumbaugh and the Pennsylvania German intelligentsia saw brighter days ahead, while poets and authors turned out more and more printed tales and stories in the dialect. Newspapers printed dialect contributions whose orthography varied fiercely. Those who read *Boonastiel* found Thomas Harter's progressive reform ideas in his dialect epistles, but most material was entertainment, or just folksy.[4]

Then came the shock of the Wilson years, of 1914 and 1917. For the Pennsylvania Dutchman, who was most aware of affairs at the local level, national political philosophy and international imperial competition were beyond his ken. He did recall that Teddy Roosevelt and the German Kaiser often exchanged harsh words. Between Teddy and Kaiser William he never hesitated in his choice. The American of German origin felt no attachment to political Germany, although he did retain a fondness for the German language and old German ways. German propaganda sometimes did make the Pennsylvania German seem suspect.

These Dutch, who had found their niche as a compliant minority in American society, now suffered a shock. They were sufficiently individualistic to retain their language and some other customs, but they had conformed enough to be ignored by the larger society around them—until World War I, that is. Vigorously, enthusiastically American, they shouted and sang their good fortune in a dialect German strictly their own. Suddenly, in the crisis of World War I, it was insufficient.

Had they looked around them, they would have found that all America faced dilemmas of choice. Although legally neutral, the whole country took sides. Progressives of domestic reform opposed progressives of international goals and missionary programs. Both major parties split. President Wilson and Secretary of State Bryan differed on the application of legally mandated neutrality, until in the Lusitania incident Wilson accepted the British interpretation of matters and Bryan resigned.[5] While the Pennsylvania Dutch had cast the majority of their presidential votes for neither Wilson nor Bryan, they tended to favor Bryan's "evenhanded neutrality."

Some of the Dutch leaders and intellectuals, having immersed themselves in German scientific history and the methodical analysis of language dialects and folk customs, joined the New Germans of later arrival in Missouri or Nebraska to ask that Germany's position be fairly assessed. As late as January, 1915, the American Neutrality League of Philadelphia met, saw Governor Martin Brumbaugh preside, heard anti-British speeches by three congressmen, and sang German songs. There is very little evidence that rank-and-file Pennsylvania Germans gave any credence or support to such efforts. They considered the war a hangover from older European dynastic wars (with more than a little justification) from which their ancestors had escaped generations before.[6]

Then, as the American effort became transmuted from furnishing supplies and funds for the Allies to an all-out war to save the world for democracy, the price became apparent. Propaganda, both British and American, reported exaggerated incidents and fabricated German grossness and atrocities. Doctored propaganda flowed into America from British sources. To be sure, German submarines and policy in occupied territories offered no rebuttal. Campaigns to vilify the "Huns" succeeded in making some Americans suspicious of other Americans who spoke German. Once the spirit of George Creel's Committee on Public Information spread, "pro-German sentiments" were subject to investigation.

Provisions were quite broadly interpreted. Government reference to "hyphenates," or to "German-Americans" were nearly all derogatory, with Woodrow Wilson personally leading the attack.[7] Julio Camba, an Iberian novelist traveling through the United States in 1916, commented on the contradictions he saw. In a United States whose one hundred million population included fifteen to twenty million persons of German descent (including the Pennsylvania Dutch), many people feared these millions had not been sufficiently assimilated. "The stomach of the United States," wrote Camba, "had not digested the German hyphen." America not only heard the slogan of Wilson's partisans, "He kept us out of war," but also the charge that "Hughes was the candidate of the German-Americans," though one British intelligence officer observed that "there is no more difference between [Hughes and Wilson] than a barber could remove in ten minutes."[8]

Pennsylvania Germans, along with others of similar origins, noted with astonishment the efforts to purge America of the taint of Teutonism. German as a foreign language was eliminated from most secondary schools and virtually all college curricula. *Deutsche Sommerschule* of Middlebury College, pioneer in oral German studies at the university level in 1915, and first of that college's cluster of summer language schools, suspended operation in 1918 and did not reopen until 1931. "Reflecting the animus against everything German that swept the country," as they put it, in May, 1917, the Ursinus College Board of Directors, in the heart of the Dutch Perkiomen Valley, made German optional and introduced Spanish and Italian as alternatives. Professor Calvin D. Yost, whose ancestors arrived in Philadelphia in 1738, continued teaching German without interruption, a triumph for his untiring efforts and stubborn insistence.[9]

In Philadelphia, public evening-school instruction in English for German-speaking migrants, was abruptly halted in 1917. Fashion conscious New York women dressed in blacks and whites in the absence of German chemical dyes. Citizens who in 1914 had patronized twelve hundred German language periodicals, in wartime found fewer available. By 1920 scarcely thirty important German language daily newspapers survived. The nation, in a surge of patriotism, supported a new age of euphemisms. German sausage became liberty pork, and knockwurst, liberty bologna. German fried potatoes disappeared from printed menus. Sauerkraut was dignified on restaurant menus as "liberty cabbage." Sport was not exempt from this linguistic amelioration. "Germany" Schultz of the Washington Senators, the only left-handed catcher in professional baseball, became more acceptable as "Liberty" Schultz. Even card games were not exempt. Pinochle was rechristened "Liberty."

More than fifty years later, a woman who grew up in Germantown vividly recalls a boarded-up statue on her daily walk to school. The newly completed statue of Francis Daniel Pastorius (the work of a German sculptor), honoring the first German and Dutch immigration to Pennsylvania, stood crated in the public square until unpacked for belated dedication ceremonies in 1920.[10] Charles Lindbergh, shortly before his death, commented upon "the bitterness we had in World War I, when you couldn't even play Beethoven."[11]

Some German-Americans, especially first or second generation ones, who had looked disdainfully upon anglicized family names, now found strength to do the same to avoid further embarrassment and bad jokes. Strangely enough, very few Pennsylvania Dutch changed the spelling of their names in World War I, although many had done so earlier. As government pressure intensified and Congress passed the toughest sedition laws ever, repression and fear led many of the Dutchmen, some of them sixth and seventh generation Americans, to renounce interests which might now prove embarrassing. The United States, embarked upon a war to save the world for democracy, found little time for democratic choice at home.

Actually, allowing for the value they attached to German regional culture, the Pennsylvania Dutch were as loyal and quietly patriotic as any ethnic group in the nation. Twenty-five years later, one observer succinctly stated the position of Americans of German descent.

At the same time that they maintained an unquestionable loyalty to the United States, they kept alive an affection for . . . the German way of doing things. . . . [Subsequently] opposition to German-Americans was whipped up until "hyphenate" and "traitor" became synonymous. . . . German-Americans found themselves vilified and discredited. Of all the people who suffered during the years of the war, few drank more deeply of the bitter dregs of humiliation and disgrace.[12]

The Keystone State expanded food production as Lancaster County turned out some of the highest per acreage yield of any farm counties throughout the country. Lancaster was almost solidly Dutch. Financial and industrial contributions marked Pennsylvania's concerned participation as well. Although the

Pittsburgh area became "the arsenal of the world," with some Pennsylvania Germans employed there, major production of coal, iron, and steel in the Delaware, Lehigh, Schuylkill, and Susquehanna Valleys counted a much higher percentage of workers of Pennsylvania Dutch descent. Charles Schwab, one Pennsylvania German who rose to corporate leadership in Bethlehem Steel, headed the Emergency Fleet Corporation of World War I. He supervised construction of the largest shipyard in the world at Hog Island, on the Delaware River, where early prefabricated steel ships were assembled and the ill-fated concrete ships were cast of portland cement, quarried in the Dutch country of eastern Pennsylvania.[13]

Indeed the extent to which small farmers held two jobs—that of farmer and steel worker—provided a preview of major new sociological work patterns for twentieth-century America. Similarly many sons and a surprising number of daughters of the Dutch farmers went into war work, the women on a temporary basis, of course. War plants in the state utilized available manpower to produce cannon, rifles, helmets, ships, locomotives, trucks, and airplane engines. They also supplied coal and oil for the newly mechanized war effort. Richard Shryock, an eminent historian, later mused about his experiences in a military unit stationed in Allentown. From there his battalion toured Berks and Lancaster Counties on Liberty Loan drives. Before visiting these areas, the soldiers were advised that a special effort was in order there, for these people were Germans. After the tour, Shryock noted, "They responded just as other citizens."[14]

The Keystone State supplied 8 percent of national military manpower needs, sending some three hundred seventy thousand into the armed forces. Some were drafted, but Pennsylvania continued to furnish large numbers of volunteers as in previous American wars. Manpower from the state served in many units, but the Twenty-eighth Division, national guard units from Pennsylvania, included a great many of the Dutch, and became almost a symbol of state participation.

Men of Pennsylvania Dutch origin served in the United States Army at home and in France and Belgium, in ranks ranging from buck private to the highest echelons of command. A conservative estimate places the number of German-origin troops in the American Expeditionary Force (AEF) at "from ten to fifteen percent." Dutch country soldiers found little adventure in pitching manure for the cavalry horses, when many of them performed such duties daily in civilian life.

John J. Pershing, whose versatility in command had placed him in command of black regiments in the Pacific and then of Pennsylvania Dutch national guard units in Mexico in 1916, was of German immigrant descent himself. It was Pershing, Commander of the AEF, who insisted on deploying Americans into battle only as units, not as replacement soldiers as Marshal Foch preferred. General J. Hunter Liggett, second in command, was born in Reading, center of the Berks County Germans. Notwithstanding such participation, high and low, reports persisted that Provost General Enoch Crowder had solicitously asked Governor Brumbaugh whether he felt federal troops were needed in the state to suppress the Pennsylvania Germans. Specific action did result when an officer in a Midwest training camp in 1917 overheard one of his men singing a dialect folksong. Suspecting the man was a spy, he quickly transferred him to another company.[15]

In France they faced the realities of a war both traditional and ultramodern. High-level communications were extremely sophisticated, but numerous Pennsylvania Dutch privates from villages and small towns found themselves designated as runners, carrying messages from one unit to another, often from one French village to another. Hervey Allen, junior officer in the 111th Regiment of the Twenty-eighth Division, who commanded some of these Dutchmen in his unit, probably spoke for all, "Hell is not paved with good intentions but with mud."[16]

Lehigh County officers of the AEF found their French to be defective, as was the English spoken by French officers. They communicated better if the Americans used Pennsylvania German and the French officers, High German. Captain Ralph Schwalm told of an incident late in the war. His troops, reconnoitering, reached a small bridge. He called to them to see if the stream might be forded, to avoid crossing the bridge. After some time behind German lines they returned without casualty. In a few days they learned from German prisoners how fortunate they were. German artillery, prepared to stand off any advancing column, were alerted by the activity at the bridge. When they discerned the orders and response, they allowed the unit to pass, assuming it was one of their own. Obviously, without conscious thought, the captain and his men had spoken Pennsylvania Dutch.[17]

A new special unit of World War I was the Aviation Section of the Signal Corps, later called the Division of Military Aeronautics. The use of airplanes for reconnaissance and intelligence was another of the novel developments of that war. A few men from southeastern Pennsylvania took part in early affairs of the Air Service, which contained just over a thousand men and three airfields (including one at Essington, Pennsylvania) in April, 1917. Most of the combat aviators in American uniform trained under French and British fliers, benefiting greatly from prior Allied experience. Carl Spaatz, whose father had published the German language *Boyertown Democrat*, was attached to the Thirteenth Aero Squadron in 1918 under disguised rank, so as to gain some combat experience before returning to America to train U.S. pilots. In France, he commanded the Third Aviation Instruction Center at Issoudun. Spaatz joined his fellow Pennsylvanian Henry Harley (Hap) Arnold in pioneering efforts in United States military aviation.[18]

Another active leader in aviation, though less publicized than Spaatz or Arnold, was Captain Samuel B. Eckert, Pennsylvania Dutchman of Chester County, Pennsylvania. He trained with the British, saw combat in both 80th and 84th Squadrons of the RAF, near Chateau-Thierry. As American forces arrived in France, Eckert first commanded the 9th Aero Squadron, AEF, at Dijon, and subsequently comanded the 17th Aero Squadron, AEF, in support of British units near Dunkirk. French-trained Americans of the Lafayette Escadrille, after February, 1918, flew as the U.S. 103rd Pursuit Squadron, though one, Edward C. Parsons, continued in French service.[19]

Many of the Liberty engines used in military planes were made in Bethlehem, Philadelphia, and Evansburg, Pennsylvania. Dutch soldiers served in the ground service crews, while others of similar origin were training for aerial activity when the armistice was declared. Eddie Rickenbacker, one of the Army Air innovators, was New German, not Pennsylvania German, whose parents came to Ohio from Germany in the second half of the nineteenth century.[20]

Women not only reported for war work in Bethlehem, Allentown, Palmerton, Lancaster, and other cities, but served as army nurses and civilian volunteers with units or with recuperating soldiers. Elsie Janis, "songbird of the A.E.F.," was originally Elsie Birbauer, and her family first settled in Pennsylvania before the War for Independence. A contribution of a different kind was made by Dorothy and Lillian Gish, whose Waltz and Gish ancestors had arrived in Lancaster County as early as 1733. They performed in *Hearts of the World* and other war films of D. W. Griffith.[21]

The campaign of hatred, a conscious governmental policy in World War I, exerted massive pressure against Germans and German corporations. The entire German-American community, including the Pennsylvania Dutch, lived under this cloud. Of course some felt Germany was justified, whereas others simply honored German culture or traditions reflected by the monuments to Goethe and Schiller in Philadelphia's Fairmount Park. During the early stages of the European conflict, the German Society of Pennsylvania sent funds to Germany to care for war widows and orphans and for the relief of German prisoners of war in Siberia. This ceased entirely when the United States entered the war. Further German-American efforts are illustrated by activities of Louis H. Schmidt, organizer and officer of the "Liberty Loan Committee of Americans of German Birth and Descent." Their slogan gave expression to their difficulties:

> Deutsche-Amerika tut seine Pflicht,
> und wenn dabei das Herz auch bricht.[22]

> German-Americans do their duty
> even though their hearts may be breaking.

In that same mood, Hamburg, Berks County, became the first American town to exceed sales quotas for Liberty Bonds in 1917.[23]

Vast numbers of Pennsylvania Germans resorted to the same solution they had used in the past: they simply retreated into their shell. Society was content to regard them as "dumb Dutch."

There was a profound internal and personal conflict. That they were loyal Americans, not bound by German origins, should have been obvious to all. Faced with the reality that it was not, many Pennsylvania Dutch felt the need to apologize. The apologies took numerous, varied forms. Without realizing all the implications, and without rationalizing his actions, the Dutchman found himself profoundly affected by his second-class status. Many resolved that the old ways and culture were not worth the social ostracism. They determined that their children, seventh or eighth generation Americans as they were, should not be similarly handicapped by accent or educational limitations. Thousands of young parents who had heard no language but Pennsylvania Dutch in their own childhood, forbade their children to learn the dialect, and punished them when they did. Many were still branded verbally by a thick Dutch accent in their English speech.

With the end of fighting, American troops joined with French, English, and Belgians in occupation duties in the Rhineland. American soldiers, enjoying the hospitality of the region, commented on the apparent contradiction between the "Hun" war propaganda and the beer and pretzels *Gemütlichkeit* of the occupation years. No Americans were given any finer reception than those whose origins and Pennsylvania Dutch speech made them the favorites of the local population. From 1919 to 1924, a food-relief program for blockade-starved German children was sponsored by Pennsylvania's Germans. Having no relief organization in Germany, their generous donations were handled through Herbert Hoover and governmental agencies, or through the Friends' Service Committee.[24]

The Pennsylvania Dutch nonetheless fit very well into the isolationist mood of the twenties and early thirties. Some remained on the family farms, but more and more of the children went off to factories and business houses. The mood of the twenties in economic matters preeminently suited the Dutch value system. A very few from the Dutch country protested the imposition of immigration quotas in 1923. Some were actively hostile to any further general immigration, but the majority appeared disinterested. To these citizens, "Normalcy" meant a renewed acceptance of old values. "Liberty cabbage is again known as Sauerkraut, and it tastes as fine as ever." The Gish sisters returned to serious drama in *Way down East* and *Orphans of the Storm*.[25] In 1923, the United States Supreme Court declared Nebraska laws prohibiting use of German in public and private elementary schools to be unconstitutional and a violation of the Fourteenth Amendment.

The Dutch tended to vote against Al Smith, a wet, a Catholic, and a New Yorker. On the other hand, Herbert Hoover had been the agent of prosperity. His was a familiar name. For those who cared, he had earned a good reputation dispensing food to the starving Germans. His people were Hubers before they became Hoover and had lived in Switzerland, the Palatinate, and Colonial Pennsylvania. Despite the crash during Hoover's presidency, large numbers still voted for him and against Franklin Roosevelt in 1932. They didn't know where Roosevelt stood, but were aware of his New York connections.[26]

The folksiness of FDR won over some Pennsylvanians, and his early isolationism, ignoring affairs abroad to solve problems at home, appealed to them. Despite the pressures brought to the state by agricultural hard times as early as 1927, Pennsylvania's Amish and Mennonite farmers rejected the Roosevelt farm programs of artificial scarcity and subsidies to farmers. They still esteemed the value of hard work and rejected the principle of something for nothing. Indeed these self-sufficient Pennsylvania German farmers refused to accept payments for crops they had not grown, just as they fought against compulsory social security shortly after.

During the 1930s German-born Fritz Kuhn and a handful of partisans of the Hitler Movement, organized a *Deutsch-Amerikanisch Bund* in Pennsylvania and New Jersey. Avowedly Nazi, the *Bund* held rallies aimed at the old German population in both areas. Reading, Pennsylvania, and Lakewood, New Jersey, became local centers for the movement. The *Bund* issued anti-Semitic propaganda, which appealed to dormant anti-Jewish sentiments of the Dutch. Outside of a few who felt particularly economically oppressed, some local bigots, and a small number who were politically unstable, a convincing majority of Pennsylvania Germans rejected the *Bund* solutions and attacked Fritz Kuhn as an ingrate and a fraud. However, those few who attired themselves in brown-shirt imitation of the new party in Germany caused a renewal of some of the adverse attitudes of World War I.

Harold L. Ickes, cabinet member and sometime confidant of the president, derived from Pennsylvania Dutch origins. Citizens from this area gradually warmed to the FDR program, if with some reservations. In his subsequent campaigns they gave him a majority of their votes. Try as they might to tend to their own surroundings, the Dutch (with the rest of America) found their nation increasingly drawn toward the vortex of a growing European storm. Most of them knew little of developments in Hitler's Germany, but what they heard distressed them more than it pleased them.[27]

The Dutch country shared the general political inertia of other citizens. Pennsylvania Germans had come to believe that the entry of the United States into World War I had been a mistake. As Europe geared up for an even more gigantic clash, Dutch country folk, when they considered it at all, thought America's neutrality laws and pacific mood made a great deal of sense.

As the late 1930s turned into the forties, the Dutch were torn. Charles Lindbergh and the America First movement appealed to them. But Mr. Roosevelt was president, and he leaned more and more actively toward support of the Allies, though he did insist American boys would not be sent again to fight Europe's wars. Gradually as Lindbergh and the peace movement became discredited, Pennsylvania Dutch regions of the state stood with Roosevelt. The first peacetime draft in American history went almost unopposed, except among the outright pacifist pietist sects. They also worked to have the exemption of farm personnel adopted as a policy in applying conscription, with some success at least.

Then in December, 1941, events at Pearl Harbor effectively limited alternatives of action. With the declaration of war against Germany and Italy as well as Japan, Americans realized they were in it again and closed ranks to support the war effort. In World War II both government and private sectors demonstrated they had no intention of again subjecting the German-American population to the extremes of 1918 but then proceeded to treat Japanese-Americans even more harshly.

Pennsylvania supported the war effort with enthusiasm, although the thought of destruction of elements of German regional culture and tradition caused anguish to thoughtful citizens. Many shared the sentiments of the oldest organization of the Pennsylvania Germans:

Within the brief span of one generation, Americans of German birth or descent witnessed their beloved country engaged in two gigantic and bitter wars with the old homeland. Where their duty lay, was and is clear—it was and is demonstrated not by lip service but by unmistakable deeds and sacrifices. What anguish of heart and soul beset many of them, no historian will ever be able to gauge. To be distressed by the suffering of one's kith and kin, of those of the same blood, the same language and the same cultural heritage, and to bear this grief in silence, is no sin in the sight of heaven.[28]

In manpower, Pennsylvania demonstrated its support. Nearly a million and a quarter men and women served in the armed forces and thirty-three thousand of them died. It is impossible to state precisely how many in both categories were of Pennsylvania Dutch origin, but they certainly constituted a very large proportion.

Individuals high in military command who came from families of Colonial German arrivals included Arnold and Spaatz of the Air Force; Jacob Devers, Lyman Lemnitzer, George Grennert, and Homer Groninger of the U.S. Army; and Edward Kalbfus among the admirals in the navy. Dwight Eisenhower, though not a Pennsylvanian, traced his ancestry to River Brethren of the Susquehanna Valley who had migrated to the Great Plains. Thousands of Pennsylvania Dutch served in middle- and lower-officer ranks and tens of thousands more as noncommissioned officers.

A few of the Pennsylvania Dutch had served in Hawaii or the Philippines in peacetime between the wars. Others had absorbed some idea of the need for organization and command in the late New Deal Civilian Conservation Corps. They constituted only a very small minority of both groups. Pennsylvania Germans served in army and navy units throughout the world in the very earliest days of United States involvement as a result of peacetime conscription and a rush to enlist after Pearl Harbor. Some of the Dutch fought briefly at Bataan and Corregidor, only to spend the entire war in Japanese prison camps, while others served in North Africa. They hit Sicilian beaches with Patton and wormed their way northward to Rome with Clark.

Alton Knappenberger won the admiration of the nation with singlehanded attacks against machine-gun nests at Anzio. "The one-man army" was publicly acclaimed in Army and civilian publications. After more such exploits he was awarded the Congressional Medal of Honor. A check of the sources reveals that the first Knappenberger in Pennsylvania arrived among settlers from Württemberg and Alsace in the great migration of 1749, and had settled not far from Frederick Antes and Jost Pannebecker in Montgomery County.[29]

Individual Pennsylvania Germans from Carbon County served with the Fifth Army and Seventh Army Artillery in North Africa, Italy, and southern France. Schuylkill County Dutch served as infantrymen replacements in Texas and Oklahoma divisions at Anzio and Monte Cassino, while Lehigh County *landsmenner* were among the island hoppers from Guadalcanal to Iwo Jima. Dutch personnel from Carbon, Northampton, and York Counties took part in signal and intelligence operations with the First, Third, and Ninth Armies.

An infantryman from central Montgomery County with the Seventh Army, who conversed easily with Alsatians upon arrival in France, was captured, and held in a POW camp in the Rhineland close enough to *Vergeltungswaffen* (V-2) installations that he saw rockets fired against distant targets in Antwerp. A number of Pennsylvania Germans served in army language-training programs as assignment personnel or instructors. At least one, from Wind Gap, Northampton County, steered fellow Dutch into the ASTP language-school program.

For many army personnel from the Pennsylvania Dutch country, the most impressive event of their war service was the Normandy Invasion directed by General Dwight Eisenhower. In the heavy fighting that ensued, high casualties resulted among both regular and special service units.

Still, just as in World War I, the experience of the Twenty-eighth Division, composed of Pennsylvania National Guard units, was taken as a kind of summary of service by Pennsylvanians in the Second World War. From July until November, 1944, the Twenty-eighth, known familiarly to the Germans as "Bloody Bucket" (because of the crimson keystone shoulder patch), was continually in the line, moving rapidly. Untried units who replaced the 28th in December caught the main thrust of German tank units in the Battle of the Bulge. Recalled on short notice from rest centers, units of the Keystone Division were thrown right back into combat to help plug holes punched in the line by German armor.

In preparation for that attack, English-speaking special troops were culled from all German armies. This Special Force, including Germans who had lived in the United States, dressed in captured American uniforms to spearhead the attack. They were finally stopped and the entire offensive ground to a halt. German units failed to capture gasoline depots necessary to refuel their long-range tanks. Pennsylvania Dutch soldiers of the 28th Division finally helped expose German troops in American uniforms and carrying American equipment. Complicated recognition procedures were required because the attacking Germans had learned passwords and code names. Thus detailed questions about sports, movies, or comic-strip characters helped verify American personnel and apprehend German soldiers in U.S. Army uniforms.[30]

Familiar and unconscious use of *Pennsylfawnisch Deitsch,* and the easy response to conversation in *Hoch Deutsch,* brought a month of trouble to Corporal Gilbert Beamesderfer of Ephrata and the 35th Division. Wounded near Nancy, he was handled in routine fashion until a captured German medic, assisting in the evacuation hospital, came to his bedside. "Konscht mich verstenne?" asked Beamesderfer. "Ja," answered the German, and for several minutes the Lancaster County soldier found his *Deitsch* completely adequate for conversation. He did not notice an army nurse nearby taking it all in.

For the next thirty-one days, Corporal Beamesderfer, wounded when he wrestled down a German machine-gunner, was detained by the American Army as a German prisoner of war. He finally realized the dilemma he was in when he was moved into a ward of captured Germans, put on a POW work detail and after ten days, flown to England with them. He complained so loudly and gave American officers so much backtalk, even the Germans seemed to think he was one of them. Finally, after he discussed minutiae of Lancaster County life, his interrogators began to have their doubts, and they reluctantly agreed to send Beamesderfer's fingerprints to Washington, D.C. After some delay the lieutenant interrogator returned and said, "I am happy to inform you that you are an American," and they sent the corporal to a hospital in Massachusetts.[31]

As in both previous major wars, those Pennsylvania Germans of pietist origins who did object to military service on the basis of their pacifist beliefs registered as conscientious objectors. Most of them had to perform substitute service as hospital orderlies or otherwise make up for their failure to perform military duties. Throughout the war conscientious objectors experienced difficulties, as public opinion exerted a strong pressure. Pay for such duties was set at the very lowest rank of equivalent military pay, and no fringe benefits accrued. Pennsylvania Dutch areas on the whole, however, actively supported the war effort.

It became apparent in the aftermath of war that, despite the vigorous increase in production, Pennsylvania had lost ground relatively and stood third or fourth among the states in production of war material, whereas in World War I, Pennsylvania had headed the list of states in total production. Just as obviously, new factors were at work and new solutions would be not only appropriate but necessary.[32]

Pennsylvania Germans actively participated in the occupation of Germany after V-E Day, though many of them had difficulty understanding the policy decisions at the top and the practical effect all this would have upon Germany. A Pennsylvania Dutchman in uniform, elated by the successes of United States forces in battle, was likely to feel doubt and chagrin as he stood in Weimar, near the Goethe-Haus, and watched Russian occupation forces march in. He might have felt outraged that he could not buy a Leica or Zeiss optical items at Jena, because the Zeiss-Works had been promised as reparations to the Soviets.

Because of the war, larger numbers of Pennsylvania Germans than ever before traveled abroad under military orders. Thousands of other Dutchmen followed the urgent call for factory workers both in Pennsylvania and in other states, which were often at a distance. The homogenizing effects of mass media radio and universal compulsory education seemed to spell doom for the ethnic island of Dutch culture which had withstood encroachment or had absorbed intruding forces for two hundred years. As many wartime travelers returned to their home soil, and as they noted the peculiarities and the values of the *Deitsch lond,* they also became aware that cultural amalgamation was only one of the possible solutions. The new mood of cultural pluralism accepted and honored the inevitable differences in ethnic groups. Many individuals and some organizations took advantage of this new understanding to try to retain ethnic and cultural distinctions before they disappeared once and for all.

CHAPTER XIV

Ethnic Tradition Today: The Legacy

IN A LIMITED SENSE, THE PENNSYLVANIA DUTCH WERE THOSE "who spoke the dialect," but most German and American historians would prefer Richard Shryock's view that "'Pennsylvania Germans' are the English-speaking as well as the German-speaking descendants of the original settlers."[1] I accept the broad definition stated by Judge James Henninger of Lehigh County:

A Pennsylvania German is a descendant of German immigrants, who migrated to America from the Rhenish Palatinate or from Switzerland before the Revolutionary War and who has retained the characteristics—in language, accent, character and customs, or any of them—of his German ancestors; or also any other person of predominantly German ancestry, who, by reason of his association ... with the Pennsylvania Germans, has been so influenced by [them] as to be practically indistinguishable from the descendants of the pre-Revolutionary Germans.[2]

Three hundred thousand persons now speak the dialect and four hundred thousand others understand it, mostly in Pennsylvania, but also in enclaves in Virginia, Maryland, North Carolina, Florida, and Ontario, and smaller groups in ten other states.[3]

Thomas Harter observed in 1904, "Dutch is English for *Deitsch*"; then he added "Take the 'Pennsylvania German' out of the history of the state and you remove Hamlet from the play."[4]

However, the Pennsylvania Dutch have been overlooked as an important segment of American history; a fair judgment is that they have been

the unintended victims of nearly every point of view that has motivated historical writing in this country.... They seemed a relatively local group, and general historians aspired to national rather than local themes. They were relatively inactive in politics, and most historians ... overlooked them in consequence.[5]

Their achievements were in areas the historians ignored: music, science, the arts. In theology, where their concerns might have been studied as were New England Puritans, they wrote in German. The historians, ignorant of this regional culture, imputed that ignorance to the culture itself. They were not familiar with Dutch accomplishments, so the historical record stands almost entirely mute.[6]

A hoary tradition in Pennsylvania is the categorization of the "dumb Dutch," almost a single word like "damn Yankee." They were dumb in a literal sense (*stumm* in High German) for they could not speak English, and some of them never learned. They simply conversed in dialect with their kind. It was one mechanism of cultural unity in a vastly different world. *Deitsch* was legal and acceptable in deeds, wills, and court testimony under Pennsylvania English law, so why bother with English.

In a second sense, these Pennsylvania settlers grew out of a continental tradition that assumed their stupidity (*dummköpfig* or *dickeppich*) because of their Swabian origins. In old German tradition as in modern Germany, the Swabians were the hillbilly mountaineers. German and Pennsylvania Dutch told jokes about the silly, slow *Sivva Schwowe* or *Sieben Schwaben* ("seven Swabians"). One example, told on both sides of the Atlantic, was the predicament of the seven Swabians carrying a twelve-foot plank across their shoulders; when they came to a foot-bridge with two-feet clearance from side to side they couldn't cross. After consultation they cut the plank into two-foot lengths, whereupon they crossed the bridge with ease.[7]

There are other traditions of the crafty Dutch, the Pennsylvania counterpart of the New England Yankee, and his competitor. In their shrewdness the Dutch epitomized the poker-faced trader, failing to comprehend unfavorable terms, but concurring rapidly (and as it appeared, luckily) when they had the best deal. Tales of real-estate purchase involve a farmer who, when buying a separate farm for one of his sons, worked the price down by crying poor and then paid the agreed amount of thirty-five thousand dollars by peeling off the cash from the battered cigar box he carried. Less adventurous Dutch would rather deal with their own kind, even if they lost in the bargain, than to trade favorably with an outsider. Pennsylvania Germans grudgingly respected the Jewish merchant peddler for his business acumen. To the Dutch, German Yiddish was just another local dialect.

Much has been made of the differences between the plain Dutch and the gaudy Dutch. *Papa is All* and *Plain and Fancy*, two Broadway successes of the 1940s and 1950s, exaggerated existing misunderstandings. Differences between plain and gaudy Dutch do exist, of course. But both plain sects and nonpietist *Deitsch* make use of brilliant colors.[8]

Even from the earliest settlements, Pennsylvania Dutch values were American values. Whatever their cultural baggage from the German valleys, their Pennsylvania experience had so many novel ingredients that it was literally a different world. They shed few tears for the Old Country, refugees and outcasts as they were. Many had to pay tax or feudal duty before they left, or they were required to pay a fee for a permit to emigrate. These costs constituted a final added insult after years of financial and social restrictions. They had no regrets and they recalled those obligations quite unkindly.[9] Moreover, they could identify with no real Germany in any political sense.

The Pennsylvania Germans retained some useful characteristics which they had acquired in their homeland. Adaptability in the face of political and economic restrictions had enabled them not only to survive but, under similar pressures in America, to flourish. The Dutchman retained his individuality while cooperating in community efforts.

Toleration of religious differences, hard-earned by pietist and by minority Church Germans in unfriendly states of post-Reformation Europe, survived in the New World. They proved that toleration need not emanate from weakness but that it was a sign of strength and confidence. In order to enjoy certain rights, the Pennsylvania Dutch had to insist upon similar rights for others, though such mutual toleration was no proof against occasional intolerant individuals.

An often surprising religious intercommunication resulted in Pennsylvania. Doctrinally divergent Lutheran and Reformed denominations joined pragmatically in Union Churches, almost unique in their time. Modern church mergers and ecumenical movements have drawn support from former Pennsylvania German denominations. Organic differences in structure were overcome as German Reformed elements joined Congregational Christian units in the United Church of Christ in 1959. Other Pennsylvania Dutch denominations have taken the lead in additional mergers.[10]

The Pennsylvania Dutch were legendary for their frugality and extremely modern in their ecology, and the two were intimately related. They had refined to an art the technique of not spending money. Products of land-poor, overpopulated Europe, they had spent their lives wringing every ounce of value from the materials they had, for they could not afford to waste. They used the natural bounties, cut forests and dammed streams, but they used efficiently what they took from nature, sharing the concern of the Indian tribes in that respect. They honored nature's balance. In Pennsylvania, the dung pile (*misthaufen*) was important, though never the status symbol it was in Europe. The German farmer in Pennsylvania practiced soil conservation as he valued "the well dunged field" and rotated crops. He made the most of the limestone soil he found in central and southeast Pennsylvania. As a result they became food and grain producers for America. Their simple society was an efficient one and represented the "puritan ethic" at work, as though salvation and survival depended upon it. They literally enjoyed hard work, a hearty appetite, and a clear conscience.

A major contribution of these Pennsylvania Dutch to the American scene is the sense of community they engendered. Undoubtedly any ethnic settlement surrounded by unfamiliar, hostile forces, develops some community responses. But in a very special sense, the common effort of Amish, Mennonites, or Brethren provided initial needs of a home for the newly married couple and barn raisings for families that stood in need of that essential building for any reason. They also joined resources in farm harvesting cooperation. So intense has been their feeling, that they reject the modern concept of insurance, certain that common efforts by all available workers, volunteering to assist, will achieve the same ends without financial strings.

The Pennsylvania Dutchman remains committed to a system of private, volunteer charities, though he continues to trust that, when he finds himself in need, his fellows will also respond personally and helpfully. The Pennsylvania German distrusts impersonal government. "He believes in personal responsibility; he does not feel that any government owes him a living."[11]

Archaic as it sounds, the Pennsylvania Germans continue to value "the old ways." In some novel procedures they occasionally see outcroppings of the old value-system. In a social group where essentials of education were transmitted from parent to child in a one-to-one teaching situation, they see merit in individualized education and personal concern for young children.

The family itself has come under major contemporary stresses, and other institutions, particularly the public schools, have assumed responsibilities previously carried by the family. Social Security combined with a more mobile society has curtailed the custom of grandparents living with the young family. That has also halted the natural flow of stories and traditions from the older generation to the grandchildren. Radio, television, and mass-media news have standardized modes and values, and in turn, have de-emphasized regional and ethnic particularism. An analogy may be found in modern France, where Provençal has been relegated to a matter of antiquarian curiosity. Similar insistence on homogeneous American national models has increasingly eliminated Pennsylvania German localisms. For the group which valued voluntary participation without subjugation of the individual, the conversion to mass values appears destructive.

In the aftermath of World War II, the German origin churches continued to promote missionary enterprises in China, Japan, and Africa in a new context. In the era of superpowers, when atomic weapons only emphasized the destructive mission of so many governments, the churches (or more accurately church men and women) expressed a brotherly concern for humanity. Church World Service attempted to restructure the form of American charitable efforts, tailored to most urgent needs in the wake of the most destructive general war in history. Reginald

Helfferich, a seventh-generation pastor of a single Pennsylvania
German family, adopted the Brethren-initiated "Heifer Project"
as a Church World Service venture, cutting red tape appreciably.
By that plan, registered cattle were airlifted to devastated farms
of German war victims. If the Morgenthau Plan of the Allied
governments really meant to reduce Germany to agricultural
status, people of the church could at least assure them seeds
and livestock.[12]

For the Japanese people, shaken by atomic bombs and by
the new fallibility of the divine emperor, a new emphasis on
education turned small denominational North Japan College into
impressive Tohoku Gakuin University, with its twelve thousand
students. George and Christopher Noss, Gertrude Hoy, and
Philip Williams, all of Pennsylvania Dutch descent, have been
participants in that program.[13]

Moravians, Mennonites, and Schwenkfelders joined the Quakers in internal and international efforts to bring peace to the
world. True to the pacific traditions of their founders, men and
women of these groups defied governments and risked censure
to work toward nonviolent solutions. In a world of vigorous
national competition, these minority Pennsylvania Dutch denominations actively work to promote moral and ethical responsibilities.

Scholars, antiquarians, and old timers with a concern for roots
and traditions have attempted to salvage the remainders of the
old culture. True, they have not yet agreed on proper spelling
of Pennsylvania Dutch words, and the hoped-for definitive
dictionary has bogged down in the early alphabet, and many
old buildings and artifacts have been destroyed in the name
of progress.

And of course there are the visible remains. Conspicuous by
their abhorrence of novelty, the Plain Folk of Lancaster and
Lebanon Counties, of Ohio, Nebraska, Iowa, and Ontario are
easily noted in modern America despite their efforts to avoid
publicity. The Amish and Old Order Mennonites hold to old
methods and procedures, the values of the past. Nonetheless
they have accepted some new improvements along the way, for
their lives are surely not carbon copies of their sixteenth-century
forebears. The strictest among them insist upon the horse as

transportation and as motive power, despite the fact that most of their ancestors of even two centuries ago used oxen, if fortunate enough to own them. The horse drawn buggies of the Amish and Old Order Mennonites on the roads of south central Pennsylvania are a daily reminder of the determination of these people to avoid worldly interference.

Of course they have been discriminated against in the name of progress and of safety. Divided highways are built "for motor traffic only." But then, under ordinary circumstances those who drive the buggies are content to use smaller back roads. Some Amish on the move to the Dakotas recently found dual lane bridges the only available crossings of major rivers. Their horse drawn vehicles had to be convoyed by State Policemen, who diverted faster traffic during the crossing. After numerous traffic accidents involving the black buggies in the gathering dusk, Pennsylvania law now requires them to be equipped with reflectors and blinking turn signals. Since buggies have neither batteries nor electrical systems built in, a new accessory, the battery operated turn signal, was invented. Although such interference approaches sacrilege to some people, the casualty rate has dropped.

The prosperous plain farms of Lancaster County have a strange look, with no electric wires connecting the house or farm buildings with the pole lines along the highways. The most severe Plain People continue to value freedom from electricity, just as they avoid use of internal combustion engines. Many appliances and modern conveniences thereby remain unavailable, of course. Their horses continue to pull farm machinery which has been motorized nearly everywhere else in the United States.

Some compromises have occurred. Some of the Dutch use windmill-generated local electric current for illumination, or use farm machinery to earn a living, but not for luxury or frivolity. To others, electricity from ordinary sources may be used in the barn but not in the house; its use is permissible for a trade, as for a woodturning lathe, but not for a television set. Among some Mennonites, automobiles may be used, but all the chrome must first be painted black, like the auto itself. For others, a car may be used as purchased, without accessories, so long as it avoids colors other than black and white. Discipline is required to retain restrictions in an acquisitive neon-lighted society.

Theirs is an anachronistic society. In their concern for avoiding images, graven or otherwise, Plain Folk refused for years to submit to photography. Children were trained to turn their heads or to seek the shelter of the nearest building. All that has become much harder to control because the area has become a tourist attraction replete with instant cameras and tape recorders. Amish, Mennonites, and Brethren place exceedingly demanding requirements upon themselves.

Though shunning is still imposed upon offenders against the society, there has been less tendency toward such social ostracism than in years past.[14] Brotherhood feelings were very strong among the faithful, and refusing to assist a brother in need carried appropriate punishment. This rigidity and clannishness has been an obstacle in itself. Many people have simply rejected Plain Folk as narrow-minded, thick-headed, pinchpenny old men, whatever their age or station. Others who have made friendly overtures have been chagrined and offended by stern rejections.

The world does intrude in many ways but rarely more directly and more forcibly than in areas of governmental social welfare and of schooling. Plain farmers have avoided financial and legal complications under government subsidy programs simply by not applying. At first, Social Security did not cover farm occupations. Revisions in 1954 still left them unaffected, and professional coverage, as teachers in private schools, was optional for sectarians as for other teachers. The 1961 extension to cover self-employed individuals placed the issue squarely before them. Most refused to comply, not because of the tax factor, but because it was insurance. Any insurance was a gamble and was furthermore unnecessary because of their mutual assistance to members in need. For a time the Kennedy government forced compliance and, in western Pennsylvania, auctioned off their farm horses at sheriff's sales to extract the funds for needed Social Security coverage. Within a short time the Congress passed a bill introduced by Pennsylvania Representative Richard Schweiker, himself a Schwenkfelder, specifically exempting from participation religious groups with scruples against insurance, provided they cared for their own aged and unemployed. That ended the sheriff's sales.[15]

The question of compulsory education has been a much tougher question. The state is properly concerned that each child shall have equal educational opportunity; the sects object to its worldly aspects—from electric kitchen equipment to busing. As late as the middle 1960s, the spectacle of law enforcement officers pursuing unwilling scholars through nearby cornfields to force them to enjoy the advantages of public school facilities has made headlines.[16] The legality of government funds for private parochial education remains doubtful, but for the most part, the Amish and Mennonite schools have refused to touch such monies, even those forced upon them. Both public and private forces contend they act in the best interests of the children, but it poses interesting moral and legal questions. The children are the pawns.

Problems do arise for the tightly regulated sects as young people observe the world around them. They question their elders. Many of them disagree with the invariable limitations, especially because acquaintances and nonsect neighbors enjoy a more permissive childhood. Plain denominations lose many of their youth, who will simply not comply with so strict a code. Lack of electricity would seem to settle the question of television, in their view suggestive and misleading, but the availability of battery powered mini-sets for a few dollars has became a temptation for a new generation.

Amid the bad jokes, the raised eyebrow, and the open contempt for such restrictive living, Amish and Old Mennonite have held out remarkably under the circumstances. Today, turnpikes and tourism are a reality, giving all manner of tourists and strangers easy access to the Dutch Country. Plain People can no longer entirely isolate themselves. And so the question arises, what is to be done? The foothills of the Pocono Mountains, as Dutch as Lancaster County for almost as long, are now within an easy two and a half hour drive from Manhattan. People come as tourists, buy land at ridiculous prices, and become residents. The net result has been a new scarcity of land and inflated prices for that which is available.

Country auctions are no longer private sales to a local clientele.

Publicity and facile transportation have combined with the diminishing supply of authentic country Dutch antiques. A farm sale at a country crossroads, twenty years ago, might have drawn fifty or sixty persons living within a radius of three miles from the sale. Outsiders or tourists who "just happened by" were most conspicuous. In the 1970s no such sale is too small to escape the attention of antique dealers (or their representatives) from Philadelphia and New York, and prices for quite ordinary items have skyrocketed.

Over the years most Pennsylvania Dutch, despite their plainness and the routine of their lives, have enjoyed festivals and holidays. They joined in festivities with undisguised pleasure. If the jokes became too earthy and the cider (or whiskey) flowed too freely, they knew the minister, after recovering from his participation, would build his next Sunday sermon on the excesses of loose living. Everyone participated in high spirit. Competitions were keen. Victors were not always gracious. This social safety valve had its roots in the medieval mid-European village fair and religious holiday festival. In Pennsylvania both religious and secular diversions provided an acceptable excuse for holiday gaiety. Such festivals have been the easiest folkways to revive. We see them burgeoning today.

Among the most unique of their folk days is the Pennsylvania Dutch attention to *Grundsau-Daag* ("Groundhog Day"). Legend insisted that, on the day the groundhog emerged from his six-week hibernation (February 2 came to be the fixed day), his actions would forecast the weather for the remainder of the winter. If the sun shining on him cast a shadow, then he retreated for six weeks more of harsh snowy weather. On a cloudy day, the groundhog saw no shadow, which signified mild weather and a virtual end to winter. In continental Germany, the badger (*dachs*) has been credited with similar powers.[17] In Pennsylvania some local Germans who scoff at the groundhog legend insist that the configuration and color of goosebones offer similar weather evidence. Others observe caterpillars.

Gradually the groundhog legend has grown from local into general tradition, to be accepted by non-German neighbors. In the twentieth century in several Pennsylvania Dutch centers,

Grundsau Lodges have been organized, to celebrate the day with large banquets and storytelling. Meetings, conducted in dialect only, set the mood for the celebration and give all present an occasion to converse in the disappearing tongue.[18]

In the tradition of frugality, the Dutch country auction became a festive occasion also. Auctions were usually occasioned by death, business failure, or consolidation of holdings through favorable marriage. Surplus went on sale. Purchasers added to their stock of horses or cattle and promised to put purchased equipment to use, which might otherwise stand idle. Dutch language auctioneers presided. Old Jacob Fries had owed much of his prestige to the social prominence of auctioneers. To the present day, the bilingual commission-sales auctioneer of the Dutch country is a synthesis of town father, supersalesman, philosopher, and magician.

Many of the country folk marvel at the items which bring good prices. Horses, solid wood furniture, and tall clocks have usually gone high. More recently powder horns, down quilts, sleighbells and mason jars have brought outlandish amounts. The Pennsylvania Dutch farmer who puts out his goods for sale may shake his head or cluck his tongue at the lack of discernment of auction purchasers, but he walks off counting his money at the end of the day.

To the Pennsylvania Dutch, for whom trading for goods and haggling over prices was both an economic challenge and social occasion, markets and fairs were particularly welcome. In Colonial days, Philadelphia held market twice a week and larger productions in May and November. From the tip of Philadelphia County (later Montgomery) it meant a two-day trip. As markets became more commercialized, the nineteenth-century farmer found his direct outlet limited. In time agricultural fairs offered him new opportunities, and from 1851 annual country fairs gave him a chance to enter his grain, produce, and livestock in competition with those of his peers.

The calendar was . . . built around fair week. . . . For thirty days before the great event, work was planned to have the wheat sowed, the corn shocked, the Sunday vehicles washed . . . the harness blacked and nothing left in the way of an early-morning start to the fair. . . .

More than one farm wagon, bedded with timothy or fresh straw
and carrying a cargo of wide-eyed family and home-grown food,
rolled out of the barnyard soon after midnight and rumbled into
the fair ground at break of day.[19]

Some county fairs continue to emphasize farmers' participation, but more have survived on their sideshow carnivals. Others
have simply disbanded.

Recently, Americans are collecting antiques and artifacts with
a slightly different motivation. Distinctive ethnic concerns have
achieved status. The Pennsylvania Dutch have become much
more open about their distinctive heritage and desire to learn
about it.

Local historical societies of the Dutch country have burgeoned in the past decade or fifteen years, celebrating local
heroes or events. They attempt to preserve estates as open
spaces, houses or churches as museums, and have begun to
institutionalize many of the minutiae and artifacts of times past.
Some are simply antiquarians who merely indulge a personal
interest. Others, in particular local societies like the Goshenhoppen Historians, combine professional and amateur talents
in an effort to retain old skills and provide insights into historical
methods and possibilities.[20]

The Folk Fair and Folk Festival have celebrated the ways
of the past while providing welcome entertainment. The Pennsylvania Dutch have come to be known to many people in the
annual Kutztown Folk Festival, begun a quarter century ago.
Blacksmiths, coopers, shingle-splitters, pewterers, and Fraktur
artists demonstrate the old skills, while shoo-fly pie, cinnamon
buns, pickle cabbage, funnel cake, and cider feed the hungry
visitor with foods that have delighted Dutch palates for centuries. Moreover, as alternatives in entertainment, the festivals
and fairs have proved to be financially profitable. The two-day
Goshenhoppen Folk Festival, now an August fixture, attempts
to provide entertainment while endorsing preservation in a
spirit pioneered by Williamsburg and Sturbridge Village some
years ago.[21]

Scholarly study of folklore has recently achieved new status.
National and ethnic tales are no longer considered objection-

able. The University of Pennsylvania has pioneered in folklore studies, which survived the days of sneering condescension to reach its current level of scholarly acceptance. Professor Don Yoder has acted as coordinator of folklore information on the Pennsylvania Dutch at that institution, in the tradition of Edwin M. Fogel.

Of periodical publications in Dutch, devoted to folk activities, Preston Barba's "Pennsylfawnisch Deitsch Eck" of the Allentown *Morning Call* was one of the most durable and most distinguished. Today, Clarence G. Reitnauer continues the tradition of dialect columnist as "Der Shdivvel Knecht" ("Bootjack") in the Pennsburg *Town and Country*. In a more formal offering and a larger format, *The Pennsylvania Dutchman* and *Pennsylvania Folklife*, organ of the Pennsylvania Folklife Society, offer a variety of historical, biographical, and cultural articles. Its purpose is to disseminate interesting, accurate, readable scholarly material on "architecture, cookery, costume, customs of the year, folk art and antiques, folk dancing, folk medicine, folk literature, folk religion, folk speech, homemaking lore, recreation, superstitions, traditional farm and craft practices, transportation lore," and other similar subjects.[22]

Preservation of songs and stories of the Pennsylvania German tradition is the concern of organizations and publications previously mentioned, and of a small group of dedicated individuals armed with tape recorders, note pads, and hiking shoes. Folksongs in general have enjoyed a revival in recent years. A surprising number of local items have survived. To be sure, very few professional folksingers have managed correct or believable *Deitsch* renditions of those surviving pieces. A few dialect speakers, in the tradition of the late Theodore Reichenbach as "Professor Schnitzel," continue on a modest entertainment circuit. In that category are the Reverend Clarence Rahn, Clarence C. Reitnauer, and Merritt Freeman, when the latter takes time from his regular occupation as mortician.[23]

Historic preservation has entered a new era in the America of the sixties and seventies. Hundreds of people in Dutchland have found new interests and opportunities in that rewarding field. Log and frame houses as well as barns and pig pens dating from the eighteenth century have been saved, and others have been thoroughly documented when beyond restoration or when demolition could not be halted.[24] As a civic effort, historic preservation has brought unity and purpose to communities which had forgotten the old values. Buildings which remain represent nostalgia for the old and instruction for the young. Factually, many people are not aware of their own history, and historic preservation in its best sense, properly funded and open to tourist and scholar alike, offers to teach them.

Numerous personalities of the Pennsylvania Dutch community or among its descendants, appearing in this study, have helped make American history, in the best sense. A few disavowed their background, while others were apparently unaware of it. Public figures from that heritage include many governors, numerous senators and congressmen, and three recent presidents— Hoover, Eisenhower, and Nixon. Industrial leaders and businessmen in profusion may be included, such as Kress, Kresge, and Woolworth of the department stores and John Wanamaker, the "merchant prince." Charles Goodyear, tire manufacturer, and Harry Studebaker, who first made carriages, then automobiles, are likewise of Dutch origin. Countless college professors and some college presidents are among them, including Abraham Fetterolf and George Omwake, Daniel Luke Biemesderfer, Theodore Distler, and Donald Helfferich. John Omwake was for years chairman of the board of United States Playing Card Company.

Amelia Earhart, pioneer in women's aviation, was of Dutch descent. Conrad Richter wrote his Lutheran and German predecessors into his novels, while Owen Wister, who first coined the phrase, "Smile when you say that," in *The Virginian*, and Katherine Drinker Bowen, premier biographer, also came from Pennsylvania Dutch stock.

Recent American painters of the tradition of Jacob Eichholtz and Lewis Miller, include Charles Demuth, Walter Baum, and Franz Kline, the latter a modernist innovator born in Lehighton, Pennsylvania, and a talented student at Girard College. Cliff Arquette made "Charlie Weaver" a national figure on stage and on television. He was the most recent type of Dutch cousin making fun of the idiosyncrasies of his people in classic slapstick tradition.

Thus the Pennsylvania Dutch, approaching three hundred years on the American scene, remain the persistent minority. Many thousands still speak "Dutch," although the number who speak and understand the dialect has dramatically diminished with the prominence of radio and television. Historians and folklorists try to preserve what remains of the heritage, or to reconstruct the past for present and future enlightenment. Devotees of the folkways, knit and spin, hammer and mould, bake and whittle, in the old style, using old tools when that is possible. An adz cuts, hand looms move in rhythm, flax hatchels separate hull from fiber, though for years those activities had entirely ceased. We find new satisfaction in old accomplishments.

Change in the outlook of American society has improved minority acceptance. While not everyone agrees upon the values of a pluralistic society, there is certainly less pressure for total cultural amalgamation. The urge to conform is still present, and will remain, perhaps indefinitely. But the person who is different is not necessarily an outcast. He may even earn some respect as an individualist. In a sense, many Americans have applied our traditional sympathy for the underdog to minority groups, separately and as a whole. Witness the newly discovered concern for the Blacks and the Indians.

The Pennsylvania Dutchman who for years scratched his head and wondered, "Is it wrong to be different?" may today more likely find a sympathetic response than he did fifty or sixty years ago. Mastering the dialect today is considered a badge of merit, a mark of scholarship. That in itself should please the shades of countless Pennsylvania Germans discounted as "dumb Dutch." The admirer of Dutch arts and culture today, the practitioner of their mongrel language, may well feel himself the epitome of today's ideal of unity in diversity.

Notes and References

Readers who wish to consult full footnote references to material in this book, including complementary sources, additional references, and content footnotes, may consult the original in the Ursinusiana Collection, Myrin Library, Ursinus College, Collegeville, Pennsylvania. Copies may be obtained from the archivist there.

Key to Abbreviations

Bulletin HSMCo	*Bulletin of Historical Society of Montgomery County*
HSMCo	Historical Society of Montgomery County
HSP	Historical Society of Pennsylvania
LCP at HSP	Library Company of Philadelphia on deposit at the Historical Society of Pennsylvania
Pa. Archives	*Archives of the Province and State of Pennsylvania*
PGS	Pennsylvania German Society
PGSP	*Pennsylvania German Society Proceedings*
PGFS	Pennsylvana German Folklore Society
PGFSP	*Pennsylvania German Folklore Society Publications*
PMHB	*Pennsylvania Magazine of History and Biography*
Votes	*Votes of the House of Representatives of the Province of Pennsylvania*
WMQ	*William and Mary Quarterly*

Chapter I

1. Matthew S. Anderson, *Europe in the Eighteenth Century 1713–1783* (New York: Holt, Rinehart & Winston, 1961), p. 23.

2. Helmut G. Koenigsberger and George L. Mosse, *Europe in the Sixteenth Century* (New York: Holt, Rinehart & Winston, 1968), pp 21–22.

3. Ibid., pp. 54–57.

4. Ibid., pp. 57–58.

5. Preserved Smith, *The Age of the Reformation* (New York: Holt, Rinehart & Winston, 1920), pp. 96–98.

6. G. R. Elton, *Reformation Europe 1517–1559* (Cleveland: Meridian Books, 1964), pp. 55–61, 86–89.

7. Ibid., pp. 66–74, 216–21.

8. Koenigsberger and Mosse, *Europe in the Sixteenth Century*, pp. 127–28.

9. Elton, *Reformation Europe*, pp. 89–93.

10. Gillian L. Gollin, *Moravians in Two Worlds: A Study of Changing Communities* (New York: Columbia University Press, 1967), pp. 1–22.

11. Elton, *Reformation Europe*, pp. 265–67.

12. Karl Brandi, *The Emperor Charles V* (London: J. Cape, 1954), pp. 324–29, 589, 629.

13. Cicely V. Wedgwood, *The Thirty Years War* (New Haven: Yale University Press, 1949), pp. 11–15, 203–8, 505–26.

14. Henry S. Lucas, *The Renaissance and Reformation* (New York: Harper & Bros., 1934), pp. 525–31.

15. Ibid.

16. Julius F. Sachse, *The Fatherland (1450–1700)* (Philadelphia: Pennsylvania German Society, 1897), pp. 94–101.

17. Albert B. Faust, *The German Element in the United States* (Boston: Houghton, 1909), I, 56–57.

18. Andrew S. Berky, ed. and trans., *The Journals and Papers of David Shultze* (Pennsburg, Pa.: Schwenkfelder Library, 1952), I, 3.

19. Abbot E. Smith, *Colonists in Bondage: White Servitude and Convict Labor in America 1607–1776* (Gloucester, Massachusetts: Peter Smith, 1965), pp. 50–51.

CHAPTER II

1. Charles II, *Charter of the Province of Pennsylvania*, March 4, 1681, *Minutes of the Provincial Council of Pennsylvania* (Harrisburg: T. Fenn, 1838), I, ix–xviii (hereafter cited as *Colonial Records*).

2. William Penn. *Certain Conditions or Concessions Agreed upon by William Penn . . . and those who are the Adventurers and Purchasers in the same Province*, July 11, 1681, *Colonial Records*, I, xxiii.

3. Ibid.

4. Samuel Hazard, ed., *The Register of Pennsylvania* (Harrisburg: T. Fenn, 1828), I, 305–8.

5. Edwin B. Bronner, *William Penn's "Holy Experiment," the Founding of Pennsylvania 1681–1701* (New York: Columbia University Press, 1962), pp. 28–30.

6. Mary M. Dunn, *William Penn, Politics and Conscience* (Princeton: Princeton University Press, 1967), pp. 100–102.

7. Francis Daniel Pastorius, "Description of Pennsylvania, 1700," *Old South Leaflets* 4, no. 95, 4–6, 7–8, 12–13.

8. Ibid., pp. 12–13.

9. William E. Woodward, *The Way our People Lived* (New York: Washington Square Press, 1963), p. 129.

10. Fredric Klees, *The Pennsylvania Dutch* (New York: Macmillan, 1951), pp. 61–68.

11. Francis Daniel Pastorius, Gerrit Hendericks, Derick Op den Graeff, and Abraham Op den Graef, "Petition . . . April 18, 1688," Samuel W. Pennypacker, "Settlement of Germantown and Causes which led to it," *Pennsylvania Magazine of History and Biography* 4 (1880), 28–30.

12. William Allen and Robert Turner to John Griffiths, Jr., October 6, 1760, William Allen Letters 1753–70, Burd-Shippen-Hubley Papers, Historical Society of Pennsylvania.

13. William Penn, "Charter of Privileges of October 28, 1701," *Colonial Records*, II, 56–59.

14. Ibid., II, 59.

15. William Penn to James Logan, September 14, 1705 and March 2, 1705/6, Edward Armstrong, ed., *Correspondence between William Penn and James Logan, 1700–1750* (Phila.: Historical Society of Pennsylvania, 1872), II, 64–74, 109–11.

16. Klaus Wust, *The Virginia Germans* (Charlottesville: University Press of Virginia, 1969), pp. 50–65.

17. Walter A. Knittle, *Early Eighteenth Century Palatine Emigration* (Phila.: University of Pennsylvania, 1937), pp. 65–77, 123–35.

18. Winthrop P. Bell, *The "Foreign Protestants" and the Settlement of Nova Scotia* (Toronto: University of Toronto Press, 1961), pp. 17–32, 95–102, 397ff.

CHAPTER III

1. *Nachrichten von den vereinigten Deutschen Evangelisch-Lutherischen Gemeinden in Nord-America, absonderlich in Pennsylvanien* (Halle, Hallische Gemeinschaft, 1787), II, 194–96 (hereafter cited as *Hallische Nachrichten*).

2. William Keith to Provincial Councillors, February 1717, *Colonial Records*, III, 27–29.

3. Ralph B. Strassburger and William J. Hinke, *Pennsylvania German Pioneers* (Norristown, Pennsylvania: Pennsylvania German Society, 1934), I, xviii–xxi.

4. Abbott Smith, *Colonists in Bondage*, pp. 314–23.

5. Frank R. Diffenderfer, *The German Immigration into Pennsylvania through the Port of Philadelphia from 1700 to 1775* (Lancaster: Pennsylvania German Society, 1900), pp. 190–91.

6. Strassburger and Hinke, *Pennsylvania German Pioneers*, I, 57–58.

7. Gottlieb Mittelberger, *Journey to Pennsylvania* (Cambridge, Massachusetts: Harvard University Press, 1960), p. 17.

8. Frederick Tolles, *Meeting House and Counting House* (New York: W. W. Norton and Co., 1963), p. 88.

9. Berky, *Journals of David Shultze*, I, 267–71; Mittelberger, *Journey to Pennsylvania*, pp. 12–14.

10. Berky, *Journals of David Shultze*, I, 272–73.

11. Carl and Jessica Bridenbaugh, *Rebels and Gentlemen; Philadelphia in the Age of Franklin* (New York: Oxford University Press, 1962), pp. 3–13.

12. Berky, *Journals of David Shultze*, I, 273.

13. Mittelberger, *Journey to Pennsylvania*, p. 36.

14. Diffenderfer, *German Immigration into Pennsylvania*, p. 94.

15. Ibid., pp. 171–72.

16. Peter Kalm, *Travels in North America* (New York: Dover Publications, 1964), I, 16–17.

17. Diffenderfer, *German Immigration into Pennsylvania*, pp. 302–3.

18. James T. Lemon, *The Best Poor Man's Country* (Baltimore: Johns Hopkins Press, 1972), pp. 106–7; Flour Accounts 1735–1741, Norris Account Book no. 1, and Bread Accounts 1720–1721, Norris Account Book no. 3, Norris Papers, Library Company of Philadelphia, on deposit at The Historical Society of Pennsylvania (hereafter cited as LCP at HSP).

19. Lee L. Grumbine, *The Pennsylvania-German Dialect* (Lancaster, Pennsylvania: Pennsylvania German Society, 1902), pp. 39–43.

20. David Zeisberger, *Essay of a Delaware-Indian and English Spelling-Book* (Philadelphia: Henrich Miller, 1776), pp. 3–5.

21. Paul A. W. Wallace, *Conrad Weiser 1696–1760: Friend of Colonist and Mohawk* (Phila.: University of Pennsylvania Press, 1945), pp. 65–75, 184–95; Julian P. Boyd, *Indian Treaties Printed by Benjamin Franklin* (Phila.: Historical Society of Pennsylvania, 1938), pp. ix–xi, lxiv–lxvii, 6, 31–79, 241.

22. Patrick Gordon to Provincial Councillors, September 1727, *Colonial Records,* III, 280–83.

23. Strassburger and Hinke, *Pennsylvania German Pioneers*, I, xxvi–xxvii.

24. Diffenderfer, *German Immigration into Pennsylvania*, pp. 90–92; *Colonial Records,* III, 246–92.

25. Strassburger and Hinke, *Pennsylvania German Pioneers*, I, xxx–xxxii; *Pensylvanische Berichte*, September 16, 1749.

26. Mittelberger, *Journey to Pennsylvania*, pp. 7, 9–14.

27. Benjamin Franklin, "Observations Concerning the Increase of Mankind, Peopling of Countries, &c.," in *The Benjamin Franklin Papers*, ed. Leonard Labaree, IV, 225–34; [William Smith,] *A Brief State of the Province of Pennsylvania* (London: n.p., 1755), pp. 18, 30, 36.

28. "Petition," November 22, 1749, *Votes of the House of Representatives of the Province of Pennsylvania* (Philadelphia: Franklin and Hall, 1756), IV, 121 (hereafter cited as *Votes*).

29. James Hamilton to Thomas Penn, September 24, 1750, Penn Papers: Off. Corr. V, 53, HSP.

Chapter IV

1. Franklin, "Observations Concerning the Increase of Mankind," *Franklin Papers*, IV, 234.

2. David Hawke, *The Colonial Experience* (Indianapolis: Bobbs-Merrill, 1966), p. 364.

3. Franklin, *Franklin Papers*, IV, 234.

4. C. Lee Hopple, "Spatial Development of the Southeastern Pennsylvania Plain Dutch Community to 1970," *Pennsylvania Folklife* 21, no. 2 (1971–72), 18–40; no. 3, 36–45; Lemon, *Best Poor Man's Country*, pp. 51–55.

5. James I. Good, *History of the Reformed Church in the United States, 1725–1792* (Reading, Pennsylvania: Daniel Miller, 1899), pp. 102–19.

6. Theodore Tappert and John W. Doberstein, trans., *The Journals of Henry Melchior Muhlenberg* (Philadelphia: Muhlenberg Press, 1942), I, 70–84 (hereafter cited as Muhlenberg, *Journals*).

7. Ibid., I, 359–60, 381–85; Mittelberger, *Journey to America*, pp. xii–xiv, 7–8.

8. R. L. Winters, *John Caspar Stoever, Colonial Pastor and Founder of Churches* (Norristown, Pennsylvania: Pennsylvania German Society, 1948), pp. 1–2, 20, 24–31.

9. Good, *History of the Reformed Church*, pp. 100–103, 249–51, 308–13.

10. *Minutes and Letters of the Coetus of the German Reformed Congregations in Pennsylvania 1747–1792* (Philadelphia: Schaff, 1903), pp. 6–8, 18–19 (hereafter cited as *Minutes of Coetus*).

11. John B. Frantz, Jr., "Role of the German Churches in the Great Awakening," *Yearbook of the American Philosophical Society, 1966*, pp. 425–27.

12. Wallace, *Conrad Weiser*, pp. 30–32, 250, 305.

13. Gollin, *Moravians in Two Worlds*, pp. 27–39.

14. Elma E. Gray, *Wilderness Christians: The Moravian Mission to the Delaware Indians* (Ithaca: Cornell University Press, 1956), pp. 21–27.

15. Meniolagomekah Diary 1752–1754, MS, box 122, Moravian Archives, Bethlehem, Pa.

16. Gollin, *Moravians in Two Worlds*, pp. 133–41, 156–59.

17. Walter C. Klein, *Johann Conrad Beissel: Mystic and Martinet 1690–1768* (Philadelphia: University of Pennsylvania Press, 1942), pp. 79–88.

18. John K. Heyl, Architecture of the Pennsylvania Dutch, address given at Annual Meeting of the Pennsylvania German Society, May 6, 1972, at Pennsburg Pa.

19. Klein, *Johann Conrad Beissel*, pp. 103–4.

20. Oscar Kuhns, *The German and Swiss Settlements of Colonial Pennsylvania* (New York: Abingdon, 1914), pp. 46–48, 55–56, 206.

21. James Hamilton to Thomas Penn, September 24, 1750, Penn Papers: Off. Corr., V, 53, HSP.

22. William Parsons to Richard Peters, December 8, 1752, *Archives of the Province and State of Pennsylvania*, ed. Samuel Hazard (Harrisburg: T. Fenn, 1848), 1st ser., II, 97–98 (hereafter cited as *Pa. Archives*).

23. Benjamin Franklin to Peter Collinson, May 9, 1753, *Franklin Papers*, IV, 485.

CHAPTER V

1. David Hawke, *In the Midst of a Revolution* (Phila.: University of Pennsylvania Press, 1961), p. 188.

2. William T. Parsons, "Isaac Norris II, the Speaker, 1701–1766," University of Pennsylvania, Ph.D. dissertation, 1955, pp. 121–49.

3. William T. Parsons, "William Allen as Seen by a Contemporary," *Proceedings, Lehigh County Historical Society* 25 (1964), 162–63; "Petition of Palatines against the Head Duty," January 15, 16, 1729/30, *Votes*, III, 99.

4. Journal of Isaac Norris I, 1730, bound with *Leeds Almanack*, 1730, HSP.

5. Flour Accounts and Bread Accounts, Norris Account Books no. 1, no. 3, Norris of Fairhill Papers, LCP in HSP.

6. Isaac Norris II to Lawrence Williams, April 6, 1739, Norris Letters 1733–39, Norris Papers, HSP.

7. Norris to Williams, August 4, 1739, Ibid., p. 58.

8. Ibid.

9. Norris to Williams, April 6, August 4, and November 20, 1739, Ibid., pp. 53, 58, 63.

10. Workers and Tenants Accounts, Norris Account Book no. 6, 1–24, Norris Papers, LCP in HSP.

11. Ibid., pp. 59–64, 68, 81.

12. Isaac Norris II to Robert Charles, March 31, 1741, Norris Letters 1719–56, p. 5, Norris Papers, HSP.

13. John J. Zimmerman, "Benjamin Franklin and the Quaker Party 1755–1756," *WMQ*, 3rd ser., 17 (1960), 292–93.

14. William T. Parsons, "The Bloody Election of 1742," *Pennsylvania History* 36 (1969), 291–93.

15. Conrad Weiser, *Ein Wohl-gemeindter und Ernstlicher Rath an unsere Lands-Leute, die Teutschen* (Philadelphia: B. Franklin, 1741).

16. Hermann Wellenreuther, *Glaube und Politik in Pennsylvania 1681–1776* (Köln: Böhlau Verlag, 1972), pp. 136, 141–46, 152; *Votes*, III, 390–400, 500–502, and Appendix, pp. 568–86.

17. "A Petition from divers Inhabitants of Chester County . . . for the Destruction of Squirrels," *Votes*, II, 215; Ibid., IV, 84–94; Kalm, *Travels in North America*, I, 168–69.

18. Isaac Norris II to Robert Charles, April 29, 1755, Norris Letters 1719–56, p. 70, HSP; Christopher Schultz to [?], September 28, 1752. The Schwenkfelder Library, Pennsburg, Pennsylvania.

19. James Hamilton to Thomas Penn, September 24, 1750, Penn Papers: Off. Corr., V, 53, 83, HSP.

20. William Reichel Papers, Miscellaneous Manuscripts: Box, Northampton County Papers, HSP; Labaree, ed., *Franklin Papers*, IV, 234, 483–85.

21. William Allen to A. Griffiths, Jr., March 25, 1761, Allen Letters 1753–70, Burd-Shippen-Hubley Papers, HSP.

22. Stevenson W. Fletcher, *Pennsylvania Agriculture and Country Life, 1640–1840* (Harrisburg: Pennsylvania Historical & Museum Commission, 1950), pp. 46–51, 109.

23. Anthony F. C. Wallace, *King of the Delawares, Teedyuscung 1700–1763* (Philadelphia: University of Pennsylvania Press, 1949), pp. 24–29.

24. E. Dingwall and Elizabeth Ann Heard, *Pennsylvania 1681–1756: The State without an Army* (London: C. W. Daniel Co., Ltd., 1937), pp. 52–57, 87.

25. Northampton County Land Warrants, III, 62–85, Northampton County Papers, HSP.

26. Ibid., III, 65–75; IV, 20–40.

27. Julian P. Boyd, editor, *The Susquehannah Company Papers* (Wilkes-Barre, Pennsylvania: Wyoming Historical & Geological Soc., 1930), I, ix–xiii, xx–xxviii, 6–17.

28. James Hutson, "Benjamin Franklin and Pennsylvania Politics, 1751–1755: A Reappraisal," *PMHB* 93 (1969), 312–16.

29. William S. Hanna, *Benjamin Franklin and Pennsylvania Politics* (Stanford: Stanford University Press, 1964), pp. 96–97, 113–14.

30. Sister Joan deLourdes Leonard, "Elections in Colonial Pennsylvania," *WMQ*, 3rd ser., 11 (1954), 399–400.

31. Christopher Sauer, Jr., *Anmerckungen über Ein noch nie erhört und gesehen Wunder thier in Pennsylvanien....* (Germantown: C. Sauer, 1764), pp. 3, 7, 13–14, 16.

CHAPTER VI

A slightly different version of this chapter and a portion of chapter 5 appears as my contribution to *Pfälzer-Palatines*, ed. Karl Scherer (Kaiserslautern: Heimatstelle Pfalz, 1975).

1. Lawrence H. Gipson, *The British Empire before the American Revolution*, vol. VI, VII, *The Great War for the Empire* (New York: Alfred A. Knopf, Inc., 1946, 1949), VI, vii–ix, 1–6; VII, 428–30, 467.

2. Robert L. D. Davidson, *War Comes to Quaker Pennsylvania 1682–1756* (New York: Columbia University Press, 1957), pp. 33–46.

3. Ibid., pp. 113–29

4. Tolles, *Meeting House and Counting House*, pp. 23–25.

5. Gipson, *The Great War for Empire*, VI, 67.

6. Davidson, *War Comes to Quaker Penna.*, pp. 166–67.

7. Isaac Norris II to Robert Charles, October 7, 1754, Norris Letters 1719–1756, p. 56, Norris Papers, HSP.

8. Paul A. W. Wallace, *Indians in Pennsylvania* (Harrisburg, Pennsylvania: Pennsylvania Historical & Museum Commission, 1961), pp. 141–47.

9. Vernon H. Nelson, "The Moravian Contribution to the Tulpehocken Region," *Der Reggeboge* 7 (July, 1973), 3–16; William A. Hunter, "German Settlers and Indian Warriors," Ibid. 3 (September 1969), 5–6.

10. Smith, *A Brief State*, pp. 18, 28–29, 36.

11. Ibid., pp. 18, 26–36; *REASONS Humbly offered for including Those of the MORAVIAN BRETHREN, who scruple the Taking of an Oath, in the Bill for Naturalizing Foreign Protestants*, Broadside, Reichel Papers (Box), Northampton County Misc. MSS, HSP.

12. Michael Schlatter to Thomas Penn, June 3, 1750, Penn Papers: Off. Corr., V, 17, HSP.

13. "Petition of the German Protestants in Pennsylvania to Robert Hunter Morris," November 20, 1754, Schwenkfelder Library, Pennsburg, Pennsylvania.

14. *Franklin Papers*, VI, 19–22, 24–26.

15. Gipson, *The Great War for Empire*, VI, 62–98.

16. Ralph L. Ketcham, "Conscience, War and Politics in Pennsylvania, 1755–1757," *WMQ*, 3rd ser., 20 (1963), 418–19.

17. William Allen to William Beckford, November 28, 1755, Allen Letters 1753–70, Burd-Shippen-Hubley Papers, HSP.

18. Thomas Graeme to Thomas Penn, November 6, 1750, Penn Papers: Off. Corr., V, 83.

19. Glenn Weaver, "Benjamin Franklin and the Pennsylvania Germans," *WMQ*, 3rd ser., 14 (1957), 547–48.

20. Jacob Ehrenhardt, "An Account of the Carriage of Indian Corn for the Indians, from Gnadenhütten to Bethlehem," November 30, 1755, Reichel Papers (Box), Northampton County Misc. MSS, HSP.

21. Gray, *Wilderness Christians*, p. 39.

22. Henry M. M. Richards, *The Pennsylvania German in the French and Indian War* (Lancaster, Pennsylvania: Pennsylvania German Society, 1905), pp. 139–45.

23. William A. Hunter, *Forts on the Pennsylvania Frontier 1753–1758* (Harrisburg, Pennsylvania: Pennsylvania Historical & Museum Commission, 1956), pp. 214–300.

24. Papers of the Provincial Council, May 26, 1757, Penna. Historical and Museum Commission, Harrisburg.

25. Richards, "Some Service Rolls of the War," *Penna. Germans in French and Indian War*, pp. 223–48.

26. Capt. George Reynolds to Col. Conrad Weiser, February 5, 1757, box I, Northampton County Misc. MSS, HSP.

27. Hunter, "German Settlers and Indian Warriors," p. 15.

28. Berky, *Journal of David Shultze*, I, 163–65.

29. *Franklin Papers*, VI, 362–68.

30. Melville Boyer, *American Boyers* (Allentown, Pa.: Lehigh County Historical Society, 1940), pp. 184–86; "A List of the Captives' Names delivered by Beaver [Tamaqua]" August 3, 1762, Archives relative to Pennsylvania, HSP.

31. Richards, *Penna. Germans in French and Indian War*, pp. 79–106, 107–26; John Birmelin, "Regina Hartmann," *Gezwitscher* (Allentown, Pennsylvania: PGFS, 1938), pp. 89–94.

32. Valentine Probst to Jacob Levan [February, 1756], Berky, *Journal of David Schultze*, I, 167–69.

33. Hunter, "German Settlers and Indian Warriors," p. 14.

34. Henry J. Kauffman, *Early American Gunsmiths 1650–1850* (New York: Bramhall House, 1952), pp. ix–xix. Gunsmiths are identified by location and dates in this valuable directory.

35. Hunter, "German Settlers and Indian Warriors," pp. 10–11, 16.

36. Ibid., pp. 17–18.

37. "Return of English Children delivered up by the Indians and Canadians, that were taken in the Province of Pennsylvania and colony of Virginia [1762 or 1763]," A. F. C. Wallace Collection, Papers relative to William Parsons, APS.

38. Arthur L. Jensen, *The Maritime Commerce of Colonial Philadelphia* (Madison, Wisconsin: University of Wisconsin, 1963), pp. 114–21, 130–31; Nicholas Wainwright, "Governor William Denny in Pennsylvania," *PMHB* 81 (1957), 192–94.

39. Jensen, *Maritime Commerce of Phila.*, pp. 144, 146–47.

40. Howard Peckham, *Pontiac and the Indian Uprising* (Princeton: Princeton University Press, 1947), pp. 198–203, 214–17, 220, 282–83.

41. James Hamilton to Thomas Penn, September 24, 1750, Penn Papers: Off. Corr., V, 53, HSP.

42. Christopher Schultz to Israel Pemberton, April 4, 1764, Schwenkfelder Library, Pennsburg; Wellenreuther, *Glaube und Politik*, pp. 370–83.

43. J. Philip Gleason, "The Scurrilous Election of 1764 and Benjamin Franklin," *WMQ*, 3rd ser., 18 (1961), 75–77.

44. William Allen to David Barclay and Sons, November 20, 1764, Allen Letters 1753–70, Burd-Shippen-Hubley Papers, HSP.

45. *The Plain Dealer* (Philadelphia: W. Dunlap, 1764); *An Address to Freeholders and Electors of the Province of Pennsylvania, in Answer to a Paper called The Plain Dealer* (Philadelphia: A. Armbruster, 1764), p. 11.

46. Joseph Galloway, *Speech delivered before the Assembly* (Philadelphia: W. Dunlap, 1764); [John Dickinson], *Advertisement and not a Joke* (Philadelphia: W. Bradford, 1764) (broadside).

47. [Benjamin Franklin], *Cool Thoughts on the Present Situation of our Publick Affairs* (Philadelphia: W. Dunlap, 1764), p. 20; *An Die Freyhalter und Einwohner der Stadt und County Philadephia, Deutscher Nation* (Philadelphia: A. Armbruster, 1764); *Eine Anrede an die Deutschen Freyhalter der Stadt und County Philadelphia* (Philadelphia: A. Armbruster, 1764), pp. 1–3; *The Scribler* (Philadelphia: A. Armbruster, 1764), pp. 12–14.

48. [Sauer], *Anmerckungen über Ein . . . Wunder Thier*, pp. 3, 16; *Ein Andere Anrede an die Deutschen Freyhalter* (Philadelphia: A. Armbruster, 1764), pp. 1–8.

49. Benjamin Franklin to Richard Jackson, October 11, 1764, *Franklin Papers*, XI, 397; [David J. Dove], *The Counter-Medly* (Philadelphia: A. Armbruster, 1765).

50. "The Stamp Act, March 22, 1765," in *Prologue to Revolution, Sources and Documents on the Stamp Act Crisis, 1764–1766*, by Ed-

mund S. Morgan (Chapel Hill: University of North Carolina Press, 1959), p. 41.

51. Ibid., pp. 40–41.

52. Journal of Isaac Norris II, 1765, bound with *Poor Richard's Almanack*, Rosenbach Collection.

53. Morgan, *Prologue to Revolution*, pp. 155–56; John Adams to Hezekiah Niles, February 13, 1818, in *The Selected Writings of John and John Quincy Adams*, ed. Adrienne Koch and William Pedeñ (New York: Alfred A. Knopf, 1946), pp. 203–5.

CHAPTER VII

1. George W. Norris, Manuscript History of the Norris Family, p. 107.

2. *Philadelphische Zeitung*, May 6 and June 24, 1732; *Franklin Papers*, I, 230–31, 232–33; Julius F. Sachse, "The First German Newspaper published in America," *PGSP* 10 (1899), 41–46; Karl J. R. Arndt and May E. Olson, *German-American Newspapers and Periodicals 1732–1955*, 2nd rev. ed. (New York: Johnson Reprint Corp., 1965), p. 5.

3. *Der Hoch-Deutsch Pensylvanische Geschicht-Schreiber, Oder, Sammlung Wichtiger Nachrichten, aus dem Natur-und Kirchen-Reich*, no. 1, August 20, 1739. Microfilm copies of *Hoch-Deutsch Geschicht-Schreiber* and *Pensylvanische Berichte* courtesy of the HSP.

4. Edward W. Hocker, *The Sower Printing House of Colonial Times* (Norristown, Pennsylvania: Pennsylvania German Society, 1948), pp. 3, 7–9, 40.

5. Benjamin Franklin to Peter Collinson, May 9, 1753, and partial letter [1753], *Franklin Papers*, IV, 484, and V, 158–60.

6. Hocker, *Sower Printing House*, pp. 19–25.

7. Ibid., pp. 37–58, 65; *Biblia . . . Nebst dem Gewöhnlichen Anhang* (Germantown, 1743).

8. *Pensylvanische Berichte*, September 30, 1758.

9. Hocker, *Sower Printing House*, pp. 63–84.

10. Ibid., pp. 85, 90–93.

11. Arndt and Olson, *German-American Newspapers*, pp. 501–605.

12. Charles F. Dapp, *The Evolution of an American Patriot . . . John Henry Miller* (Philadelphia: Pennsylvania German Society, 1924), pp. 35–47.

13. *Heinrich Millers Pennsylvanischer Staatsbote*, July 9, 1776 (copy in HSP); Dapp, *John Henry Miller*, pp. 51–52.

14. Arndt and Olson, *German-American Newspapers*, p. 567.

15. *Die Pennsylvanischer Gazette, oder der Allgemeine Americanische Zeitungs-Schreiber*, February 3, 1779.

16. Eugene E. Doll, *The Ephrata Cloister, An Introduction* (Ephrata: Ephrata Cloister Associates, 1958), pp. 8–10. *Zionitischer Weyrauchs-Hügel, oder MyrrenBerg* . . . (Germantown: C. Sauer, 1739); Christopher Sauer, *Ein Abgenöthiger Bericht: oder zum öfftern begehrte Antwort, denen darnach fragenden dargelegt* . . . (Germantown: C. Sauer, 1739).

17. James E. Ernst, *Ephrata, A History* (Allentown: Pennsylvania German Folklore Society, 1963), pp. 218–20, 282.

18. Ibid., pp. 282, 293–94; *Der Blutige Schau-Platz, oder Martyrer Spiegel der Tauffs Besinken* (Ephrata, 1748).

19. [Johann Bunjan], *Eines Christen Reise nach der Seeligen Ewigkeit Anderer Theil* (Ephrata, Brotherhood Printing, 1754); *Johann Bunians Pilgrims- oder Christen-Reise* (Germantown, C. Sauer, 1755); [Anthony Benezet], *Eine Kurtze Vorstellung des theils von AFRICA, Welches bewohnt wird von NEGROES.*... (Ephrata: Brotherhood Printing, 1763), pp. 3ff.

20. Carl Bridenbaugh, *The Colonial Craftsman* (New York: Oxford University Press, 1950), pp. 54–57, 61–63.

21. *Pensylvanische Berichte*, November 13, 27, 1756; Norris-Fairhill Accounts, Account Book, 76, and Great Leidger, 35, Norris Papers, HSP, Norris-Fairhill Accounts, Account Book no. 4, pp. 23, 185, and Account Book no. 6, p. 64, Norris Papers, LCP at HSP.

22. Muhlenberg, *Journals*, I, 145, 152.

23. Reverend Abraham Blumer, President, Coetus, to Very Reverend Fathers, Holland, June 6, 1774, *Minutes of Coetus*, pp. 347–48.

24. Journal of Isaac Norris II, 1750, bound with *Poor Richards Almanack*, 1750, Rosenbach Collection; Norris Ledger 1736–65, p. 145, and Account Book no. 4, pp. 24, 53, 57, Norris Papers, LCP at HSP.

25. Andrew S. Berky, *The Schoolhouse near the Old Spring* . . . *1735–1955* (Norristown, Pennsylvania: Pennsylvania German Society, 1955).

26. Edward W. Hocker, *Germantown, 1683–1933* (Germantown: author, 1933), pp. 46, 79–81.

27. Gerald Studer, *Christopher Dock, Colonial Schoolmaster* (Scottdale, Pa.: Herald Press, 1967), pp. 101, 121–23.

28. Ibid., pp. 124–27, 131–32, 336–38.

29. Christopher Dock, *Eine Einfältige und gründlich abgefaszte Schul-Ordnung* (Germantown: C. Sauer, 1770), pp. vi–vii; Studer, *Christopher Dock*, p. 266.

30. Dock, *Schul-Ordnung*, pp. 7–12, 14–27; Studer, *Christopher Dock*, pp. 274–78, 281–97, 410–11.

31. Studer, *Christopher Dock*, pp. 151–53; (Appendix) pp. 261ff.;

S. Alexander Rippa, *Educational Ideas in America. A Documentary History* (New York: David McKay Co., Inc., 1969), p. 52–57.

32. Samuel E. Weber, *The Charity School Movement in Colonial Pennsylvania* (Phila.: University of Pennsylvania Press, 1905), pp. 1–21.

33. Michael Schlatter to Thomas Penn, June 3, 1750, Penn Papers, Off. Corr., V, 17, HSP.

34. Ibid.

35. Joseph H. Dubbs, "The Founding of the German Churches of Pennsylvania," *PMHB* 17 (1893), 256.

36. Petition of German Protestants in Pennsylvania to Robert Hunter Morris, November 30, 1754, Schwenkfelder Library, Pennsburg, Pa.

37. Thomas Penn to Richard Peters, July 31, 1754, Peters Papers, III, 107, HSP.

38. Weber, *Charity School Movement*, pp. 22, 29, 31, 41.

39. Ibid., pp. 41–44; Trustees-General for the Management of the said Charitable Scheme, *A Brief History of the Rise and Progress of the Charitable Scheme Carrying on By a Society of Noblemen and Gentlemen in London, for the Relief and Instruction of poor Germans and their Descendants, Settled in Pennsylvania and the Adjacent British Colonies in North America* (Philadelphia: Franklin and Hall, 1755), pp. 6–8, 10–14.

40. Weber, *Charity School Movement*, pp. 44–45; William Parsons to Richard Peters, November 23, 1754, and Poor German Settlers of Easton and Northampton County to Trustees-General [sic] of the Charitable School at Easton, [1755] and Engagement of Services for School, Easton, July 1, 1755, Northampton County Papers, Misc. MSS, 1727–58, pp. 154, 159, 161, HSP.

41. Weber, *Charity School Movement*, pp. 32, 38–39, 49–53; Hocker, *Sower Printing House*, pp. 59–61.

42. Alan Tully, "Literacy Levels and Educational Development in Rural Pennsylvania, 1729–1775," *Pennsylvania History* 39 (1972), 310–11.

43. *Pensylvanische Berichte*, September 1, 1754; Christopher Sauer, Sr., to "A Friend" [Conrad Weiser] September 16, 1755, and William Smith to Bishop of Oxford, November 1, 1756, Weber, *Charity School Movement*, pp. 50, 53, 59, 61.

44. Weber, *Charity School Movement*, p. 50; William Parsons to Richard Peters, July 3, 1755, Northampton County Papers: Misc. MSS. 1727–58, 157, HSP.

45. Weber, *Charity School Movement*, p. 47; *Minutes of Coetus*, pp. 129–30, 157.

46. Weber, *Charity School Movement*, pp. 47, 53–55; *Minutes of Coetus*, pp. 198–99.

47. Weber, *Charity School Movement*, pp. 57–64.

48. Ibid., p. 47.

49. *Die Regeln der Teutschen Geselschaft* (Germantown: C. Sauer, 1764), pp. 1–8; Harry W. Pfund, *A History of the German Society of Pennsylvania* (Phila.: German Soc. of Pa., 1944), p. 9.

50. Carl Haussmann, *Kunze's Seminarium and the Society for the Propagation of Christianity and Useful Knowledge among the Germans in America* (Philadelphia: University of Pennsylvania Press, 1917), pp. 9–11, 15.

51. Ibid., pp. 78–83, 137–38.

CHAPTER VIII

An earlier, longer version of this chapter was presented as a paper at the Forty-Third Annual Meeting of the Pennsylvania Historical Association, Mercer, Pennsylvania, October 25, 1974.

1. "Petition of Mennonites and German Baptists," November 7, 1775, *Votes*, VI, 645.

2. Hocker, *The Sower Printing House*, p. 85.

3. Owen S. Ireland, "The Ethnic-Religious Dimension of Pennsylvania Politics, 1778–1779," *WMQ*, 3rd ser., 30 (1973), 425–28.

4. Wayne Bockelman and Owen S. Ireland, "The Internal Revolution in Pennsylvania: An Ethnic-Religious Interpretation," *Pennsylvania History* 41 (1974), 125.

5. *Schreiben des Evangelisch-Lutherischen und Reformierten Kirchen-Raths* (Philadelphia: Henrich Miller, 1775), pp. 2–3, 21.

6. Ibid., p. 10; H. M. J. Klein, *The History of the Eastern Synod of the Reformed Church in the United States* (Lancaster: The Eastern Synod, 1943), p. 69.

7. Klein, *History of the Eastern Synod*, p. 69; *Pennsylvania Archives*, 5th ser., 3, 783–832.

8. *Minutes of Coetus*, p. 352.

9. Wallace, *The Muhlenbergs of Pennsylvania*, pp. 106–9; 115.

10. Ibid., pp. 116, 118–21.

11. Henry Melchior Muhlenberg to Emanuel Schultze, March 7, 1776, as quoted in Wallace, Ibid., p. 123.

12. Ibid., pp. 123–24; Family Accounts 1746–1789, folder 1766, Norris-Fairhill Papers, HSP.

13. William W. Condit, "Christopher Ludwick, The Patriotic Gingerbread Baker," *PMHB* 81 (1957), 367–68, 370–74.

14. Ibid., p. 378.

15. Ibid., pp. 379–83.

16. Whitfield J. Bell, Jr., "Addenda to Watson's Annals: Notes by Jacob Mordecai, 1836," *PMHB* 98 (1974), 146.

17. Theodore Tappert and John Doberstein, eds., *The Notebook of a Colonial Clergyman* (Philadelphia: Muhlenberg Press, 1959), pp. 160–61; Wallace, *Muhlenbergs of Pennsylvania*, pp. 124–25.

18. *Pennsylvanischer Staatsbote*, July 5, July 9, 1776.

19. Wallace, *Muhlenbergs of Pennsylvania*, pp. 124–26.

20. Muhlenberg, *Notebook*, p. 162.

21. Ibid., pp. 162–63.

22. Ibid., pp. 161, 166–68.

23. Peggy Kuntze to Betsy Schultze, July 11, 1776, in Wallace, *Muhlenbergs of Pennsylvania*, p. 127.

24. Rosenberger, *Intimate Glimpses of Penna. Germans*, p. 25.

25. Wallace, *Muhlenbergs of Pennsylvania*, pp. 131–34, 138–42.

26. Condit, "Christopher Ludwick," p. 280; Thomas A. Posen, "Washington Along the Skippack," *Bulletin, HSMCo.* 19 (1974), 246.

27. Condit, op. cit., pp. 380–81.

28. Wallace, *Muhlenbergs of Pennsylvania*, pp. 160–63; Henry M. M. Richards, *Valley Forge and the Penna.-Germans* (Lancaster: Pa. German Soc., 1917), pp. 22–32.

29. Robert Mentzell, *The Liberty Bell's Interlude in Allentown* (Sellersville, Pa.: Sellersville Historical Achievement Authority, 1974), pp. 1–10; John B. Stoudt, *The Liberty Bells of Pennsylvania* (Phila.: William J. Campbell, 1926), pp. 49–54, 80–84.

30. Hocker, *The Sower Printing House*, pp. 94–95.

31. *Selections from Arthur Graeff's Scholla* (Breinigsville, Pennsylvania: Pennsylvania German Society, 1971), p. 102.

32. Edward J. Lowell, *The Hessians and the Other German Auxiliaries of Great Britain in the Revolutionary War* (Williamstown, Massachusetts: Corner House, 1970), pp. 21–22, 37–45.

33. Ernst Kipping, *The Hessian View of America 1776–1783* (Monmouth Beach, New Jersey: Philip Freneau Press, 1971), pp. 24, 31–33.

34. Ibid., pp. 23–24, 29.

35. Charles H. Metzger, *The Prisoner in the American Revolution* (Chicago: Loyola University Press, 1971), pp. 109–11.

36. Condit, "Christopher Ludwick," *PMHB* 81 (1957), 375.

37. Ibid., pp. 374–77.

38. Bell, "Addenda to Watson's Annals," *PMHB* 98 (1974), 157.

39. Metzger, *The Prisoner*, pp. 58–60; Lowell, *The Hessians*, pp. 180–86.

40. Metzger, *The Prisoner*, pp. 216–21; Kipping, *Hessian View*, pp. 30–31, 43–46, 58–60.

41. Metzger, *The Prisoner*, pp. 111–13, 119; Christopher Ludwick to the Continental Congress, March 8, 1777, in "Christopher Ludwick," pp. 377–78.

42. Hocker, *The Sower Printing House*, pp. 93–101; William H. Nelson, *The American Tory* (Boston: Beacon Press, 1964), pp. 89–90.

43. Chambers, *Early Germans of New Jersey*, p. 40.

44. Gilbert, *The Pennsylvania Germans*, p. 33.

45. Ibid., p. 32.

46. Wallace, *Muhlenbergs of Pennsylvania*, pp. 202–3, 205.

47. Carl Van Doren, *Secret History of the American Revolution* (New York: Viking Press, 1968), pp. 407–11.

48. Wallace, *Muhlenbergs of Pennsylvania*, pp. 207–12.

49. Ibid., pp. 227–29, 231–33, 237; Henry P. Johnston, *The Yorktown Campaign and the Surrender of Cornwallis 1781* (New York: Harper & Bros., 1881), pp. 32, 113, 116.

50. Metzger, *The Prisoner*, p. 148.

51. Muhlenberg, *Notebook*, pp. 163, 166.

52. Brooke Hindle, *David Rittenhouse* (Princeton: Princeton University Press, 1964), pp. 134–35, 175–76.

53. Ibid., pp. 208–9.

54. Gilbert, *The Pennsylvania Germans*, pp. 35–36.

55. Ibid., pp. 37–39.

56. As quoted in Ibid., p. 41.

57. Condit, "Christopher Ludwick," *PMHB* 81 (1957), 385–86.

58. Arthur D. Graeff, "The Pennsylvania Germans in Ontario, Canada," *PGFSP* 11 (1946), 11–13, 22, 30.

Chapter IX

1. John Joseph Stoudt, *Pennsylvania German Folk Art: An Interpretation* (Allentown: PGFS, 1966), pp. 5–7, 10, 13, 15.

2. Henry C. Mercer, *The Bible in Iron*, 3rd ed. (Doylestown: Bucks County Historical Society, 1961), pp. 37–44, 77–79.

3. Amos Long, Jr., *The Pennsylvania German Family Farm* (Breinigsville, Pennsylvania: Pennsylvania German Society, 1972), pp. 37–48.

4. Donald A. Shelley, *The Fractur-Writings or Illuminated Manuscripts of the Pennsylvania Germans* (Allentown: PGFS, 1961), pp. 2, 22–23, 25; Carroll Hopf, "Calligraphic Drawings and Pennsylvania German Fraktur," *Pennsylvania Folklife* 22 (Summer, 1972), 2–9.

5. Shelley, *Fractur-Writings*, pp. 23–28.

6. Ibid., pp. 121, 179–80; Monroe H. Fabian, "The Easton Bible Artist Identified," *Pennsylvania Folklife* 22 (Winter, 1972), 2-14.

7. Studer, *Christopher Dock*, pp. 189–96.

8. Shelley, *Fractur-Writings*, pp. 28–29, 70, 175–76.

9. John J. Stoudt, *Early Pennsylvania Arts and Crafts* (New York: A. S. Barnes, 1964), p. 200.

10. George S. and Helen McKearin, *American Glass* (New York: Crown Publishers, 1941), pp. 82–83; Rhea M. Knittle, *Early American Glass* (Garden City: The Century Co., N. Y., 1948), p. 119.

11. Stoudt, *Early Penna. Arts and Crafts*, pp. 200–203.

12. McKearin, *American Glass*, pp. 87–88.

13. Knittle, *Early American Glass*, pp. 84–96, 152–53.

14. Edwin A. Barber, *Tulip Ware of the Pennsylvania German Potters* (New York: Dover Publications, 1970), pp. 112–15, 136–39; Stoudt, *Early Penna. Arts and Crafts*, pp. 206–18.

15. Ledlie I. Laughlin, *Pewter in America: Its Makers and their Marks* (Boston: Houghton Mifflin, 1940), II, 35–50.

16. Ibid., I, plates X, XVII, XXVII; II, 40, 44–55.

17. Frances Lichten, *Folk Art of Rural Pennsylvania* (London: Scribner, 1946), pp. 81–92.

18. George H. Eckhardt, *Pennsylvania Clocks and Clockmakers* (New York: Devin-Adair, 1955), pp. 17–18, 168–222.

19. Hindle, *David Rittenhouse*, pp. 14, 25–26, 33–35, 48–52.

20. Eckhardt, *Penna. Clocks and Clockmakers*, pp. 67–70.

21. Oliver W. Larkin, *Art and Life in America*, revised and enlarged ed. (New York: Holt, Rinehart & Winston, 1960), pp. 488–89.

22. Stoudt, *Early Penna. Arts and Crafts*, pp. 143–44; Nicholas B. Wainwright, *Paintings and Miniatures at the Historical Society of Pennsylvania* (Phila.: Historical Society of Pennsylvania, 1974), pp. 36, 172–73, 324.

23. Stoudt, *Early Penna. Arts and Crafts*, pp. 144–48.

24. Garth A. Howland, "John Valentine Haidt, A Little Known Eighteenth Century Painter," *Pennsylvania History* 8 (1941), 304–6, 313.

25. Rebecca J. Beal, *Jacob Eichholtz 1776–1842* (Phila.: Hist. Soc. of Pa., 1969), pp. x–xv, xxv.

26. As quoted in E. P. Richardson, "Jacob Eichholtz," in ibid., pp. xxi, xxiii.

27. Earle Newton, "Jacob Eichholtz," *Pennsylvania History* 26 (1959), 115.

28. Beal, *Jacob Eichholtz*, pp. xxv–xxxi, 58–62, 277, 290, 302, 309.

29. Robert P. Turner, ed., *Lewis Miller, Sketches and Chronicles* (York: York County Historical Society, 1969), xiii–xvii, 101–17, 123–31.

30. Donald A. Shelley, "Lewis Miller, An Introduction," in ibid., pp. xxi–xxii, 30.

31. Helen M. Wolfe, "Some Kern Notes, Written for Members of the Family . . . ," Kern Papers, Bancroft Library, University of California, Berkeley, pp. 1–2.

32. Robert V. Hine, *Edward Kern and American Expansion* (New Haven: Yale University Press, 1962), p. 19.

33. Wolfe, "Kern Notes," pp. 3, 6–8; Leroy and Ann Hafen, *Fremont's Fourth Expedition* (Glendale, Calif.: A. H. Clarke, 1960), pp. 29–30.

34. Hine, *Edward Kern*, pp. 81, 155–56, 201, 203–6, 208–10.

35. *Norristown Times Herald*, September 17, 1973.

36. Preston A. Barba, *Pennsylvania German Tombstones* (Allentown: PGFS, 1954), pp. 1–30, 33–228 passim.

37. Stoudt, *Early Penna. Arts and Crafts*, pp. 141, 190–91.

38. Mittelberger, *Journey to Pennsylvania*, pp. 40–41, 45; Robert B. Whiting, "John Ziegler, Montgomery County Organ Builder," *Bulletin of HSMCo.* 19 (1973), 46–53.

39. Ernst, *Ephrata, A History*, pp. 234–37, 241–48.

40. Stoudt, *Early Penna. Arts and Crafts*, p. 190; Carl Bridenbaugh, ed., *Gentleman's Progress . . . 1744* (Chapel Hill: University of North Carolina Press, 1948), p. 191; James Sullivan et al., eds., *Sir William Johnson Papers* (Albany: University of the State of New York, 1921–1965), I, 265; IV, 638, 840; XIII, 647–48.

41. Stoudt, *Early Pennsylvania Arts and Crafts*, p. 191.

42. Donald M. McCorkle, *John Antes/Three Trios: the Birth of Chamber Music in America* (program notes for Columbia Records) MS–6741; see also Donald McCorkle, "John Antes, 'American Dilettante,' " *The Musical Quarterly* 42 (1956), 486–99.

43. *The Unknown Century of American Classical Music: Arias, Anthems and Chorales of the American Moravians, 1760–1860,* Columbia Records, I, MS–6102.

44. John J. Stoudt, *Pennsylvania German Poetry 1685–1830* (Allentown, Pennsylvania: PGFS, 1955), pp. xxxiii, 3–13.

45. Ibid., pp. xxxiii–xxxiv, 148–52, 188–90, 266–68.

46. Earl P. Robacker, *Pennsylvania German Literature: Changing Trends from 1683 to 1942* (Philadelphia: University of Pennsylvania Press, 1943), pp. 64, 77–79; [Henry Harbaugh], *Harbaughs Harfe: Gedichte in Pennsylvanisch-Deutscher Mundart* (Philadelphia: Reformed Church Publications Board, 1870), pp. 25–35.

47. Edwin M. Fogel, *Beliefs and Superstitions of the Pennsylvania Germans* (Philadelphia: American Germanica Press, 1915), pp. 267–306: William S. Troxell, ed., *Aus Pennsylfawnia: An Anthology of*

Translations into the Pennsylvania German Dialect (Philadelphia: University of Pennsylvania Press, 1938), pp. 23–27.

CHAPTER X

1. Charles Beard, *An Economic Interpretation of the Constitution of the United States* (New York: Macmillan, 1913), pp. 27–28.
2. Forrest McDonald, *We, the People: The Economic Origins of the Constitution* (Chicago: University of Chicago Press, 1958), pp. 163–64, 169.
3. Robert L. Brunhouse, *The Counter-Revolution in Pennsylvania 1776–1790* (Harrisburg: Pennsylvania Historical & Museum Commission, 1942), pp. 2–3.
4. Hindle, *David Rittenhouse*, pp. 144–45, 209–10, 273, 311.
5. McDonald, *We the People*, p. 54.
6. Beard, *Economic Interpretation*, pp. 19–25, 27, 34–37, 216; McDonald, *We the People*, pp. 173–82, 398–401.
7. Hindle, *David Rittenhouse*, pp. 293–99.
8. Brunhouse, *Counter-Revolution*, pp. 209–11, 221–27.
9. Wallace, *Muhlenbergs of Pennsylvania*, pp. 274–76.
10. Ibid., p. 275.
11. Harry M. Tinkcom, *The Republicans and Federalists in Pennsylvania 1790–1801* (Harrisburg: Pennsylvania Historical & Museum Commission, 1950), pp. 28–29.
12. Ibid., pp. 47, 188–89; Wallace, *Muhlenbergs of Pennsylvania*, pp. 280–89.
13. Tinkcom, *Republicans and Federalists*, p. 65; Anonymous contributor, *General Advertiser*, July 5, 1793, as quoted in Tinkcom, p. 136.
14. Tinkcom, *Republicans and Federalists*, pp. 76–77, 81–86; Harry Ammon, *The Genêt Mission* (New York: W. W. Norton and Company, 1973), pp. 55–57, 106–7.
15. Leland Baldwin, *Whiskey Rebels, The Story of a Frontier Uprising* (Pittsburgh: University of Pittsburgh Press, 1968), pp. 221–23, 231–41.
16. Tinkcom, *Republicans and Federalists*, pp. 106–7, 109–10, 135–36.
17. James Morton Smith, *Freedom's Fetters: The Alien and Sedition Laws and American Civil Liberties* (Ithaca: Cornell University Press, 1956), pp. 22–34, 49–52.
18. Raymond Walters, Jr., *Alexander James Dallas, Lawyer-Politician-Financier 1759–1817* (Philadelphia: University of Pennsylvania Press, 1943), p. 82; Thomas Carpenter, *The Two Trials of John Fries*

on an Indictment for Treason . . . (Philadelphia: Thomas Carpenter, 1800), pp. 220–21.

19. Wood, *The Pennsylvania Germans*, pp. 20–21; Tinkcom, *Republicans and Federalists*, p. 218.

20. Carpenter, *Two Trials of John Fries*, pp. 177, 226.

21. "A Citizen of Dauphin," *Aurora*, July 30, 1799, as cited in *Republicans and Federalists*, by Tinkcom, 233.

22. Ibid., pp. 238–39, 271–73.

23. Sanford W. Higginbotham, *The Keystone in the Democratic Arch: Pennsylvania Politics 1800–1816* (Harrisburg: Pennsylvania Historical & Museum Commission, 1952), pp. 18, 26.

24. Philip S. Klein and Ari Hoogenboom, *A History of Pennsylvania* (New York: McGraw–Hill Book Co., 1973), p. 112; Tinkcom, *Republicans and Federalists*, pp. 207–8.

25. Klein and Hoogenboom, *History of Penna.*, pp. 112–13; Sylvester K. Stevens, *Pennsylvania, Birthplace of a Nation* (New York: Random House, 1964), p. 169.

26. Klein and Hoogenboom, *History of Penna.*, p. 113.

27. Higginbotham, *Keystone in the Democratic Arch*, pp. 18–19, 26.

28. Stevens, *Pennsylvania*, p. 170; *Pennsylvania Archives*, 6th Ser., 7, pp. 3–963 passim., and 8, pp. 5–1423 passim., and 9, 1–243, 605–924, and 10, 1–246.

29. Philip S. Klein, *Pennsylvania Politics 1817–1832, A Game Without Rules* (Phila.: Historical Society of Pennsylvania, 1940), pp. 4–5.

30. Ibid., pp. 5–6.

31. Ibid., pp. 273–83.

32. Stevens, *Pennsylvania*, pp. 170–71.

33. Klein, *Pennsylvania Politics*, p. 93.

34. Ibid., pp. 138–39.

35. Ibid., pp. 139–46.

36. Register of Deeds, Northampton County Records, Easton, Pa.; Register of Deeds, Carbon County Records, Jim Thorpe, Pa.

37. Klein, *Pennsylvania Politics*, p. 250.

38. Ibid., pp. 287–88; Wood, *The Pennsylvania Germans*, pp. 116–21.

39. Klein, *Pennsylvania Politics*, p. 367; Stevens, *Pennsylvania*, pp. 172–75.

40. J. G. Kohl, *Travels in Canada and through the States of New York and Pennsylvania* (London: n.p., 1861), II, 321.

41. Stevens, *Pennsylvania*, pp. 175–76.

42. Elizabeth M. Geffen, "Violence in Philadelphia in the 1840's and 1850's," *Pennsylvania History* 36 (1969), 380, 399, 403–4; Pitts-

burgh *Mercury* [?] May 18, 1897; *Greensburg Tribune Review,* November 5, 1964.

43. John Omwake, *The Conestoga Six-Horse Bell Teams of Eastern Pennsylvania* (Cincinnati: Ebbert & Richardson Co., 1930), pp. 15–20, 47–49, 51–61.

44. James W. Livengood, *The Philadelphia-Baltimore Trade Rivalry 1780–1860* (Harrisburg: Pennsylvania Historical & Museum Commission, 1947), p. 49.

45. Ibid., pp. 100–109; Hindle, *David Rittenhouse,* pp. 94–96, 357–59.

46. Kohl, *Travels in Canada . . . New York and Penna.,* II, 225–75, 301, 313.

47. Klein, *Penna. Politics,* pp. 367–68; Stevens, *Pennsylvania,* pp. 369–70.

CHAPTER XI

1. John J. Stoudt, "Daniel and Squire Boone—A Study in Historical Symbolism," *Pennsylvania History* 3 (1936), 27–40; LeRoy R. Hafen, *The Mountain Men and the Fur Trade of the Far West* (Glendale, Calif.: A. H. Clarke, 1964–1972), III, 249–62.

2. Mathias Young Journal 1819–1821, HSMCo.

3. Henry N. Smith, *Virgin Land: The American West as Symbol and Myth* (Cambridge, Mass.: Harvard University Press, 1950), pp. 121–32.

4. Omwake, *Conestoga Six-Horse Bell Teams,* pp. 119–24, 157–62.

5 Hafen, *Mountain Men,* I, 337–54, 367–71; II, 351–62, 379–401; III, 49–53, 119–30, 189–96; IX, 187–92, 385–91.

6. Ibid., IX, 386–91; Meriwether Lewis, *The Lewis and Clark Expedition* (1814; reprint ed., Phila.: J. B. Lippincott, 1961), III, 633–40, 834.

7. Hine, *Edward Kern,* pp. 11–13, 30–31, 46–68, 78–81; Wolfe, "Kern Family Notes," Bancroft Library, Berkeley, pp. 7–8; LeRoy R. Hafen and Ann W. Hafen, eds., *Frémont's Fourth Expedition: A Documentary Account of the Disaster of 1848–1849* (Glendale, Calif.: Arthur H. Clarke Co., 1960), pp. 102–6, 132, 229.

8. Hine, *Edward Kern,* xi, 17–26, 41–44; Hafen and Hafen, *Frémont's Fourth Expedition,* p. 29; George McKinstry to Edward Kern, March 4, 1847, Fort Sutter Papers, Huntington Library, San Marino, Calif.; *California Star* (Yerba Buena), March 18, 1847.

9. Hafen, *Mountain Men,* III, 191–96; Hine, *Edward Kern,* pp. 30–33.

10. *Pennsylvania Archives,* 6th Series, 10, 247–458, especially 351–54.

11. John A. Markle to John L. Markle, January 26, 1850, Private Collection of Robert Markle Blackson, Altoona, Pennsylvania.

12. Isaac J. Wistar, *Autobiography . . . 1827–1905* (Phila.: Wistar Institute, 1937), pp. 15–21, 50, 81, 121–23, 225, 337–39.

13. Hafen, *Mountain Men*, III, 196.

14. Hine, *Edward Kern*, pp. 112–18; John M. Brooke to John Rodgers, June 22, 1855, Alan B. Cole, ed., *Yankee Surveyors in the Shogun's Seas* (Princeton: Princeton University Press, 1947), pp. 87–98.

15. John Rodgers to James C. Dobbin, October 19, 1855, and January 29, 1856, Cole, ed., *Yankee Surveyors*, pp. 134–35, 160–61; Alexander W. Habersham, *My Last Cruise; or Where we Went and What we Saw* (Philadelphia: J. B. Lippincott, 1857), pp. 317–42, 412–19.

16. *San Francisco Herald*, March 18, 1850, Kern Papers, Bancroft Library.

17. Hine, *Edward Kern*, p. 145, figures 41–50 following page 180.

18. Kohl, *Travels in Canada . . . New York and Pennsylvania*, II, 317–18.

19. Homer T. Rosenberger, "Montgomery County's Greatest Lady: Lucretia Mott," *Bulletin of HSMCo.* 6 (1948), 112–13, 142.

20. Elizabeth Clarke Kieffer, *Henry Harbaugh, Pennsylvania Dutchman, 1817–1867* (Norristown: Pennsylvania German Society, 1945), p. 224.

21. John R. Reed, "Montgomery County's 'Bivouac of the Dead,'" *Bulletin of HSMCo.* 13 (1961), 57–58.

22. Arndt, *German American Newspapers*, pp. 515–18; Kieffer, *Henry Harbaugh*, pp. 224, 309.

23. Kenneth Stampp, *The Causes of the Civil War* (Englewood Cliffs, New Jersey: Houghton Mifflin Company, 1959), p. 135. Originally stated in the Concord, New Hampshire, *Independent Democrat*.

24. Charles Hunsicker to Joseph Hunsicker, May 18, 1861, Hunsicker Family Letters, HSMCo.

25. Edward N. Wright, *Conscientious Objectors in the Civil War* (Philadelphia: University of Pennsylvania Press, 1931), pp. 102–7, 168–71; Samuel Horst, *Mennonites in the Confederacy* (Scottdale, Pennsylvania: Herald Press, 1967), pp. 28–44, 62–65, 75–80, 91–93.

26. Samuel W. Pennypacker, "The Pennsylvania Dutchman," *Year Book of the Pennsylvania Society of New York, 1901* (New York, 1901), p. 29.

27. Klees, *The Pennsylvania Dutch*, pp. 187, 265.

28. FitzGerald Ross, *Cities and Camps of the Confederate States* (Urbana: University of Illinois, 1958), p. 13.

29. Bruce Catton, *Glory Road* (Garden City: Doubleday and Company, Inc., 1952), pp. 182–85.

30. Ibid., pp. 186–93.

31. Pennypacker, "The Pennsylvania Dutchman," p. 30.

32. Thomas H. Parker, *History of the 51st Regiment of P. V. and V. V.* (Philadelphia:: King & Baird, 1869), pp. 694–95.

33. Wistar, *Autobiography*, pp. 352–63.

34. Wood, *Pennsylvania Germans*, p. 233.

35. John Schillich, MS Diary, HSMCo.; William T. Parsons, ed., "Letters from the Fifty-First," *Bulletin of HSMCo.*, 13 (1962), 195–238.

36. Parker, *History of the 51st*, pp. 230–37; Wistar, *Autobiography*, 399–405; R. Ernest Dupuy and Trevor N. Dupuy, *Military Heritage of America* (New York: McGraw–Hill Book Company, 1956), pp. 252–57.

37. Pennypacker, *Autobiography*, pp. 93–97; Reed, "Montgomery County's 'Bivouac of the Dead,'" pp. 56–57.

38. Reed, "'Bivouac of the Dead,'" pp. 54–55, 59–60.

39. Otto Eisenschiml and Ralph Newman, *Eyewitness: The Civil War as we Lived it* (New York: Grosset & Dunlap, Inc., 1956), pp. 211, 222; Obituary (1863), Kern Papers, Bancroft Library; Richard O'Connor, *The German-Americans, An Informal History* (Boston: Little, Brown and Company, 1968), pp. 57, 152–53.

40. Klein and Hoogenboom, *History of Pennsylvania*, p. 250.

41. Elinor and James A. Barnes, eds., *Naval Surgeon; Blockading the South 1862–1866* (Bloomington, Indiana: University of Indiana Press, 1963), pp. 7–14, 288–92, 299, 329–33.

42. A. M. Stewart, *Camp, March, and Battlefield*, p. 248, as quoted in *Glory Road*, by Catton, p. 1.

43. Stevens, *Pennsylvania, Birthplace of a Nation*, pp. 200–202.

44. Minutes of Army Aid Society, 1862–1865, HSMCo.; Anna Holstein, *Three Years in Field Hospitals of the Army of the Potomac* (Philadelphia: J. B. Lippincott Company, 1867), pp. 38–51.

45. *The Norristown Herald*, April–June, 1865; *National Defender* (Norristown), April–June, 1865.

CHAPTER XII

1. Reed, "'Bivouac of the Dead,'" pp. 55, 58.

2. Elinor and James A. Barnes, *Naval Surgeon: Revolt in Japan 1868–1869* (Bloomington, Indiana: University of Indiana Press, 1963), pp. xxiii, xxviii, 29–33, 78–87, 99–103, 181–88, 226–29.

3. Wistar, *Autobiography*, pp. 458–66, 475–77.

4. George Korson, *Black Rock: Mining Folklore of the Pennsylvania Dutch* (Baltimore: The Johns Hopkins University Press, 1960), pp. 64–69, 72–74, 178–79.

5. Rodman W. Paul, *Mining Frontiers of the Far West 1848–1880* (New York: Holt, Rinehart & Winston, Inc., 1963), pp. 159–60; *The Private Journal of George Whitwell Parsons* (Tucson: Arizona Historical Associates, 1936), pp. 44–84.

6. Beth K. Harris, *The Towns of Tintic* (Denver: Sage Books, 1961), pp. 13, 39, 100–101.

7. Wood, *Pennsylvania Germans*, pp. 212–21.

8. Wayland F. Dunaway, *A History of Pennsylvania*, 2nd ed. (New York: Prentice, Hall, 1948), p. 560; Klein and Hoogenboom, *History of Penna.*, pp. 297–302.

9. Wood, *Penna. Germans*, pp. 119–25.

10. Pennypacker, *Autobiography*, pp. 16–20, 264–72.

11. Klein and Hoogenboom, *History of Penna.*, pp. 379–81, 384–86; Stevens, *Pennsylvania, Birthplace of a Nation*, pp. 272–73.

12. Mittelberger, *Journey to Pennsylvania*, pp. 74–75.

13. Ibid., pp. 38–41, 70–71, 93.

14. Kenneth and Anna M. Roberts, *Moreau de St. Méry's American Journey [1793–1798]* (Garden City, N.Y.: Doubleday & Co., Inc., 1947), pp. 295–97.

15. Journal of Isaac Norris, 1764, 1765, Rosenbach Museum; Norris Account Book no. 6 (Workers' Accounts), p. 81, Norris of Fairhill MSS, LCP in HSP.

16. Hector St. John de Crevecoeur, *Letters from an American Farmer* (London, 1782), p. 82.

17. Michel Chevalier, *Society, Manners and Politics in the United States* (Ithaca: Cornell University Press, 1969), p. 331.

18. James G. Leyburn, *The Scotch-Irish* (Chapel Hill: University of North Carolina Press, 1962), pp. 260–64; Klees, *The Pennsylvania Dutch*, pp. 201–2.

19. Crevecoeur, *Letters from an American Farmer*, p. 82.

20. Nettles, *Roots of American Civilization*, p. 448.

21. Wood, *Pennsylvania Germans*, pp. 212–15; Clarence Iobst, *En Quart Millich un En Halb Beint Raum* (Allentown: PGFS, 1939), pp. 30–63.

22. Thomas Harter, *Boonastiel, A Volume of Legend, Story and Song in "Pensylvania Dutch"* (Bellefonte: The Keystone Gazette, 1904), pp. 198–200, 208–9.

23. Birmelin, *Gezwitscher*, pp. 58–65, 90–94, 102–10.

24. Klees, *The Pennsylvania Dutch*, pp. 201–2; Helen Reimensnyder Martin, *Tillie, A Mennonite Maid* (New York: Grosset & Dun-

lap, Inc., 1904), and *Sabina, A Story of the Amish* (New York: New York Century, 1905); Elsie Singmaster, *Ellen Levis* (Boston: Houghton Mifflin Company, 1921), and *A High Wind Rising* (Boston: Houghton Mifflin, 1942); Joseph W. Yoder, *Rosanna of the Amish* (Huntingdon, Pennsylvania: Mennonite Press, 1940), and *Rosanna's Boys* (Huntingdon, Pennsylvania: Mennonite Press, 1948).

CHAPTER XIII

1. Oscar Handlin, *The Uprooted* (New York, 1951), pp. 4–6.

2. Wood, *Pennsylvania Germans*, pp. 141–42.

3. Pennypacker, *Autobiography*, pp. 246–47, 318–19, 366–68.

4. Harter, *Boonastiel*, pp. 30–31, 39–42, 100–101.

5. J. Joseph Huthmacher, *Twentieth Century America, An Interpretation with Readings* (Boston: Twentieth Century, 1965), pp. 97–100.

6. Klein and Hoogenboom, *History of Pennsylvania*, pp. 386–87.

7. Ray Stannard Baker, *Woodrow Wilson Life and Letters* (Garden City, New York, 1937), VI, 289–90; VII, 22, 201; H. C. Peterson, *Propaganda for War, The Campaign against American Neutrality 1914–1917* (Norman, Oklahoma: University of Oklahoma Press, 1939), pp. 173–74, 240, 277; Carl Wittke, *German-Americans and the World War* (Columbus, Ohio, 1936), pp. 41–43.

8. Julio Camba, *Un año en el otro mondo*, translated in *This Was America*, by Oscar Handlin (New York: Harper and Row, 1964), pp. 457–62; Peterson, *Propaganda for War*, p. 274; Wittke, *German-Americans*, pp. 94–96.

9. Wittke, *German-Americans*, pp. 147–48, 163, 180–82, 189; Calvin D. Yost, Jr., "Ursinus College: A History of its First Hundred Years," unpublished MS, 1973, Vol. III, p. 7, Ursinusiana Collection, Myrin Library, Ursinus College, Collegeville, Pennsylvania. Ursinus was founded by German Reformed clergymen in 1869.

10. Interview with Elizabeth Schofield Yost, August 9, 1973; Harry Pfund, *History of the German Society*, pp. 15–16.

11. *The National Observer* (Silver Spring, Maryland), June 30, 1973.

12. Peterson, *Propaganda for War*, p. 173; *New York Times*, August 23, 1918; January 8, March 4, 31, 1920.

13. Klein and Hoogenboom, *History of Pennsylvania*, p. 388.

14. Wood, *Penna. Germans*, pp. 239–40.

15. Ibid., pp. 233–35; Wittke, *German-Americans*, p. 162.

16. Hervey Allen, *Toward the Flame, A War Diary* (Pittsburgh: University of Pittsburgh Press, 1968), p. 165.

17. Wood, *Pennsylvania Germans*, pp. 235–36.

18. James J. Hudson, *Hostile Skies: A Combat History of the American Air Service in World War I* (Syracuse: Syracuse University Press, 1968), pp. 8–9, 35–36, 183; Lawrence Driggs, "Aces Among Aces," *National Geographic* 33 (1918), pp. 568–80.

19. Hudson, *Hostile Skies*, pp. 198–201; Frederick M. Clapp, *A History of the 17th Aero Squadron* (n.p., 1918), pp. 15, 55ff; Edwin C. Parsons, *I Flew with the Lafayette Escadrille* (Indianapolis: The Bobbs-Merrill Co., Inc., 1963), pp. vi–vii, 8–12, 333–35.

20. Driggs, "Aces Among Aces," pp. 570–74; Hiram Bingham, "Building America's Air Army," *National Geographic* 33 (1918), 48–86.

21. Lillian Gish and Ann Pinchot, *The Movies, Mr. Griffith and Me* (Englewood Cliffs, New Jersey: Prentice-Hall, Inc., 1969), pp. 2, 192, 199–203.

22. Wittke, *German-Americans*, pp. 141, 188; Pfund, *History of the German Society*, pp. 17–20.

23. Wood, *Pennsylvania Germans*, p. 234.

24. Klees, *The Pennsylvania Dutch*, p. 280; Pfund, *History of the German Society*, p. 19; [I. L. Hunt], *American Military Government of Occupied Germany, 1918–1920* (Washington: U.S.G.P.O., 1943), pp. 43–52, 63–81, 344–65.

25. Gish and Pinchot, *The Movies, Mr. Griffith and Me*, pp. 233–37, 244–47.

26. Wittke, *German-Americans*, pp. 181–82, 209; "'s Pennsylfawnisch Deitsch Eck," *Allentown Morning Call*, October 12, 1935.

27. Gilbert, *Penna. Germans*, p. 26.

28. Scott F. Brenner, *Pennsylvania Dutch, The Plain and the Fancy* (Harrisburg: Stackpole & Co., 1957), pp. 141–47; Pfund, *History of the German Society*, p. 18.

29. *New York Times*, May 26, August 10, 21, 24, 1944; Strassburger and Hinke, *Pennsylvania German Pioneers*, I, 400.

30. A. Russell Buchanan, *The United States and World War II* (New York: Harper & Row, 1964), II, 381–82, 432; Interview with Robert Albright, August 20, 1973.

31. Walter Bernstein, "They Thought he was a Kraut," *Yank, The Army Weekly* 4, no. 8 (August 10, 1945), 16–17.

32. Klein and Hoogenboom, *History of Penn.*, pp. 424–26.

Chapter XIV

A preliminary version of this chapter is my "Ethnic Tradition: The Legacy of the Pennsylvania Dutch," *The Picket Post* (Valley Forge) (Fall, 1974), pp. 24–31, and (Winter, 1975), pp. 17–18, 38–43.

1. Wood, *Pennsylvania Germans*, pp. 246–48.

2. Gilbert, *Pennsylvania Germans*, p. 13.

3. Ibid., p. 14.

4. Harter, *Boonastiel*, pp. 255–56.

5. Wood, *Pennsylvania Germans*, p. 255.

6. Ibid.

7. Interview with Thomas A. Greene, March, 1968. He related the story as he heard it from his father, the author's grandfather.

8. *New York Times*, January 7, 18, 1942; January 23, 28, February 6, 26, 1955.

9. Friederich Krebs, "Palatine Emigrants to America from the Oppenheim Area, 1742–1749," *Pennsylvania Folklife* 22 (Autumn, 1972), 46–48.

10. *Acts and Proceedings of the Eleventh Meeting of the General Synod of the Evangelical and Reformed Church*, July 1–5, 1959, Oberlin, Ohio, pp. 8, 49–50, 436–38; *Minutes of the Second General Synod of the United Church of Christ*, July 5–9, 1959, Oberlin, Ohio, pp. 5–13, 27–29, 81–110.

11. Gilbert, *Penna. Germans*, p. 57.

12. Klees, *The Penna. Dutch*, pp. 66–67; *New York Times*, December 20, 1951; July 6, 1957.

13. Christopher Noss, *Tohoku the Scotland of Japan* (Philadelphia: Reformed Church in the United States, 1918), pp. 185, 188–91; Philip Williams, "Japan Today," *Youth* 23 (June, 1972), 48–62.

14. Klees, *The Pennsylvania Dutch*, pp. 31–32; Yoder, *Rosanna of the Amish*, p. 249.

15. Yoder, *Rosanna of the Amish*, pp. 231–32; *New York Times*, May 2, 22, 1961; November 7, 1963; September 10, 1964; July 31, 1965.

16. *New York Times*, November 23, 28, December 18, 21, 1965.

17. Gilbert, *Penna. Germans*, pp. 64–65.

18. Klees, *The Pennsylvania Dutch*, p. 342.

19. Klein and Hoogenboom, *History of Pennsylvania*, p. 302.

20. In Montgomery County, Pa., the County Historical Society was, until recently, the only historical society in the county. During the past fifteen years, no less than eighteen local historical societies have organized.

21. Ken Britt, "Pennsylvania's Old-time Dutch Treat," *National Geographic* 143 (1973), 564–78.

22. *Pennsylvania Folklife* 21 (1971), 50.

23. Mac E. Barrick, "Pulpit Humor in Central Pennsylvania," *Pennsylvania Folklife* 19 (Autumn, 1969), 28–36; *Pennsylvania Dutch Spoken Here Abouts*, BR-1, and *As I Was Saying*, BR-2, Buch Records,

Lincoln, Pennsylvania, 1961, 1962; *Pennsburg Town and Country*, Friday issues.

24. The National Trust for Historic Preservation, Washington, D.C., has taken the lead in systematizing preservation projects.

Selected Bibliography

PRIMARY SOURCES

1. Books

An Address to Freeholders and Electors of the Province of Pennsylvania, in Answer to a Paper called The Plain Dealer. Philadelphia: A. Armbrüster, 1764.

An die Freyhalter und Einwohner der Stadt und County Philadelphia, Deutscher Nation. Philadelphia: A. Armbrüster, 1764.

ALLEN, HERVEY. *Toward the Flame, A War Diary.* Pittsburgh: University of Pittsburgh Press, 1968.

BARNES, ELINOR, and BARNES, JAMES A. *Naval Surgeon.* 2 vols. Bloomington, Ind.: Indiana University Press, 1963.

BEAM, C. RICHARD. *Abridged Pennsylvania German Dictionary.* Kaiserslautern: Heimatstelle Pfalz, 1970.

BEISSEL, J. CONRAD. *Zionitischer Weyrauchs-Hügel Oder: Myrrhen Berg, Worinnen allerley liebliches und wohl riechendes nach Apotheker-Kunst zu bereitetes Rauch-Werck zu finden.* Germantown: Christopher Sauer, 1739.

BIRMELIN, JOHN. *Gezwitscher: A Book of Pennsylvania German Verse.* Allentown: Pennsylvania German Folklore Society, 1938.

————. *E bissel vun dem un e bissel vun sellem.* Kaiserslautern: Heimatstelle Pfalz, 1960.

BORNEMAN, HENRY S. *Pennsylvania German Illuminated Manuscripts.* New York: Dover Publications, 1973.

CARPENTER, THOMAS. *The Two Trials of John Fries on an Indictment for Treason; together with a Brief Report of the Trials of Several Other Persons for Treason and Insurrection. In the Counties of Bucks, Northampton and Montgomery, in the Circuit Court of the United States.* Philadelphia: William Woodward, 1800.

CHEVALIER, MICHEL. *Society, Manners and Politics in the United States.* Ithaca: Claremont, 1969.

CLAPP, FREDERICK. *A History of the 17th Aero Squadron.* N.p.: 17th Aero Squadron, 1918.

CLAUS, C. DANIEL. *A Primer for the Use of Mohawk Children, To acquire the Spelling and Reading of their own; As well as to get acquainted with the English Tongue.* Montreal, 1781.

COLE, ALAN B. *Yankee Surveyors in the Shogun's Seas.* Princeton: Princeton University Press, 1947.

Colonial Records of Pennsylvania. Compiled by Samuel Hazard. 16 vols. Philadelphia: Joseph Severns, 1851–1852.

CREVECOEUR, HECTOR ST. JOHN DE. *Letters from an American Farmer.* London: Dent, 1782.

Der Blutige Schau-Platz, oder Martyrer Spiegel der Tauffs Besinken. (Martyr's Mirror.) Ephrata: Drucks und Verlags der Brüderschaft, 1748.

Die Regeln der Teutschen Gesellschaft. Germantown: C. Sauer, Jr., 1764.

DOCK, CHRISTOPHER. *Eine Einfältige und gründlich abgefaszte Schul-Ordnung.* Germantown: C. Sauer, Jr., 1770.

EISENSCHIML, OTTO, and NEWMAN, RALPH. *Eyewitness: The Civil War as We Lived it.* New York: Grosset and Dunlap, 1956.

FOGEL, EDWIN M. *Beliefs and Superstitions of the Pennsylvania Germans.* Philadelphia: American-Germanica Press, 1915.

FRANKLIN, BENJAMIN. *Cool Thoughts on the Present Situation of our Publick Affairs.* Philadelphia, 1764.

————. *Indian Treaties Printed by Benjamin Franklin.* Edited by Julian P. Boyd. Philadelphia: Historical Society of Pennsylvania, 1938.

————. *The Papers of Benjamin Franklin.* 18 vols. to date. Edited by Leonard Labaree et al. New Haven: Yale University Press, 1958–.

FREY, J. WILLIAM. *Pennsylvania Dutch Grammar.* Clinton, S. C.: Jacobs Press, 1942.

GALLOWAY, JOSEPH. *Speech delivered before the Assembly.* Philadelphia: B. Franklin, 1764.

GISH, LILLIAN and PINCHOT, ANN. *The Movies, Mr. Griffith and Me.* Englewood Cliffs, N. J.: Prentice Hall, 1969.

GRAEFF, ARTHUR. *Selections from Arthur Graeff's Scholla.* Edited by Frederick Weiser. Breinigsville, Pa.: Pennsylvania German Society, 1971.

GRUMBINE, LEE L. *Der Dengelstock.* Lancaster: New Era, 1903.

————. *The Pennsylvania German Dialect.* Lancaster: Pennsylvania German Society, 1902.

HABERSHAM, ALEXANDER. *My Last Cruise; or Where we Went and What we Saw.* Philadelphia: J. B. Lippincott, 1857.

HANDLIN, OSCAR. *This Was America.* New York: Harper & Bros., 1964.

————. *The Uprooted.* New York: Harper & Bros., 1951.

HARBAUGH, HENRY. *Harbaughs Harfe: Gedichte in Pennsylfawnisch-Deutscher Mundart.* Philadelphia: Reformed Church Publication Board, 1870.

HARTER, THOMAS. *Boonastiel, A Volume of Legend, Story and Song in "Pennsylvania Dutch."* Middleburg: T. Harter, 1893.

HELLER, EDNA EBY. *The Art of Pennsylvania Dutch Cooking.* Garden City, N. Y.: Doubleday & Co., 1968.

HOHMAN, JOHAN GEORG. *Der Lang Verborgene Freund.* Harrisburg: J. G. Hohman, 1843.

HOLSTEIN, ANNA. *Three Years in Field Hospitals of the Army of the Potomac.* Philadelphia: J. B. Lippincott, 1867.

HORNE, A. R. *A Pennsylvania German Manual.* Kutztown, Pa.: Urick & Gehring, 1875.

IOBST, CLARENCE F. *En Quart Millich un En Halb Beint Raum.* Allentown: Pennsylvania German Folklore Society, 1939.

KALM, PETER. *Travels in North America.* 2 vols. New York: Dover Publications, 1964.

KLOSS, HEINZ. *Lewendiche Schtimme aus Pennsilveni.* Stuttgart: B. Westermann, 1929.

KOHL, J. G. *Travels in Canada and through the States of New York and Pennsylvania.* 2 vols. London, 1861.

KORSON, GEORGE. *Black Rock: Mining Folklore of the Pennsylvania Dutch.* Baltimore: Johns Hopkins Press, 1960.

LAMBERT, MARCUS BACHMAN. *A Dictionary of the Non-English Words of the Pennsylvania German Dialect.* Norristown, Pa.: Pennsylvania German Society, 1924.

LEWIS, MERIWETHER. *The Lewis and Clark Expedition.* 3 vols. Philadelphia: J. B. Lippincott, 1961.

MILLER, DANIEL. *Pennsylvania German.* 2 vols. Reading: D. Miller, 1903–1911.

Minutes and Letters of the Coetus of the German Reformed Congregations in Pennsylvania 1747–1792. Philadelphia: Reformed Church Publishing Board, 1903.

MITTELBERGER, GOTTLIEB. *Journey to Pennsylvania.* Cambridge, Mass.: Harvard University Press, 1960.

MORGAN, EDMUND S. *Prologue to Revolution, Sources and Documents on the Stamp Act Crisis, 1764–1766.* Chapel Hill: University of North Carolina Press, 1959.

MOYER, EARL H., and KRICK, KAY MOYER. *Almanac Lore of the Pennsylvania Dutch.* Collegeville, Pa.: Institute for Pennsylvania Dutch Studies, 1975.

MUHLENBERG, HENRY M. *The Journals of Henry Melchior Muhlenberg.* Edited by Theodore Tappert and John W. Doberstein. 3 vols. Philadelphia: Evangelical Lutheran Ministerium of Pennsylvania, 1942–1958.

––––––. *The Notebook of a Colonial Clergyman.* Edited by Theodore Tappert and John W. Doberstein. Philadelphia: Muhlenberg Press, 1959.

MYERS, ALBERT C. *Hannah Logan's Courtship.* Philadelphia: Ferris & Leach, 1904.

––––––. *Narratives of Early Pennsylvania. West New Jersey and Delaware 1630–1707.* New York: Charles Scribner's Sons, 1912.

Nachrichten von dem vereinigten Deutschen Evangelisch-Lutherischen Gemeinen in Nord-America, absonderlich in Pennsylvanien. Halle: Evangelish-Lutherischen Gemein, 1787.

PARKER, THOMAS. *History of the 51st Regiment of P. V. and P. V. V.* Philadelphia: King & Baird, 1869.

PARSONS, EDWIN C. *I Flew with the Lafayette Escadrille.* Indianapolis: E. C. Seale & Co., 1963.

PARSONS, WILLIAM T. *The Preachers' Appeal of 1775.* Collegeville, Pa.: Pennsylvania South East Conference, United Church of Christ, 1975.

PASTORIUS, FRANCIS DANIEL. *A New Primmer, or Methodical Directions to attain the True Spelling, Reading and Writing of English.* New York: Wm. Bradford, 1698.

––––––. *Pastorius' Description of Pennsylvania, 1700, Old South Leaflets,* no. 95. [Boston: Directors of the Old South Work], 1898.

PENN, WILLIAM, and LOGAN, JAMES. *Correspondence between William Penn and James Logan, Secretary of the Province of Pennsylvania, and Others. 1700–1750.* Edited by Edward Armstrong. 2 vols. Philadelphia: Historical Society of Pennsylvania, 1870–1872.

Pennsylvania Archives, Selected and arranged from Original Documents. Edited by Samuel Hazard. 9 Series, 119 vols. Philadelphia and Harrisburg: Joseph Severns, 1852–1914.

PENNYPACKER, SAMUEL. *Autobiography of a Pennsylvanian.* Philadelphia: Winston, 1918.

REICHMANN, FELIX, and DOLL, EUGENE. *Ephrata as Seen by Contemporaries.* Allentown: Pennsylvania German Folklore Society, 1952.

REITNAUER, CLARENCE G. *So Shreibt der Shdivvel Knecht.* Collegeville, Pa.: Institute for Pennsylvania Dutch Studies, 1975.

RUSH, BENJAMIN. *An Account of the Manners of the German In-*

habitants of Pennsylvania (1789). Edited by William T. Parsons. Collegeville, Pa.: Institute for Pennsylvania Dutch Studies, 1974.

SAUER, CHRISTOPHER. *Ein Abgenöthiger Bericht: Oder, zum öfftern begehrte Antwort, denen darnach fragenden dargelegt. In sich haltende: Zwey Brieffe und deren Ursach. Dem noch angehaenget worden eine Historie von Doctor Schotte und einige Breiffe von demselben zu unseren Zeiten nöthig zu Erwegen.* Germantown: Christopher Sauer, 1739.

SAUER, CHRISTOPHER, JR. *Anmerkungen über Ein noch nie erhört und gesehen Wunder Thier in Pennsylvanien, genannt Streitund Strauss Vogel, Heraus gegeben von einer Teutschen Gesellschaft freyer Bürger und getreuer Unterthanen Seiner Gross Brittanischen Majestät.* Germantown: Christopher Sauer, Jr., 1764.

Schreiben des Evangelisch-Lutherischen und Reformierten Kirchen-Raths, wie auch der Beamten der Teutschen Gesellschaft in der Stadt Philadelphia, an die Teutschen Einwohner der Provinzen von Neuyork und Nord-Carolina. Philadelphia: Henrich Miller, 1775.

SCHWENCKFELD VON OSSIG, CASPAR. *Passional and Prayer Book.* Translated by John J. Stoudt. Pennsburg, Pa.: Schwenkfelder Library, 1961.

SHULTZE, DAVID. *The Journals and Papers of David Schultze.* Translated and edited by Andrew S. Berky. 2 vols. Pennsburg, Pa.: Schwenkfelder Library, 1952.

SMITH, WILLIAM. *A Brief History of the Rise and Progress of the Charitable Scheme Carrying on by a Society of Noblemen and Gentlemen in London, for the Relief and Instruction of Germans and their Descendants Settled in Pennsylvania and the Adjacent British Colonies in North America.* Philadelphia: Franklin & Hall, 1755.

STRASSBURGER, RALPH B., and HINKE, WILLIAM J. *Pennsylvania German Pioneers.* 3 vols. Norristown, Pa.: Pennsylvania German Society, 1934.

TROXEL, WILLIAM S., ed. *Aus Pennsylfawnia: An Anthology of Translations into the Pennsylvania German Dialect.* Philadelphia: University of Pennsylvania Press, 1938.

TURNER, ROBERT P. *Lewis Miller, Sketches and Chronicles.* York, Pa.: Historical Society of York County, 1966.

WEISER, CONRAD. *Ein Wohl-gemeindter und Ernstlicher Rath an unsere Lands-Leute, die Teutschen.* Philadelphia: B. Franklin, 1741.

WISTAR, ISAAC J. *Autobiography of Isaac J. Wistar 1827–1905.* Philadelphia: Wistar Institute, 1937.

WOLLENWEBER, LUDWIG A. *Mountain Mary.* Translated and Introduction by John J. Stoudt. York, Pa.: Liberty Cap Books, 1974.

WOOD, RALPH and BRAUN, FRITZ. *Pennsilfaanisch deitsch.* Kaiserslautern: Heimatstelle Pfalz, 1966.

YODER, JOSEPH W. *Rosanna of the Amish.* Huntingdon, Pa.: Yoder Publishing Co., 1940.

————. *Rosanna's Boys.* Huntingdon, Pa.: Yoder Publishing Co., 1948.

ZEISBERGER, DAVID. *Essay of a Delaware Indian and English Spelling Book.* Philadelphia: Henrich Miller, 1776.

ZIEGLER, CHARLES CALVIN. *Drauss un Deheem.* Leipzig: Hesse und Becker, 1891.

2. Articles

BELL, WHITFIELD, J., JR. "Addenda to Watson's Annals: Notes by Jacob Mordecai, 1836." *Pennsylvania Magazine of History and Biography* 98 (1974), 131–70.

BINDER-JOHNSON, HILDEGARD. "The German Protest of 1688 Against Negro Slavery." *Pennsylvania Magazine of History and Biography* 65 (1941), 145–56.

DEISCHER, CLAUDE K. "My Experience with the Dialect." *Pennsylvania Folklife* 23 (Summer 1974), 47–48.

DRISCOLL, CAROLYN MATTERN. "A Pennsylvania Dutch Yankee: Civil War Letters of Private David William Mattern." Departmental Honors Typescript, History. Collegeville, Pa.: Ursinus College, 1966.

FRIEDRICH, GERHARD. "The Earliest History of Germantown [1691], An Unknown Pastorius Manuscript." *Pennsylvania History* 8 (1941), 314–16.

KREBS, FRIEDERICH. "Palatine Emigrants to America from the Oppenheim Area, 1742–1749." *Pennsylvania Folklife* 22 (Autumn 1972), 46–48.

NELSON, VERNON H., and MADEHEIM, LOTHAR. "The Moravian Settlements of Pennsylvania in 1757: The Nicholas Garrison Views." *Pennsylvania Folklife* 19 (Autumn 1969), 2–13.

PARSONS, WILLIAM T. "Letters from the Fifty-First." *Bulletin of the Historical Society of Montgomery County* 13 (1962), 195–238.

SHANER, RICHARD H. "The Oley Valley Basketmaker." *Pennsylvania Folklife* 14 (October 1964), 2–8.

YODER, DON. "25 Years of the Folk Festival." *Pennsylvania Folklife* 23 (1974), 2–7.

ZEHNER, OLIVE G. "The Hills from Hamburg." *The Pennsylvania Dutchman* 4 (February 1, 1953) pp. 16, 13.

SECONDARY SOURCES

1. Books

AMMON, HARRY. *The Genet Mission.* New York: W. W. Norton & Co., 1973.

ANDERSON, MATTHEW S. *Europe in the Eighteenth Century 1713–1783.* New York: Holt, Rinehart & Winston, 1961.

ARNDT, KARL J. R., and OLSON MAY E. *German-American Newspapers and Periodicals 1732–1795.* 2d rev. ed. New York: Johnson Reprint Corp., 1965.

BALDWIN, LELAND. *Whiskey Rebels, the Story of a Frontier Uprising.* Pittsburgh: University of Pittsburgh Press, 1968.

BARBA, PRESTON A. *Pennsylvania German Tombstones.* Allentown: Pennsylvania German Folklore Society, 1954.

BARBER, EDWIN A. *Tulip Ware of the Pennsylvania German Potters.* New York: Dover Publications, 1970.

BEAL, REBECCA J. *Jacob Eichholtz 1776–1842.* Philadelphia: Historical Society of Pennsylvania, 1969.

BELL, WINTHROP P. *The "Foreign Protestants" and the Settlement of Nova Scotia.* Toronto: University of Toronto Press, 1961.

BENRATH, GUSTAV A. *Reformierte Kirchengeschichtsschriebung an der Universität Heidelberg im 16. und 17. Jahrhundert.* Speyer: Zechnersche Buchdruckerei, 1963.

BERKY, ANDREW S. *The Schoolhouse near the Old Spring, A History of the Union School and Church Association, Dillingersville, Pennsylvania 1735–1955.* Norristown, Pa.: Pennsylvania German Society, 1955.

BITTINGER, LUCY F. *The Germans in Colonial Times.* New York: Russell & Russell, 1968.

BOYD, JULIAN P., ed. *The Susquehanna Company Papers.* 11 vols. Wilkes-Barre: Wyoming Historical and Geological Society, 1930–1971.

BRANDI, KARL. *The Emperor Charles V.* London: J. Cape, 1954.

BRENNER, SCOTT F. *Pennsylvania Dutch, The Plain and the Fancy.* Harrisburg: Stackpole & Co., 1957.

BRIDENBAUGH, CARL. *The Colonial Craftsman.* New York: New York University Press, 1950.

BRIDENBAUGH, CARL, and BRIDENBAUGH, JESSICA. *Rebels and Gentlemen: Philadelphia in the Age of Franklin.* New York: Oxford University Press, 1962.

BRONNER, EDWIN B. *William Penn's "Holy Experiment": The Founding of Pennsylvania 1681–1701.* New York: Columbia University Press, 1962.

BRUNHOUSE, ROBERT L. *The Counter-Revolution in Pennsylvania 1776–1790.* Harrisburg: Pennsylvania Historical and Museum Commission, 1942.

BUCHANAN, A. RUSSELL. *The United States and World War II.* 2 vols. New York: Harper & Row, 1964.

CATTON, BRUCE. *Glory Road.* New York: Doubleday & Co., 1952.

CHAMBERS, THEODORE F. *The Early Germans of New Jersey.* Dover: T. F. Chambers, 1895.

DAPP, CHARLES F. *The Evolution of an American Patriot: John Henry Miller.* Philadelphia: Pennsylvania German Society, 1924.

DAVIDSON, ROBERT L. D. *War Comes to Quaker Pennsylvania.* New York: Columbia University Press, 1957.

DE ANGELI, MARGUERITE. *Henner's Lydia.* Garden City, N.Y.: Doubleday & Co., 1937.

––––––. *Skippack School.* Garden City, N. Y.: Doubleday & Co., 1939.

––––––. *Yonie Wondernose.* Garden City, N. Y.: Doubleday & Co., 1944.

DENLINGER, A. MARTHA. *Real People.* Scottdale, Pa.: Herald Press, 1975.

DE SCHWEINITZ, EDMUND. *The Moravian Manual, Containing an Account of the Moravian United Brethren.* Philadelphia: Lindsay, 1859.

DIFFENDERFER, FRANK R. *The German Immigration into Pennsylvania through the Port of Philadelphia from 1700 to 1775.* Lancaster: Pennsylvania German Society, 1900.

DINGWALL, E., and ELIZABETH HEARD. *Pennsylvania 1681–1756: The State without an Army.* London: C. W. Daniel Co., 1937.

DUNN, MARY MAPLES. *William Penn, Politics and Conscience.* Princeton: Princeton University Press, 1967.

EARLE, ALICE. *Home Life in Colonial Days.* New York: Harper & Co., 1898.

ECKHARDT, GEORGE H. *Pennsylvania Clocks and Clockmakers.* New York: Devin-Adair, 1955.

ELTON, GEOFFREY R. *Reformation Europe 1517–1559.* Cleveland: Meridian Books, 1964.

ERNST, JAMES E. *Ephrata, A History.* Allentown: Pennsylvania German Folklore Society, 1963.

FAUST, ALBERT B. *The German Element in the United States.* 2 vols. Boston: Houghton, 1909.

FLETCHER, STEVENSON W. *Pennsylvania Agriculture and Country Life, 1640–1840.* Harrisburg: Pennsylvania Historical and Museum Commission, 1950.

Fox, Edith M. *Land Speculation in the Mohawk Country.* Ithaca: Cornell University Press, 1949.

Geiser, Karl F. *Redemptioners and Indentured Servants in the Colony and Commonwealth of Pennsylvania.* New Haven: Tuttle, Morehouse & Taylor, 1901.

Gerstell, Vivian S. *Silversmiths of Lancaster, Pennsylvania, 1730–1850.* Lancaster: Lancaster County Historical Society, 1972.

Gibson, James E. *Dr. Bodo Otto and the Medical Background of the American Revolution.* Springfield, Ill.: C. C. Thomas, 1937.

Gipson, Lawrence. *The British Empire in America before the American Revolution.* 15 vols. Caldwell, Idaho and New York: Caxton Printers and A. A. Knopf, 1936–1970.

Gollin, Gillian L. *Moravians in Two Worlds: A Study of Changing Communities.* New York: Columbia University Press, 1967.

Good, James I. *History of the Reformed Church in the United States, 1725–1792.* Reading: Daniel Miller, 1899.

Gray, Elma E. *Wilderness Christians: The Moravian Mission to the Delaware Indians.* Ithaca: Cornell University Press, 1956.

Hafen, LeRoy R. *The Mountain Men and the Fur Trade of the Far West.* 10 vols. Glendale, Calif., A. H. Clark, 1965–1970.

Hafen, LeRoy, and Hafen, Ann. *Frémont's Fourth Expedition.* Glendale, Calif.: A. H. Clark Co., 1960.

Hanna, William S. *Benjamin Franklin and Pennsylvania Politics.* Stanford: Stanford University Press, 1964.

Hark, Ann. *Blue Hills and Shoo-fly Pie.* Philadelphia: J. B. Lippincott, 1952.

Harris, Beth. *The Towns of Tintic.* Denver: Sage Books, 1961.

Hawke, David. *The Colonial Experience.* Indianapolis: Bobbs-Merrill, 1966.

————. *In the Midst of a Revolution.* Philadelphia: University of Pennsylvania Press, 1961.

Herrick, Cheesman A. *White Servitude in Pennsylvania: Indentured and Redemption Labor in Colony and Commonwealth.* Philadelphia: McVey, 1926.

Higginbotham, Sanford W. *The Keystone in the Democratic Arch: Pennsylvania Politics 1800–1816.* Harrisburg: Pennsylvania Historical and Museum Commission, 1952.

Hindle, Brooke. *David Rittenhouse.* Princeton: Princeton University Press, 1964.

Hine, Robert V. *Edward Kern and American Expansion.* New Haven: Yale University Press, 1972.

Hinke, William J. *Ministers of the German Reformed Congregations in Pennsylvania and other Colonies in the Eighteenth Cen-*

tury. Edited by George W. Richards. Lancaster, Pa.: Historical Commission of the Evangelical and Reformed Church, 1951.

HOCKER, EDWARD W. *Germantown 1683–1933*. Germantown: E. W. Hocker, 1933.

——. *The Sower Printing House of Colonial Times*. Norristown, Pa.: Pennsylvania German Society, 1948.

HORST, SAMUEL. *Mennonites in the Confederacy*. Scottdale, Pa.: Herald Press, 1967.

HUDSON, JAMES J. *Hostile Skies: A Combat History of the American Air Service in World War I*. Syracuse: Syracuse University Press, 1968.

HUNT, I. L. *American Military Government of Occupied Germany 1918–1920*. Washington, D. C.: Government Printing Office, 1943.

HUNTER, WILLIAM A. *Forts on the Pennsylvania Frontier 1753–1758*. Harrisburg: Pennsylvania Historical and Museum Commission, 1956.

JENSEN, ARTHUR L. *The Maritime Commerce of Colonial Philadelphia*. Madison: State Historical Society of Wisconsin, 1966.

JOHNSTON, HENRY P. *The Yorktown Campaign and Surrender of Cornwallis 1781*. New York: Harper & Brothers, 1881.

JORDAN, MILDRED. *One Red Rose Forever*. New York: A. A. Knopf, 1941.

KAUFFMAN, HENRY J. *Early American Gunsmiths 1650–1850*. New York: Bramhall House, 1952.

——. *Pennsylvania Dutch American Folk Art*. Rev. and enl. ed. New York: Dover Publications, 1964.

KEYSER, ALAN G., and HOLLENBACH, RAYMOND. *The Account Book of the Clements Family of Lower Salford Township, Montgomery County, Pennsylvania, 1749–1857*. Breinigsville, Pa.: Pennsylvania German Society, 1975.

KIEFFER, ELIZABETH C. *Henry Harbaugh, Pennsylvania Dutchman, 1817–1867*. Norristown, Pa.: Pennsylvania German Society, 1945.

KIPPING, ERNST. *The Hessian View of America 1776–1783*. Monmouth Beach, N. J.: Philip Freneau Press, 1971.

KLEES, FREDRIC. *The Pennsylvania Dutch*. New York: Macmillan, 1950.

KLEIN, H. M. J. *The History of the Eastern Synod of the Reformed Church in the United States*. Lancaster: The Eastern Synod, 1943.

KLEIN, PHILIP S. *Pennsylvania Politics 1817–1832: A Game Without Rules*. Philadelphia: Historical Society of Pennsylvania, 1940.

KLEIN, PHILIP S., and HOOGENBOOM, ARI. *A History of Pennsylvania.* New York: McGraw-Hill, 1973.

KLEIN, WALTER C. *Johann Conrad Beissel: Mystic and Martinet 1690–1768.* Philadelphia: University of Pennsylvania Press, 1942.

KNAUSS, JAMES O. *Social Conditions among the Pennsylvania Germans in the Eighteenth Century.* Lancaster: New Era, 1922.

KNITTLE, RHEA M. *Early American Glass.* Garden City, N. Y.: Century Co., 1948.

KNITTLE, WALTER A. *Early Eighteenth Century Palatine Emigration.* Philadelphia: University of Pennsylvania Press, 1937.

KOENIGSBERGER, HELMUT, and MOSSE, GEORGE L. *Europe in the Sixteenth Century.* New York: Holt, Rinehart & Winston, 1968.

KUHNS, OSCAR. *German and Swiss Settlements of Pennsylvania.* New York: Abingdon Press, 1914.

LAUGHLIN, LEDLIE. *Pewter in America: Its Makers and their Marks.* Boston: Houghton Mifflin Co., 1940.

LEMON, JAMES T. *The Best Poor Man's Country.* Baltimore: Johns Hopkins University Press, 1972.

LICHTEN, FRANCES. *Folk Art of Rural Pennsylvania.* New York: Scribner's, 1946.

LIVENGOOD, JAMES. *The Philadelphia-Baltimore Trade Rivalry 1780–1860.* Harrisburg: Pennsylvania Historical and Museum Commission, 1947.

LONG, AMOS, JR. *The Pennsylvania German Family Farm.* Breinigsville: Pennsylvania German Society, 1972.

LOWELL, EDWARD J. *The Hessians and Other German Auxiliaries of Great Britain in the Revolutionary War.* Williamstown, Mass.: Corner House, 1970.

LUCAS, HENRY S. *The Renaissance and Reformation.* New York: Harper & Bros., 1934.

MASON, HERBERT M. *Lafayette Escadrille.* New York: Random House, 1964.

McDONALD, FORREST. *We the People: The Economic Origins of the Constitution.* Chicago: University of Chicago Press, 1958.

McKEARIN, GEORGE S., and McKEARIN, HELEN. *American Glass.* New York: Crown Publishers, 1941.

MENTZELL, ROBERT. *The Liberty Bell's Interlude in Allentown.* Sellersville: Sellersville Historical and Achievement Authority, 1974.

MERCER, HENRY C. *The Bible in Iron,* 3rd ed. Doylestown: Bucks County Historical Society, 1961.

METZGER, CHARLES H. *The Prisoner in the American Revolution.* Chicago: Loyola University Press, 1971.

MONTGOMERY, MORTON L. *History of Berks County, Pennsylvania, in the Revolution, from 1774–1783.* Reading: Charles F. Haage, 1894.

MURTAGH, WILLIAM J. *Moravian Architecture and Town Planning.* Chapel Hill: University of North Carolina Press, 1967.

NASH, GARY B. *Quakers and Politics, Pennsylvania 1681–1726.* Princeton: Princeton University Press, 1968.

NELSON, WILLIAM H. *The American Tory.* Oxford: Clarendon Press, 1961.

NOSS, CHRISTOPHER. *Tohoku: The Scotland of Japan.* Philadelphia: Board of Foreign Missions, 1918.

O'CONNOR, RICHARD. *The German-Americans, An Informal History.* Boston: Little, Brown & Co., 1968.

OMWAKE, JOHN. *The Conestoga Six-Horse Bell Teams of Eastern Pennsylvania.* Cincinnati: Ebbert S. Richardson, 1930.

PARSONS, WILLIAM T. *Ethnic Tradition: The Legacy of the Pennsylvania Dutch.* Collegeville, Pa.: Institute on Pennsylvania Dutch Studies, 1975.

PAUL, RODMAN W. *Mining Frontiers of the Far West 1848–1880.* New York: Holt, Rinehart & Winston, 1963.

PECKHAM, HOWARD H. *Pontiac and the Indian Uprising.* Princeton: Princeton University Press, 1947.

PETERSON, H. C. *Propaganda for War, The Campaign against American Neutrality 1914–1917.* Norman: University of Oklahoma Press, 1939.

PFUND, HARRY W. *A History of the German Society of Pennsylvania.* Philadelphia: 1944.

RICHARDS, HENRY M. M. *The Pennsylvania German in the French and Indian War.* Lancaster: Pennsylvania German Society, 1905.

ROBACKER, EARL F. *Pennsylvania German Literature.* Philadelphia: University of Pennsylvania Press, 1943.

SACHSE, JULIUS F. *The Fatherland (1450–1700).* Philadelphia: Pennsylvania German Society, 1897.

—————. *Music of the Ephrata Cloister.* Lancaster: Pennsylvania German Society, 1903.

SAWITZKY, WILLIAM. *Catalogue Descriptive and Critical of the Paintings and Miniatures in the Historical Society of Pennsylvania.* Philadelphia: Historical Society of Pennsylvania, 1942.

SCHERER, KARL, ed. *Pfälzer-Palatines.* Kaiserslautern: Heimatstelle Pfalz, 1975.

SCHLESINGER, ARTHUR. *The Colonial Merchants and the American Revolution.* New York: F. Ungar, 1957.

SHELLEY, DONALD A. *The Fraktur-Writings or Illuminated Manuscripts of the Pennsylvania Germans.* Allentown: Pennsylvania German Folklore Society, 1961.

SHOEMAKER, ALFRED L. *Christmas in Pennsylvania.* Kutztown: Pennsylvania Folklife Society, 1959.

SINGMASTER, ELSIE. *Ellen Levis.* Boston: Houghton, Mifflin Co., 1921.

————. *A High Wind Rising.* Boston: Houghton, Mifflin Co., 1942.

SMITH, ABBOTT E. *Colonists in Bondage: White Servitude and Convict Labor in America.* New York: W. W. Norton, 1971.

SMITH, HENRY N. *Virgin Land: The American West as Symbol and Myth.* Cambridge, Mass.: Harvard University Press, 1950.

SMITH, JAMES MORTON. *Freedom's Fetters: The Alien and Sedition Laws and American Civil Liberties.* Ithaca: Cornell University Press, 1956.

SMITH, PRESERVED. *The Age of the Reformation.* New York: Holt, 1920.

STOUDT, JOHN BAER. *The Liberty Bells of Pennsylvania.* Philadelphia: W. J. Campbell, 1930.

STOUDT, JOHN JOSEPH. *Consider The Lilies How They Grow.* Allentown: Pennsylvania German Folklore Society, 1937.

————. *Pennsylvania German Poetry 1685–1830.* Allentown: Pennsylvania German Folklore Society, 1956.

————. *Sunbonnets and Shoofly Pies.* New York: A. S. Barnes, 1974.

STUDER, GERALD. *Christopher Dock, Colonial Schoolmaster.* Scottdale, Pa.: Herald Press, 1967.

TINKCOM, HARRY M. *The Republicans and Federalists in Pennsylvania 1790–1801.* Harrisburg: Pennsylvania Historical and Museum Commission, 1950.

TOLLES, FREDERICK. *Meeting House and Counting House.* New York: W. W. Norton & Co., 1963.

WAINWRIGHT, NICHOLAS B. *George Croghan: Wilderness Diplomat.* Chapel Hill: University of North Carolina Press, 1959.

————. *Paintings and Miniatures at the Historical Society of Pennsylvania.* Philadelphia: Historical Society of Pennsylvania, 1974.

WALLACE, ANTHONY F. C. *King of the Delawares, Teedyuscung 1700–1763.* Philadelphia: University of Pennsylvania Press, 1949.

WALLACE, PAUL A. W. *Conrad Weiser 1696–1760: Friend of Colonist and Mohawk.* Philadelphia: University of Pennsylvania Press, 1945.

————. *The Muhlenbergs of Pennsylvania.* Philadelphia: University of Pennsylvania Press, 1950.

WALTERS, RAYMOND, JR. *Alexander James Dallas, Lawyer-Politician-Financier 1759–1817.* Philadelphia: University of Pennsylvania Press, 1943.

WEBER, SAMUEL E. *The Charity School Movement in Colonial Pennsylvania.* Philadelphia: University of Pennsylvania, 1905.

WEDGWOOD, CICELY. *The Thirty Years War.* New Haven: Yale University Press, 1949.

WELLENREUTHER, HERMANN. *Glaube und Politik in Pennsylvania 1681–1776.* Köln: Böhlau Verlag, 1972.

WEYGANDT, CORNELIUS. *The Dutch Country.* New York: Appleton-Century, 1939.

WINTERS, R. L. *John Caspar Stoever, Colonial Pastor and Founder of Churches.* Norristown, Pa.: Pennsylvania German Society, 1948.

WITTKE, CARL. *German-Americans and the World War.* Columbus: Ohio State University Press, 1936.

WOOD, RALPH. *The Pennsylvania Germans.* Princeton: Princeton University Press, 1942.

WOODWARD, WILLIAM E. *The Way our People Lived.* New York: Washington Square Press, 1963.

WUST, KLAUS. *The Virginia Germans.* Charlottesville: University Press of Virginia, 1969.

2. Articles

BARRICK, MAC. "Pulpit Humor in Central Pennsylvania." *Pennsylvania Folklife* 19 (Autumn 1969), 28–36.

BECK, BERTON E. "Grain Harvesting in the Nineteenth Century." *Pennsylvania Folklife* 23 (Summer 1974), 43–46.

BERNSTEIN, WALTER. "They Thought he was a Kraut." *Yank, The Army Weekly* 4, no. 8 (1945), 16–17.

BINGHAM, HIRAM. "Building America's Air Army." *National Geographic* 33 (1918), 48–86.

BOCKELMAN, WAYNE, and IRELAND, OWEN S. "The Internal Revolution in Pennsylvania: An Ethnic-Religious Interpretation." *Pennsylvania History* 41 (1974), 125–59.

BRITT, KEN. "Pennsylvania's Old-time Dutch Treat." *National Geographic* 143 (1973), 564–78.

COHEN, NORMAN S. "The Philadelphia Election Riot of 1742." *Pennsylvania Magazine of History and Biography* 92 (1968), 306–19.

CONDIT, WILLIAM W. "Christopher Ludwick, The Patriotic Gingerbread Baker." *Pennsylvania Magazine of History and Biography* 81 (1957), 365–90.

DRIGGS, LAWRENCE. "Aces among Aces." *National Geographic* 33 (1918), 568–80.

DUBBS, JOSEPH H. "The Founding of the German Churches of Pennsylvania." *Pennsylvania Magazine of History and Biography* 17 (1893), 241–62.

FABIAN, MONROE H. "The Easton Bible Artist Identified." *Pennsylvania Folklife* 22 (Winter 1972), 2–14.

GEFFEN, ELIZABETH M. "Violence in Philadelphia in the 1840's and 1850's." *Pennsylvania History* 36 (1969), 380–410.

GEHRET, ELLEN J. and ALAN G. KEYSER. "Flax Processing in Pennsylvania from Seed to Fiber." *Pennsylvania Folklife* 22 (Autumn 1972), 10–31.

GLEASON, J. PHILIP. "The Scurrilous Election of 1764 and Benjamin Franklin." *William and Mary Quarterly*, Third Series, 18 (1961), 68–84.

GRAEFF, ARTHUR D. "The Pennsylvania Germans in Ontario, Canada." *Pennsylvania German Folklore Society* 11 (1946), 1–80.

HOPF, CARROLL. "Calligraphic Drawings and Pennsylvania German Fraktur." *Pennsylvania Folklife* 22 (Autumn 1972), 2–9.

HOPPLE, C. LEE. "Spatial Development of the Southeastern Pennsylvania Plain Dutch Community to 1970." *Pennsylvania Folklife* 21 (Winter 1971–72), 18–40; (Spring 1972), 36–45.

HOSTETLER, JOHN A. and BEULAH S. "Amish Genealogy: A Progress Report." *Pennsylvania Folklife* 19 (Autumn 1969), 23–27.

HOWLAND, GARTH A. "John Valentine Haidt, A Little Known Eighteenth Century Painter." *Pennsylvania History* 8 (1941), 304–13.

HUNTER, WILLIAM A. "German Settlers and Indian Warriors." *Der Reggeboge*, 3 (September 1969), 3–18.

HUTSON, JAMES. "Benjamin Franklin and Pennsylvania Politics, 1751–1755: A Reappraisal." *Pennsylvania Magazine of History and Biography* 93 (1969), 303–71.

IRELAND, OWEN S. "The Ethnic-Religious Dimension of Pennsylvania Politics, 1778–1779." *William and Mary Quarterly*, Third Series, 30 (1973), 423–48.

JORDAN, ALBERT F. "Some Early Moravian Builders in America." *Pennsylvania Folklife* 24 (Fall 1974), 2–17.

KETCHAM, RALPH L. "Conscience, War and Politics in Pennsylvania, 1755–1757." *William and Mary Quarterly*, Third Series, 20 (1963), 416–39.

KULP, I. CLARENCE, JR. "Christmas Customs of the Goschenhoppen Region." *The Goschenhoppen Region* 1 (1968), 4–11.

LEONARD, SISTER JOAN DE LOURDES. "Elections in Colonial Pennsylvania." *William and Mary Quarterly,* Third Series, 11 (1954), 383–401.

LEVINE, PETER. "The Fries Rebellion: Social Violence and the Politics of the New Nation." *Pennsylvania History* 40 (1973), 241–58.

LOKKEN, ROY N. "The Concept of Democracy in Colonial America." *William and Mary Quarterly,* Third Series, 16 (1959), 568–80.

LONG, AMOS JR. "Pennsylvania Summer-Houses and Summer-Kitchens." *Pennsylvania Folklife* 15 (Autumn 1965), 10–19.

MINDERHOUT, MARY ALICE. "Juvenile Books about Pennsylvania Germans." *Der Reggeboge* 9 (March 1975), 3–14.

MOOK, MAURICE A. "Bread Baking in Mifflin County, Pennsylvania." *Pennsylvania Folklife* 21 (Autumn 1971), 42–45.

NELSON, VERNON H. "The Moravian Contribution to the Tulpehocken Region." *Der Reggeboge* 7 (July 1973), 3–16.

NEWTON, EARLE. "Jacob Eichholtz." *Pennsylvania History* 26 (1959), 103–18.

PARSONS, WILLIAM T. "The Bloody Election of 1742." *Pennsylvania History* 26 (1969), 290–306.

————. "Isaac Norris, the Councillor, Master of Norriton Manor." *Bulletin of the Historical Society of Montgomery County* 19 (1973), 3–33.

————. "William Allen as Seen by a Contemporary." *Proceedings, Lehigh County Historical Society* 25 (1964), 161–72.

PENNYPACKER, SAMUEL. "The Settlement of Germantown and the Causes which led to it." *Pennsylvania Magazine of History and Biography* 4 (1880), 1–41.

POSEN, THOMAS A. "Washington along the Skippack." *Bulletin of the Historical Society of Montgomery County* 19 (1974), 230–48.

REED, JOHN R. "Montgomery County's 'Bivouac of the Dead.'" *Bulletin of the Historical Society of Montgomery County* 13 (1961), 49–64.

ROBACKER, EARL F., and ROBACKER, ADA F. "Quilting Traditions of the Dutch Country." *Pennsylvania Folklife* 21 (Festival 1972), 31–38.

ROSENBERGER, HOMER T. "Montgomery County's Greatest Lady: Lucretia Mott." *Bulletin of the Historical Society of Montgomery County* 6 (1948), 91–172.

SHANER, RICHARD H. "Recollections of Witchcraft in the Oley Hills." *Pennsylvania Folklife* 21 (Festival 1972), 39–43.

STOUDT, JOHN J. "Daniel and Squire Boone—A Study in Historical Symbolism." *Pennsylvania History* 3 (1936), 27–40.

TULLY, ALAN. "Literacy Levels and Educational Development in

Rural Pennsylvania, 1729–1775." *Pennsylvania History* 39 (1972), 301–12.

WEAVER, GLENN. "Benjamin Franklin and the Pennsylvania Germans." *William and Mary Quarterly.* Third Series, 14 (1957), 536–59.

WEAVER, WILLIAM WOYS. "A Blacksmith's 'Summerkich.'" *Pennsylvania Folklife* 22 (Summer 1973), 22–26.

—————. "Weizenthal and the Early Architecture of New-Strassburg: Swiss Plantations in the Province of Pennsylvania." *Historic Schaefferstown Record* 8 (1973), 2–11.

WHITING,, ROBERT B. "John Ziegler, Montgomery County Organ Builder." *Bulletin of the Historical Society of Montgomery County* 19 (1973), 46–53.

WINKLER, LOUIS. "Pennsylvania German Astronomy and Astrology." *Pennsylvania Folklife* 21 (Spring 1972), 25–31; (Summer 1972), 23–29; 22 (Autumn 1972), 35–41.

YODER, DON. "The Folklife Studies Movement." *Pennsylvania Folklife* 13 (July 1963), 43–56.

—————. "The Pennsylvania Germans: A Preliminary Reading List." *Pennsylvania Folklife* 21 (Winter 1971–72), 2–17.

—————. "The Tradition of the Dutch-English Comedian." *Pennsylvania Folklife* 21 (Festival 1972), 7–11.

ZIMMERMAN, JOHN J. "Benjamin Franklin and the Quaker Party 1755–1756." *William and Mary Quarterly,* Third Series, 17 (1960), 291–313.

Index